Praise for

Where the Seams Meet

"In his debut novel, Patrick Holcomb deftly explores the twists and turns of life, what it means to root for the ultimate outcome, and how the relationship between a father and son can be both tumultuous and a touchstone as we experience the uneven innings of our lives."

—Andrew Baggarly, San Francisco Giants beat writer for *The Athletic* and author of *A Band of Misfits: Tales of the 2010 San Francisco Giants*

"A gripping, suspenseful, cinematic view of baseball from the pitcher's mound and of kinship from within the pent-up hearts of a tragically misaligned father and son. Though not a sports fan (until now) I couldn't put this book down."

—Julene Bair, award-winning author of *The Ogallala Road: A Story of Love, Family, and the Fight to Keep the Great Plains from Running Dry*

"Holcomb's deft characterization and rich prose usher the reader through a tale in which life—like baseball—is so often a study in overcoming failure. Jump in and see this saga to its satisfying conclusion."

—Mike Murphey, award-winning author of *The Conman: A Baseball Odyssey*

"Throwing a baseball across a 17-inch plate with precise velocity and movement to fool a hitter is really hard. What can be even harder is fathers and sons finding the right words to say to each other. Sometimes a curveball is flat. Sometimes the advice falls flatter. In his debut novel, Patrick Holcomb weaves together San Francisco Giants baseball history with a tale of generations whose only real connections are their genes, their love of baseball, their desire to do the right thing (or the fun thing), and their regrets. With a wink to some Giants icons and the Bay Area's geography, Patrick's novel might break your heart one page and make you wanna play catch with your father the next page. Indeed, how about those Giants?"

—Josh Suchon, author of *This Gracious Season: Barry Bonds & the Greatest Year in Baseball*

WHERE THE SEAMS MEET

PATRICK HOLCOMB

FROM THE TINY ACORN…
GROWS THE MIGHTY OAK

This is a work of fiction. References to real people, events, establishments, organizations, or locales are intended only to provide a sense of authenticity and are used fictitiously. All other characters, and all incidents and dialogue are drawn from the author's imagination and are not to be construed as real.

Where the Seams Meet
Copyright © 2023 Patrick Holcomb. All rights reserved.

Printed in the United States of America. For information, address
Acorn Publishing, LLC
3943 Irvine Blvd. Ste. 218, Irvine, CA 92602

www.acornpublishingllc.com

Interior design by Kat Ross
Cover design by Damonza

Anti-Piracy Warning: The unauthorized reproduction or distribution of a copyrighted work is illegal. Criminal copyright infringement, including infringement without monetary gain, is investigated by the FBI and is punishable by up to five years in federal prison and a fine of $250,000.

All rights reserved. No part of this book may be used or reproduced in any manner whatsoever, including Internet usage, without written permission from the author.

ISBN-13: 979-8-88528-066-2 (hardcover)
ISBN-13: 979-8-88528-065-5 (paperback)
Library of Congress Control Number: 2023912062

For my dad. You were my first hero, my earliest coach, and—win or lose—my biggest fan. Thank you for setting the example, paving my road to success, and serving as a consummate reminder of a timeless truth: character counts.

"Love is the most important thing in the world, but baseball is pretty good, too."

— Yogi Berra

Prologue

Age 62

October 29, 2014

"Jesus Christ," Frank whispered.

The blasphemous curse escaped through clenched teeth, then diffused harmlessly into the stillness of the deserted lot.

His eyes darted to each corner of the empty expanse, confirming what he already knew to be true: he was alone. With all of the storefronts, save the donut shop, still dark—and the first fingers of sunlight curling over the hilltops in the east—there was no one to bear witness to his shame.

And as always, no one to blame but himself.

The truck's passenger door was slick with morning dew. Frank grudgingly yielded to the pain and vertigo, allowing his heavy frame to slump against the damp panel. Silently clocking the seconds, waiting for the crippling tightness in his chest to pass, he was somehow more concerned with the containers clutched in his arms than with the sheen of cold sweat blanketing his brow.

The Northern California air was crisp and cold, laden with the sweet decay of autumn. Frank forced an icy breath into the depths of his lungs, expanding his chest and trying to snap the thick cords of anxiety that had bound him since long before dawn. He'd awoken even earlier than usual, with a baseball-sized knot in his gut and thoughts about the evening's game—and more painful topics, those which he usually chose to avoid—racing unchecked through his mind.

"You're okay," he whispered, nodding as the pain and dizziness gradually passed. He waited a moment longer, just to be sure, then pulled the door wide and bent to deposit the carton of coffee and box of donuts onto the spotless floorboard below.

Frank cranked the ignition. The F-150 roared to life, filling the cab with the sounds of The Eagles, one of the six ancient CDs that lived in perpetuity within the truck's six-disc changer. With the closing notes of "Already Gone" lingering in the air, his shaky hands steered the truck back onto Piner Road, the rundown strip mall shrinking in his rear-view mirror. He knew through years of repetition that "Desperado" would follow and leaned forward to skip the song—a dutiful concession to *her*, a loving tribute he'd rendered more times than he could count—then changed his mind and flipped on the radio instead.

He was looking for World Series coverage. Though he found it on KNBR, disappointment quickly followed, and the flames of impatience licked at the frayed edges of his nerves. The sports radio pundits were traipsing noisily over well-trod ground. Even for a deciding game seven, when one pitch or swing can mean the difference between a champagne-drenched locker room and spending a long winter lamenting what could have been, there was only so much to be said. And with the issue of Bumgarner already settled—and the Giants electing to start Hudson on the road in Kansas City instead—the radio team was just rehashing old storylines, filling the airwaves with empty platitudes and telling him nothing about the night's matchup he didn't already know.

Frank had heard enough. He silenced the pundits, then cranked the wheel hard, passing the corner gas station and completing the sharp right turn onto Coffey Lane. Ahead on his left, crouched behind its well-manicured lawn and flanked by clusters of tall oaks, was the old firehouse, Santa Rosa Station 3. The one that was no longer *his*.

He eased the truck past the station's single-story administrative building, peered through the open retractable door of the adjoining maintenance bay, then parked in one of the handful of visitors' spots. He checked his reflection in the rearview mirror, smoothed the once-black mane, now noticeably thinner and mostly gray, and dug deep to unearth something akin to a smile, which looked phony and forced even to his own tired blue eyes.

These visits were a guilty pleasure, both a curse and a cure. He'd been dropping by the station more often, usually in the early morning, and usually on the days when sleep had been elusive and the silence in the house grew louder than the voice of caution. Though he craved their camaraderie, he had to be careful not to overstay his welcome. It was a fine line, he knew—having entertained his fair share of "old-timers" over the years—and one he was determined not to cross.

Frank lingered in the cab, engine off, staring through the rapidly-fogging windshield at the low row of shrubs and the gray metal siding of the building in front of him. He sucked in another gulp of air, trying to dispel the last remnants of tightness in his chest, then slid his phone from his coat pocket, debating again whether or not to call.

Baseball hadn't been the only topic on his mind as he'd stared up at the ceiling fan in the hours before dawn, his eyes tracing the uncomplicated lines of its motionless blades, before finally giving up on sleep. Try as he might to avoid them, there were thoughts of his son as well. Thoughts of Danny.

It wasn't surprising, really. Even now, after two years of gut-wrenching silence, Frank found it impossible to separate the two in his mind: *baseball and his son*.

Frank stared down at the phone in his hand, the heavy burden of his conscience contrasting with the phone's lightness in the broad expanse of his palm. He noted the time. Only 7:42, it was still too early to call. Or far too late, depending on how he chose to look at it.

He issued a jagged sigh, stared at the phone's display a second longer, then reluctantly slid it back into his pocket. He'd call later, he promised himself, though not for the first time. He'd made this promise a million times before—at least. Though it offered some small sliver of hope and kept him moving forward, he knew it was one he was unlikely to keep.

The sun was bright now, its rim rising above the grassy crest of the rolling hills. Frank squinted as he lowered himself gingerly from the cab and walked to the far side of the truck. He turned to face east, closing his eyes to let daybreak wash over his face. Despite the chill of the morning, and the layer of dew blanketing the row of shrubs, the cloudless skies held a certain promise. A promise of victory, perhaps. Of anything beyond that, he didn't dare to hope. Nor did he have the right.

Carried by the long strides of the athlete he once was, the carton of coffee in one hand and the box of donuts balanced atop the other, Frank walked toward the open maintenance bay. The front of the engine was barely visible, freshly washed, early morning sunlight gleaming off its chrome bumper.

Frank's lips curled to form a smile, a real one this time, though still tinged with sadness. In front of the bay, an assortment of equipment and tools was spread neatly across the concrete driveway, the tell-tale signs of an inventory in progress. The yearning for normalcy tugged him forward. Even the most menial tasks—the ones he and every other firefighter bitched loudly about and took for granted—assumed new meaning once they were performed by someone else. Once your time had passed and someone else stood the watch.

Just shy of the station's sturdy oak sign, Frank froze, his knees buckling from the weight of fifty years' worth of regret and words left unspoken. He balanced the carton and box atop the sign, made up his mind, and reached for his phone.

Some fences can never be mended—life's senseless brutality

had certainly taught him that—but perhaps this one could be, if he only had the courage to try.

He dialed Danny's number from memory, took one last deep breath to slow his racing heart, then moved his thumb to press send.

Before Frank could complete the call, an explosion rocked his core, igniting every nerve in his body. The phone slipped from his grasp.

He clutched at his chest with one hand, while the other clawed at the sign beside him, knocking the coffee and donuts to the sidewalk, legs failing beneath him.

As his frame crumpled to the earth, his eyes unseeing and his consciousness no longer in the present, one word—whispered in a voice that could only be hers—echoed hauntingly in the stillness of his mind: *time*.

It was a word Frank had come to despise. He'd been tortured with so much of it, been alone with his guilt and his grief for so very long, that he'd forgotten how precious a commodity it was. Now, as the darkness closed in to remind him, he finally remembered. And wished he had more of it.

PART ONE
FRANK

Chapter 1

Age 5

October 5, 1957

"Come here," his father ordered, his first words since they'd hopped off the bus and started their long march down the busy street.

Frank flinched at the sound of Pop's booming voice, then squirmed as an icy hand wrapped around the back of his neck, stopping him dead. His father lowered his bulk to one knee, forcing the mob of strangers to break around them like waves against a boulder. He gripped Frank by both shoulders, their faces only inches apart.

"None of this crying shit, you understand me?" His father fixed him with cold blue eyes that seemed to vibrate within their sockets, making Frank's knees tremble and knock.

Frank understood. Of course, he did. Salvatore Romano was always clear with his instructions, and it was not the first time this point had been made: men don't cry. And if Frank ever wanted to be one, a *real man* like his father, he'd better shape up—and fast.

"Yes, sir," Frank whispered, nodding and fighting hard not to shiver in the chill of the San Francisco morning. He sniffed loudly, then shifted his misty eyes to the red, white, and blue stripes of the electric barber's pole. He stared hard at the shop window, struggling to make sense of the fancy red letters splashed across the glass. He couldn't be certain—because letters were a maddening puzzle he'd yet to solve—but he figured the series of loops and curls spelled the name of the barbershop.

"I mean it, Francesco," his father continued, grabbing Frank firmly by the chin. "When you walk into Enzo's Barbershop, you behave like a man. He and I go back a long way, back to the war, and I *will not* be embarrassed. Got it?"

Frank stared into his father's narrowed eyes, the tops partly hidden by the furry black caterpillars that lived above them. He nodded again, this time harder and faster, trying to show his father the respect a soldier deserved. His pop almost never talked about the war, and although Frank was always curious about his father's far-away adventures, he knew better than to open his fat mouth to ask.

His father grunted, a low rumble that made the hairs on the back of Frank's neck stand on end, then leaned on Frank's shoulder as he lifted himself up from the sidewalk. He kept one heavy hand circled around the back of Frank's neck, then opened the glass door and ushered him inside.

Frank wriggled free just inside the door and pinched the sides of his icy nose, trying not to sneeze. It was pleasingly warm inside the shop, much warmer than outside, but the air was thick with strange smells, the kinds that tickle your nose and make your eyes water.

"Sally-fucking-Romano!" the barber called. A slim man with a red face, a black curtain of slicked-back hair, and a balloon-shaped head that seemed to float atop his tiny neck, the barber laughed loudly, then rushed across the empty shop to greet them.

Frank shrank from his father's side, bracing himself for the worst. It wasn't the rough language that shocked him—he'd heard his father use that word before—rather the man's disrespect, daring to call his father by a woman's name.

"How ya doin', Enzo?" his father asked with a broad smile, a far cry from the angry roar Frank had envisioned as he inched toward the door.

Frank watched Pop's reflection in the long mirror as he laughed, placed a giant hand on each of the smaller man's white-coated shoulders, then pulled him into his chest.

A hot blush exploded across Frank's face. His ears, frozen only a moment before, now burned like fiery coals on each side of his head. He wanted to look away, but he couldn't help himself, so he continued to stare at his father and this strange man instead. His dad never hugged anyone. *Ever*. Not even him or his mother.

Beckoned by the barber, his father settled his enormous frame into the first of three shiny red chairs, requested *"the usual,"* then fell into back-and-forth grown-up talk that was mostly about baseball. And mostly about Pop's favorite subject, the New York Yankees.

Frank sat stiffly in the seat closest to the door and hung on his father's every word as Pop chatted away about the afternoon's game. Speaking in the thick New York accent Frank wished he could imitate, his hands jerking excitedly beneath the barber's cloth, Pop peppered in a few names Frank recognized—Yogi Berra, for one, and the great Mickey Mantle, for another. There were few things his father became excited about, but the Yankees and the World Series topped the short list.

The black shiny chair was warm and inviting against Frank's chilled back. Just as he began to relax his shoulders into its soft leather, his curiosity turned to horror. He watched fearfully as Enzo and his sharp scissors darted from one side of the chair to the other, like a fly buzzing around an elephant, combing and cutting in turns. Frank gasped as Enzo reached into a liquid-filled jar and pulled out a straight-edge razor, a blade that looked sharp enough to cut a man—or a little boy, at least—clean in half.

"You okay, kid?" Enzo asked, glancing at Frank's reflection in the mirror while inspecting his sharp blade under the bright lights.

Frank didn't trust his voice, so he just nodded slowly and tried not to squirm in his seat. His skin crawled as the barber applied a thin layer of shaving cream to his father's neck, then slowly scraped the blade across his skin, shaving the hair into a neat black line. He cleaned the razor with a damp rag and returned it to the glass jar, then powdered his father's neck with a brush and spun him around in the chair.

Facing the mirror, which ran the entire length of the shop and had a row of bare round bulbs mounted above, Pop admired the fresh haircut. Combing his fingers through thick wavy hair, damp from the mist that the barber had sprayed from his plastic bottle, he nodded slowly in appreciation.

"Looks good, pal," he said finally, raising one eyebrow and flashing his teeth at the reflection in the mirror. "Let's do the same for the kid."

Horses galloped wildly inside Frank's chest as he eyed the empty chair from across the shop. He tugged at the collar of his sweater, which had transformed into a noose around his neck, and struggled to catch his breath, which came in ragged gasps. This was his first time at a real barbershop, and he was old enough to know what that meant: *his first step to becoming a man.*

Up to now, only his mother had cut his hair. Always done in the backyard of their house, with an old towel draped around his bare shoulders, it was a chore they both dreaded. And even she, who lost her temper far less than his father, became angry when Frank shrank away from the scissors, then burst into a fit of tears. One day, when he'd been especially bad, she threw down her scissors only halfway through, making him suffer the *indignity* of an unfinished haircut until she was ready to try again the next day.

"Well?" Enzo asked Frank, not unkindly. He took his time shaking out the black-and-white striped cloth, swept the black clumps of hair from the floor, then motioned for Frank to climb into the seat. He fastened the top of the cloth tightly around Frank's neck, then began wetting his hair with a series of cold squirts from the bottle, each angry blast feeling like punishment for a crime only Frank knew he didn't commit.

Frank slunk lower in the chair, his hands clenched beneath the cloth, sharp fingernails digging into fleshy palms. Tears welled in the corners of his eyes, but he willed them not to come.

"How old are you, kid?" Enzo asked, his lollipop head floating forward from behind the chair.

Before Frank could answer, his father, hunkered in the seat across from him, staring over the top of a magazine, spoke for him. "He's five. First time in the chair, but he knows the rules." His steely eyes said everything his mouth didn't.

With the first *clip-clip-clipping* of the scissors above his ear, Frank shuddered in the chair, fighting the urge to flee from the shop, never to return. He could feel the heat of his father's glare, but he avoided it and focused instead on the row of photos above him, hung side-by-side in matching black frames, high on the white-painted wall.

Frank counted all the frames, then counted them again just to be sure. Satisfied there were exactly nine pictures, no more and no less, Frank's attention was drawn and held by the picture in the middle. It was a face every good Catholic would recognize, and one Frank knew well from the faded photo that hung on their own wall in the hallway at home. The Pope.

Dressed in his white robes that reminded Frank more of a wizard than a priest, the Pope stared directly into Frank's soul, ready to pass eternal judgment should a single tear be shed. While the idea of embarrassing his father was shameful enough, appearing weak in the eyes of the Pope was more than Frank's heart could bear.

Frank abandoned the staring contest, knowing the Pope would surely win, and drew in a deep breath, just like his mother had taught him. He held it in his lungs for a count of five before slowly releasing it through his nose. All the while, he continued chanting the same three words in his head, as much a prayer to God Almighty as a reminder to himself: *men don't cry*.

Frank trailed his father out the door and joined the sea of people streaming up and down the sidewalk outside the shop. The morning remained cool, but the fog had begun to lift, and the bright outline of the sun burned twin circles into Frank's eyes as he stared for a second too long into the thinning wall of gray.

Safely back on the street, Frank's chest swelled with pride. He had survived Enzo's scissors and blade without a single tear being shed. He tugged at the sleeve of his father's coat and raised his voice, struggling to be heard over the overlapping conversations of strangers and the steady hum of traffic crawling up the street. "I did okay, right, Pop?"

"Yeah, you did okay," his father answered. He turned and reached for Frank's shoulder again, softer this time, and gave it a squeeze. "And that cut looks good on you, too," he added, tilting his head to the side as he admired Enzo's work. Cropped close on the sides, then left longer on the top and parted above the temple, their haircuts were identical. "You're looking a bit like your old man this morning, huh?"

Frank smiled shyly, pleased by the comparison. Though he already knew he looked like his father—even strangers pointed out the sameness of their black hair and olive skin, and especially their bright blue eyes—words of praise from Pop were few and far between, so he took a moment to bask in the warm glow of his compliment.

In truth, Frank saw little of his father. Much less than he'd like. His dad was a policeman—with a fancy uniform, a shiny badge, and a gun Frank was never allowed to touch—and it was a *very* important job. It was a job Frank was proud of, but it meant working a lot. Pop usually left the house before Frank woke and didn't return home until long after dark. While Frank couldn't remember the last time he and his father had been out together alone, he hadn't been surprised by Pop's invitation, which had come that morning over breakfast, under his mother's watchful eye.

He'd heard most of his parents' argument two nights before,

when his father returned home late from work and his mother had already put him to bed. The two had bickered for what seemed like hours, with his father angrily shouting about the *responsibilities* of his job and his mother yelling right back, stubbornly refusing to budge.

Curled in a tight ball beneath his soft royal-blue comforter, Frank had turned to face the wall of his bedroom, his eyes clenched, knowing it was naughty to eavesdrop. While the walls of the house were thin—thin enough to allow him to hear most of their conversation—some parts were drowned out by the *thud-thud-thudding* of footsteps on the hardwood floors as his mother hounded his father, her sharp words chasing him from one room to the next.

"Okay, then," his mother said finally, standing just outside Frank's door, speaking in that voice she used when her hands were pressed to her hips. "You'll take him out on Saturday and make a day of it."

He couldn't hear what his father said in return, if anything at all, but his footsteps had led him quickly down the hallway toward the kitchen, and the house was silent after that.

"Where are we going now?" Frank yelled ahead. Pop walked fast, much faster than his mother, making it hard for Frank to keep pace as he dodged and ducked through a jumble of people much taller than he.

"North," his father answered. He didn't slow down, just barked the single word back and over his shoulder. "We're on Powell Street now," he added, "on the edge of Little Italy. And that's Washington Square up ahead."

Frank broke into a jog, stayed close by his father's side as they crossed the street, and looked to the grassy park ahead. Along its outer edges, tall trees stood side by side like a row of knights keeping watch, their long shadows stretching across the broad lawn of the park.

Spotting a hotdog vendor's wheeled cart, his father marched to the edge of the square. He ordered two dogs and pulled his thick leather wallet from the back pocket of his trousers. "Go grab us a spot," he said, nodding toward a row of shaded benches inside the park. "I'll pay for these and be right over."

Frank wasn't sure which bench his father meant, but he knew better than to ask a question that had already been answered. He wandered down the path and into the park, bent to pick up a penny that someone had dropped, then paused in the shade of the trees to admire the bronze statue. Standing atop a mountain of stone, the face of the statue was familiar, with spooky eyes that seemed to follow him as he swayed back and forth in front of it.

"I know you…" Frank whispered to the statue. He realized with a start that he'd been to this park before with his mother, for some sort of party for the man who had first found America. His mother had been a schoolteacher once, sometime before he was born, which meant she knew pretty much *everything* about *everyone*, even this man with the creepy eyes.

Frank stared down at the bearded half-face on the penny, then up again at the statue. The man made of bronze wasn't a president, he didn't think, but something different. Something better. He squinched his eyes until the word exploded into his mind. *Inventor.* That was it!

While Frank couldn't remember much of what his mother had told him about the famous inventor—besides his name, Franklin, which was close to his own—there was one thing he couldn't possibly forget: the metal time capsule that was buried in the base of the statue, which had been there since before his parents were born. Frank loved puzzles and riddles, and the time capsule sparked Frank's imagination. He and his mother had traded guesses about the treasures hidden inside, then sworn a sacred oath to return together for its opening on its hundredth birthday.

"I thought I told you to wait on the bench, pal."

Frank spun around, startled to see his father, who was too big and noisy to sneak up on anybody. Hot dogs in hand, he stood almost on top of him, not even noticing the statue.

Trailing Pop to the row of benches, too excited to breathe, Frank spilled the secret of the time capsule. He rattled off a few of his guesses about what was hidden inside and invited his father to join them for its grand opening in 1970-*something-or-other*.

"I'll be a grownup by then," Frank added seriously, closing his eyes and picturing a grown-up version of himself. "Maybe I can bring my kids, too."

His father nodded slowly, considering the invitation. He gestured for Frank to sit beside him on the bench but only smiled in response. If he was excited about seeing the treasures inside the capsule, or even being there when it was opened, he sure didn't show it. That was fine by Frank, though; Mom was more fun anyway.

The two ate their hotdogs in silence. Being careful not to drip ketchup and mustard on his wool sweater and jeans, Frank stared across the park to the giant castle on the other side of the square. Rising high above the street below, with two identical towers that touched the sky, it looked like something out of a fairytale. Frank liked fairytales as much as the next kid, but he knew better than to admit as much to Pop.

His father turned to admire the white stone building. "Saints Peter and Paul Church," he explained, speaking through a half-chewed mouthful of hotdog and nodding in the church's direction. "You know, I saw you looking at the photos on the wall in Enzo's. Remember the one of the ballplayer? Wearing a Yankees cap, with a big toothy grin?"

Frank closed his eyes and dug deep into his memory box, struggling to remember each of the nine pictures in the row of black frames hanging on the wall. "Next to the Pope?" he asked brightly, able to see the smiling Yankee in his mind's eye.

"Yeah, that's right. Next to that guy." Pop rewarded Frank's guess with a wink. "Well, that was Joe DiMaggio," he continued, speaking in the same special tone that his mother saved for Jesus, God, and the Holy Mother. "One of the greatest players in the history of the game. He was married in that church, right over there, back in the late '30s. Your mother and I didn't live here yet, but it was a pretty big deal at the time."

His father stood, looked down at Frank with a strange gleam in his eye, and popped the remaining bite of hotdog into his mouth. "And a pretty big deal when he divorced the broad and married that actress, too."

Frank sucked in a breath that tasted like sin and looked left and right to see who else had heard that word. *"Divorced,"* not the other one. His mind raced as he scrambled to finish his hotdog and watched his father lumber away, back toward the park's edge.

"Divorce" was a word that scared Frank, one he would never dare to say aloud. In a Catholic house like theirs, where the Pope was always watching and listening from his spot on the wall, it was *much worse* than anything he might overhear in a barbershop.

THE TRIP HOME WAS QUIET. Too quiet. Frank had begged his father to ride the cable cars, instead of the boring city bus, but his father had stood firm. Frank almost kept pressing, then Pop had given him *the look*, and that was all he needed to see. Arguing with his mother was one thing, and sometimes it even worked, but he was more likely to end up bent over his father's knee than to change his mind once it was made up.

Crammed side by side into a seat near the back of the bus, Pop buried his nose in the morning newspaper he'd bought, along with some Lucky Strikes and a pack of gum for Frank, at a sidewalk stand next to the bus stop. The endless rows and lines of letters on the front page were a riddle Frank couldn't solve, but he got the gist of the story anyway when his father cursed aloud, complaining to the man across the aisle about the "Russians and their damn satellite."

Frank didn't understand exactly what a satellite was, but he'd heard plenty about the Russians. Enough to know that Pop didn't trust them any farther than he could throw them. And he knew that the race was underway to put a man into space. Like the time capsule hidden beneath the statue in the park, the idea of launching a man into space was one that fired his imagination.

Pinned against the cold side of the bus by his father's meaty thigh, being careful not to smack his gum, Frank raised his hand to the window often, using the sleeve of his sweater to wipe away the layer of fog made by hot breath on cool glass. He watched the city roll by—an endless parade of buildings and people and cars—until the bus jerked to a halt, and his father nudged his ribs with his elbow, then nodded to the door at the front of the bus.

Frank stepped down carefully from the green-and-white-painted bus, sidestepped to avoid a pink glob of gum someone had spit on the curb, then joined his father in the fast-moving jumble of people marching up and down Geary Street.

Frank weaved in and out of foot traffic along the busy sidewalk, then broke into a trot, struggling to match Pop's pace. He dawdled for a beat as they passed the corner butcher shop and admired the plaster models in the window—hams, turkeys, and roasts that looked good enough to eat—before trailing his father around the corner and down the lane onto Spruce.

Frank pulled even with his dad as they approached home. He stood on tiptoes, craning his neck and looking up to the second story of their white-painted house, hoping to catch a glimpse of his mother through the glass. She loved to sit in her reading chair above the street, paging through a book and watching the outside world through the large bay windows that overlooked the sidewalk below. Frank's heart sank as he peered upward into the living room. Though the shades were open, his mother was nowhere to be seen.

"Where's Ma?" Frank asked. He looked to his father, who had stooped to pick at the peeling paint on the base of the banister.

Without waiting for a response, he ducked around his father and raced up the narrow flight of steps, counting the hollow thumps in his mind as his feet struck each of the seven green-painted boards. Counting was a favorite hobby of Frank's, second only to putting together puzzles, and one he practiced often. He knew how many windows the house had, how many of the doors had locks, and how many forks, spoons, and knives were in the silverware drawer in the kitchen.

Reaching for the front door and finding it unlocked, Frank flung it wide, winced as the knob slammed into the wall behind it, and sprinted down the hall, hoping his father would let it slide.

"Whoa, hold on a second, pal."

Frank froze like he did on the playground when his teacher called *"red light,"* then walked slowly back toward the door. He searched his father's face for signs of anger but found none.

"I've got something for you before you run off and play."

Frank's heart skipped a beat. He searched his father's face again, more carefully this time. Experience had taught him that when his father *had something* for him, it wasn't always something good.

"Go look in the closet." Pop nodded toward the end of the hall before pausing by the door to remove his coat. "There should be a shoe box at the bottom."

Though he was eager to show his mother his new haircut and to remind her of the time capsule in the park and the sacred oath they'd sworn, Frank's curiosity got the best of him. *This* had not been a part of his parents' conversation two nights before.

He darted down the hallway, yanked the door open by its big brass knob, and found the shoe box near the back of the closet, hidden behind the dustpan and broom.

"Bring it to the sofa," his father told him, mussing Frank's freshly cut hair as he made his way to the kitchen. "And don't open it until I tell you."

Frank did as he was told and waited in torture on the pea-green sofa. He watched as his father flipped on the television, tuned the set to the baseball game, then lowered himself into his recliner.

Frank's body tingled with excitement as his father looked him up and down, then slowly lit a cigarette. He blew a thick cloud of smoke toward the ceiling and took a long pull from his bottle of beer.

"Okay, kid," he said finally, rewarding Frank's patience with a wink and a smile. "Let's see you open that thing."

Needing no further prompting, Frank jumped off the edge of the couch and ripped the top off the box.

He stared down into the cardboard box, admiring the brand-new mitt and baseball that were nestled inside. The leather mitt, stained a brown so dark it was almost black, nearly slipped from his shaking hands as he rushed to free it from the box.

"This is for me?" he asked, his heart swelling with doubt and wonder.

"Well, it's not going to fit my hand, so I guess so," his father replied, a smile playing at the corners of his mouth. "Get your little paw in there, let's see if it's a good fit."

Frank forced his hand into the mitt, working his fingers deeper and deeper into the stiff leather until his wrist disappeared under the strap. He dropped into a crouch, shifted his weight from side to side, then punched his fist into the pocket, imitating the older boys he'd seen playing ball at the park.

"Can you come and play catch with me, Pop?" Frank asked excitedly, already bounding across the room.

"Nah, you gotta break it in first. Wait right here."

He left for a minute, then returned with a small bottle of oil and a stained rag. After showing Frank how to put the oil on the glove, and how to use his hands to massage the stiff leather, he dropped the mitt back into Frank's eager hands.

"And for the next three days, I wanna hear you pop the ball into the pocket *and* the webbing 200 times a day. Each. And put it under the foot of your mattress, with the ball inside, when you sleep at night, too. You understand?"

Frank nodded, repeating his father's instructions in his mind as he struggled to open and close the small mitt around the hard lump of the baseball.

"All right, pal." His father's focus shifted back to the television, where a Yankee was walking toward home plate and the game was about to begin. "You go show your mom the new glove and start breaking it in, just like I told you."

Frank hesitated in the doorway, his eyes bouncing back and forth between Pop's blank face and the television. He wanted so badly to break in the new mitt with a game of catch, but he knew better than to press his luck. He left Pop to watch his Yankees instead, glove on one hand and ball in the other, already popping it hard into the webbing of the mitt.

He counted under his breath as he went in search of his mother. *One, two, three, four, five...*

Chapter 2

Age 10

July 7, 1963

His mother walked faster than usual, even in her Sunday heels, but Frank refused to let her out of his sight. He trailed her protectively, following in her wake as she carved through a sea of jostling dresses and suits, burst through the doors of the sanctuary, and made a beeline for their car, which was parked next to the curb in front of the church.

Frank arrived at the rear door of the Cadillac, the baby-blue de Ville that was his father's pride and joy. He slid into the backseat, debating for the hundredth time whether it was proper to ask. Whether it was even his place.

The heat in the car was suffocating. Frank popped the top button of his starched dress shirt and breathed freely for the first time since they'd left the house for Sunday Mass. He kneaded the sides of his neck, trying to erase the deep grooves that the restrictive collar had cut into his soft flesh.

"Are you okay, Mom?" Frank finally dared. His voice was barely a whisper, though they were alone in the heat and the stillness of the car. His eyes darted from the back of his mother's head to the brick archway of St. Vincent de Paul. His father was standing next to the door, still talking to Mr. Amato, and still wearing that phony grin, pretending nothing was wrong.

"I'm fine, honey," she assured him, her tone flat and unconvincing. She pulled down the visor, showed him the reflection of a feeble smile in the front passenger mirror, then began touching up her makeup, which was badly smeared around her puffy eyes.

Frank wasn't fooled. He'd watched her throughout Father McNamara's homily, a mind-numbingly long lecture about the *dignity of work* and the *rights of workers*. It had lasted for the better part of an hour, but Frank had known from the very beginning—when she'd reached a pale and shaky hand into her purse and retrieved her white handkerchief—that the sermon would spell trouble.

Wedged between his parents, his back pressed against the hard oak of the pew, Frank had searched his father's face for any hint of a reaction. If his dad had noticed the handkerchief, or how she'd worked it into a tight little ball in her tiny hands, occasionally lifting it to her face to dab at the corner of each eye, he'd given no indication. If anything, his old man had looked bored, constantly inspecting the face of his gold wristwatch, even stifling the occasional yawn.

Frank opened his mouth to speak, about to press the point with his mother, then clamped it shut and sat up straight in his seat. His father appeared at the driver's side of the car, looking formidable in the crisp dress blue police uniform that he'd begun wearing to church after his promotion to sergeant, then settled himself wordlessly behind the wheel. He didn't look at either of them, just cranked the ignition and eased the car away from the curb.

"Knock that shit off," his father ordered, adjusting the rearview mirror to shoot daggers into the backseat.

Frank pulled his hand away from his mouth and into his lap, hiding the collection of nails that were chewed to the quick. He focused on the hands of his watch instead, painfully aware of each passing minute as the car slogged through the maddening gridlock in Cow Hollow.

It was just past ten o'clock already, only two hours until the scheduled start of the Giants doubleheader against the Cardinals, and the odds of him finishing his lessons and chores in time to catch the first pitch were growing increasingly slim.

Worse still, although fifteen awkward minutes had passed since they'd left the church, his parents had yet to exchange a single word. Not one. Not even to complain about the traffic. As the car rounded the corner from Geary onto Spruce, with Frank all but convinced they would complete the entire ride in silence, his mother finally turned in her seat.

"It sounded pretty clear to me," she said, shattering the silence. Her Bronx accent was thicker than usual and tinged with a note of defiance that sounded like trouble. She stared across the bench seat of the Cadillac, her red-rimmed eyes burning a hole in his father's right ear.

She paused for a beat, waiting for a response that didn't come, then continued in a sarcastic tone, quoting Father McNamara word for word. "Work is not just a means to earn a living," she began, her voice booming in the closed space of the car. "It's more than that. It's our way to continue participating in God's creation."

His father jerked the Cadillac to a halt next to the curb in front of their house, then sighed, long and hard. Frank couldn't see the expression on his face from his seat in the back, but he didn't need to. The walnut-sized muscles in his father's clenched jaw told him everything he needed to know.

"*Participating in God's creation,*" his mother repeated slowly, as if Pop hadn't heard her the first time. "Well, c'mon, Sal. Let's hear it. Which plate of malarkey are you going to dish up today?" She folded her arms across her narrow chest, waiting, continuing to watch him like a hawk from across the car.

Even Frank knew the conversation wasn't really about Father McNamara's homily. It was about his mother returning to her job as a teacher—something she'd wanted to do for a long time, but his father would never allow. Frank had heard pieces of this argument many times before, sometimes in hushed tones when they thought he was asleep, other times in throaty shouts that reverberated throughout the house and rattled the windowpanes. No matter how long she argued, or the volume at which she did it, his father's response was always the same. "Not my wife, and not in my house."

Pop shifted the car into park. He turned in his seat and planted a heavy hand on the dash. The familiar vein pulsated in his father's forehead; it was a warning sign they knew well and one his mother would be wise to heed. Frank sat deathly still in the rising heat of the car, wishing he could evaporate through the back window and bracing himself for the explosion to come.

"We've talked about this already, Maria," his father growled. "We've talked, *and we've talked*, and you know goddamn well where I stand!" He punctuated the last word with a loud slap to the dashboard, making Frank flinch and his mother gasp.

"Now, are we done here?" he asked quietly, more a challenge than a question. "Or do you want to beat this dead horse some more?"

His mother shifted noisily in the leather seat. She uncrossed her arms and stared out the car window toward the front stairs of the house. "Oh, don't worry, Sal," she whispered, barely loud enough for Frank to hear. "*This horse* is alive and kicking."

His father exploded from the car, letting the slammed door serve as the final word. Frank released a huge breath, one he didn't even realize he'd been holding, as his father stomped up the front stairs and disappeared inside.

Frank leaned forward and placed a shaky hand on the back of her seat. He wanted to reassure her, to let her know he was on her side. But if the right words existed, the ones to make her believe it was going to be okay, he surely didn't know them.

"Well, what are you waiting for, Francesco?" his mother asked, the tension in her voice replaced with a cheerfulness he was sure she didn't feel. She turned to face him, sniffed loudly, and blinked back tears. "Do you think your lessons and chores will do themselves?"

"Uggghhh," Frank groaned. He watched as his mother, minus the heels but still wearing her navy-blue church dress, swapped his empty breakfast plate for a small picture book. It looked to be written for a kid half his age, its front cover adorned by a cartoonish illustration of an alligator, its mouth wrapped with a ridiculous makeshift bandage.

As far as he knew, he was the only kid his age who was required to do schoolwork over the summer. That said, he was *also* the only one of his classmates who was still struggling to read. It was embarrassing—his stuttering and stammering, and the snickering of classmates as he failed for all to see—and a problem that had nearly resulted in him failing the fourth grade.

"I'm not a baby," Frank protested. He delivered a sharp flick to the corner of the childish book, then watched with satisfaction as it spun like a top, finally coming to rest on the far side of the small Formica table in the corner of the kitchen. "And I'm not stupid." This was a line he found himself repeating often, at home and at school, but it was one even he was finding harder and harder to believe.

He stared longingly out the kitchen window, down the steep flight of stairs and into the shaded backyard below. Though he detested his Sunday chores—he told his mother once that he hated them, then she reminded him that "hate is a very strong word"—even pulling weeds in his mother's garden was preferable to this brand of torture. To *reading*.

The previous school year had been a constant battle, an endless procession of failed quizzes, poor grades, and lengthy after-school "chats" with his teacher, Mr. Weathersby. So, it came as no surprise to Frank, or his parents for that matter, when they were summoned to the principal's office during the last week of school, and his teacher "suggested" that Frank repeat the previous grade. It was only because of his father's angry protests—probably the only time Frank had enjoyed watching his father lose his cool—and his mother's promises to tutor him throughout the summer, that Principal Simmons had finally budged, reluctantly agreeing to let Frank move on to the fifth grade.

"Would you like a more difficult book instead?" his mother challenged, one slender black eyebrow raised. She slid his plate into the drying rack, turned off the tap, and wiped her hands on the front of the floral apron that was tied snugly around her narrow waist.

"I thought I was doing you a favor," she continued, pulling up a chair beside him at the small square table. "But we can grab a harder book, something more *advanced*, if that's what you'd prefer."

Frank shook his head, knowing better than to test his mother's patience. Though his father had disappeared into his workshop and skipped their usual Sunday breakfast, the argument in the car still hovered like a dark cloud over their morning. Frank reached across the table, retrieved the flimsy book, and reluctantly flipped to the first page.

They worked slowly and painfully through the book—a story about a young alligator who has a horrible toothache but is too afraid to go to the dentist—with his mother gently correcting his pronunciation along the way and occasionally reading a page for him, trying to lighten the load. Though he knew the plot of the book was embarrassingly simple for a boy his age, and the idea of a bus-riding alligator in need of dental care was absurd, he was still relieved when Alli the alligator overcame his fear at the end of the book and finally agreed to go see the dentist.

"Theeeee end," Frank announced, though the words were not actually written on the page.

"And the moral?" his mother asked. It was her standard question at the end of every story. She stared over at him, one porcelain doll cheek hidden behind a wave of jet-black hair.

Frank nibbled at his thumbnail and considered her question. "And the moral is . . . that we need to be brave enough to face our fears?" He smiled as his mother nodded, then continued with more confidence. "And sometimes, once we do face them, we'll realize there was nothing to be afraid of in the first place."

"Good boy." She laughed, tousled his hair, and climbed halfway out of her seat to plant a kiss on the top of his head. Though not yet eleven, he was already an inch taller and at least ten pounds heavier than her.

Frank rose from the table, announced that he would return with pencil and paper, and marched out of the kitchen.

"Not today," his mother called after him. She pushed in their chairs, returned to the sink, and turned on the tap. "No composition today, Frank. You did a good job. And sometimes hard work deserves a special reward—even if that reward is just getting an earlier start on your chores."

Frank returned her smile, grateful for both the compliment and the last-minute reprieve. He crossed the kitchen, gave her a quick hug, then headed for his bedroom to change into his work clothes.

"Hey, Mom?" Frank eyeballed her from the hallway. He returned to the doorway of the kitchen and waited for her to look up from the dishes. "I just want you to know . . . that you're a good teacher." Her warm brown eyes pooled with tears. Frank smiled again, happy to see her happy. "And a darn good mom, too," he tossed in for good measure.

He considered giving her another hug, then remembered what his father had said about him being *"too old for that shit."* He waved awkwardly from the doorway instead, then tore down the hallway toward his room.

Out of his dress clothes at last, Frank descended the back stairs with a new sense of purpose. His spirits were lifted by the prospect of quickly completing his chores, then retreating to his bedroom, his mother's portable Crosley radio in hand, to listen to the baseball games.

He shot a nervous glance at the door of his father's workshop, which sat at the bottom of the stairs. Occupying the first floor of the two-story house, the workshop was accessible only from the outside. Thankfully, the door was closed. His father had done them all a favor and made himself scarce.

Frank now listened to all the Giants games in the privacy of his room, as his love for the team had become an itchy scab that Pop couldn't help but pick. While his dad rarely spoke about his upbringing in the Bronx (Frank knew almost nothing about his father's childhood, the families he and his mother had left behind, or the big "falling out" that kept them from returning to New York after the war), his love for the Yankees, and baseball in general, was the one piece of his youth that was always open for discussion.

Baseball was more than a game. Like the glue on Frank's model airplanes, it was the only thing bonding him and Pop together. And his dad fully expected that his love for the Yankees would be embraced by his son. So Frank's chosen allegiance—an act of rebellion in the eyes of his father—had created a rift that only grew wider as the seasons passed. And the World Series the previous year, when the Giants had come within one snagged line drive of beating the Yankees in game seven, had been intense—so intense that his mother stepped in to keep the peace, making Frank listen to the games on the radio in his bedroom, while his irate father watched them on the living room television by himself.

Frank paused to listen outside the workshop door, then crept by on tiptoes, trying to dampen the noise as his feet crunched over the gravel path that separated one side of the yard from the other. On the left side, his father had planted a long strip of tall fescue grass, which ran the length of the yard and was where Frank had spent countless hours with Pop, learning to throw and catch a baseball and hearing stories about Pop's exploits on the field when he was a boy.

The right side of the yard was occupied by a small wooden shed, his mother's vegetable garden, and a picnic table that his father had built the summer before. Though Frank loathed weeding the garden, he loved to spend time in the backyard, particularly in the summer, when the daylight lasted into the evening and his father actually arrived home from work in time for a game of catch.

Frank stood in the doorway of the shed and waited for his eyes to adjust to the darkness, crinkling his nose as he breathed the humid air, thick with the motley stench of fertilizer, gasoline, and bags of rotting yard waste. He entered cautiously, like he always did, waving one arm in large circles in front of him. He was wary of the cobwebs that were often strung from one side of the shed to the other, some still inhabited by their eight-legged architects.

Stepping around the gasoline lawn mower and dodging to avoid a rake that leaned against the wall, Frank moved to the back of the shed to collect the trowel and work gloves that he kept in a small metal bucket next to the dusty workbench. He crouched to grasp the dented red bucket, accidentally kicking a metallic object that skidded across the concrete floor before disappearing beneath the workbench.

Frank dropped to his knees. Curious to discover the source of the noise and praying to God that he hadn't broken something of his father's, he bent at the waist to press one sweaty cheek against the dirty floor. It was hard to see anything in the shadows, but he located the source of the noise—a metal box that had come to rest near the back wall. Frank flopped down on his belly, stretched an arm beneath the bench, and pulled the box into the open. It was old and made from tin. Partially covered in peeling red paint, the lid of the box was secured by hinges and fastened in the front by a rusty latch.

Frank returned to his knees. He turned his body toward the light from the door, unfastened the latch, and opened the lid. Despite the heat in the shed, a chill ran down his spine as he examined the box's contents—a silver lighter, a pack of Lucky Strikes, and a half-empty glass bottle, the words "Old Crow" emblazoned on the label.

Frank had seen booze in the house before, but only on those rare occasions when his father brought a small bottle home after work. He'd never seen it hidden in a box in the back of the shed. Struck by curiosity, he picked up the bottle of brownish liquor, removed the top, and was about to sniff its contents when the daylight filtering in from the open door was suddenly eclipsed.

Frank froze. Clutched in a shaking hand, the bottle hovered halfway between his lap and his face, suspended in a no man's land that felt like disaster.

"What the fuck do you think you're doing?" Pop asked, his words less a question than an accusation. He didn't wait for an answer, just burst through the door. Terrifyingly large in the cramped quarters of the shed, his features were frozen somewhere between scorn and disgust.

Frank's mind sputtered. He groped in the darkness for the right words to proclaim his innocence. Coming up with nothing better than *"I found it,"* he barely managed to spit out the words before his father seized him roughly by the arm and dragged him to his feet. He yanked the bottle from Frank's hand, spilling some of the booze on Frank's arm and filling the shed with its stench.

"I'm going to ask you one time," he warned, bending at the waist, his curled upper lip exposing tobacco-stained teeth. "Is this your booze? Your smokes?"

Frank shrank from his hot breath but managed to look him in the eye.

"No, Sir. I promise. I was in here to grab my gloves. I found the box, and I opened it to see what was inside. That's it. I swear."

His father slowly released his arm. He straightened to his full height, but his cold eyes remained locked on Frank, seemingly vibrating inside their sockets.

"Grab your things," Pop said. "Finish your chores." He grasped Frank's shoulder and held it for a beat, the closest to an apology he was likely to come.

Without waiting for a response, his father ducked under the low doorway. Bottle and box in hand, he tore down the gravel path and back toward the house.

Frank tried to catch his breath, which came in ragged gasps. Not for the first time, the hot fires of injustice burned deep in his chest. He knew he hadn't done anything wrong—that he didn't deserve the treatment he'd received—but he also knew that innocence didn't always matter. Not when Sergeant Salvatore Romano was on the case.

Fighting back tears he refused to shed, Frank listened as the back stairs groaned under his father's weight, then flinched as the door crashed shut behind him.

◇

"Hello?" Frank called, his voice barely a whisper. He poked his head through a narrow gap between the kitchen door and the frame. He held his breath and counted to ten, listening for sounds of his father from within but hearing only the steady hum of the refrigerator and the *tick-tick-ticking* of the clock on the kitchen wall.

He had taken his sweet time in the garden, checking then rechecking his work, afraid to go back into the house while his parents shouted angry curses in their bedroom that overlooked the backyard. Even when he was finished—when every stubborn weed was pulled and the bucket returned to the shed—he still lingered outside, legs dangling over the edge of the picnic table, wondering if it was safe to return.

Still shaken from the encounter with Pop, he crept like a cat burglar through the deserted house. He peered out through the bay windows in the living room, then breathed a sigh of relief when he saw that the Cadillac was gone. It was better that way.

Though he hadn't been able to hear their argument word for word, he knew that his father's anger had escalated to rage after he stormed out of the shed. At first, he couldn't understand why his father had been so mad. Or why he'd turned his anger on his mother. Then the pieces of the puzzle slowly arranged themselves in his mind. His father wouldn't hide his own booze and smokes. Which meant they must be hers.

He knew it was now well past noon, but time and the game had both ceased to matter. Frank worked slowly and carefully through the rest of his chores, then walked to the end of the hallway, where the door of his parents' room was pulled shut. He paused outside, listening for sounds. Hearing none, he tapped one dirt-crusted knuckle against the frame.

"What is it?" his mother asked.

Though the door was thin, her voice sounded muffled and far away. Sad.

"I'm done with my chores, Mom. Can you come to inspect, so I can be done?"

Frank waited in the hall, listening to his own shallow breaths. His mother's inspection, and earning her official seal of approval, was an important part of their weekly routine and one that was never skipped.

He leaned his cheek against the cool wooden surface of the door, his concern mounting as the seconds crawled by and it remained closed, his mother hidden behind it.

"You're okay this week," she said at last. More seconds ticked by. "You're a good boy, Francesco; I'm sure you did fine. You always do."

Frank shifted his weight from one foot to the other, feeling hollow and confused, unsure of what to say or how to say it. He wanted to help her, to make all this better, but he didn't know where to begin.

He listened for another few seconds outside her door, raised his hand to knock again, then changed his mind and retraced his steps down the hallway.

Frank stopped in the kitchen on his way to his bedroom, washed the caked earth off his hands, and grabbed the handheld radio from its spot next to the sink. Somehow, things felt different now. *He* felt different. Sadder, maybe, and more alone.

The bed creaked as Frank stretched his body across it and clutched the radio to his chest. His eyes traced the spiderweb of cracks in the ceiling as angry words and images swirled unchecked through his mind. He didn't care how strong the word was—he *hated* it. Hated the way Pop treated them. How he treated *her*.

His breath caught in his chest.

Frank sobbed. It was a pitiful noise, one that escaped his lips before he could seal them shut. He wanted to cry, but crying was for women and babies—and he was neither—so he switched on the radio instead.

Frank's breathing slowed as the sounds of the ballpark washed over him and his anger and sadness drained away.

They were gone now: his parents and his worries, his anger and his fear. Only he and the game remained.

Chapter 3

Age 14

February 17, 1967

Frank sat at the end of the bench, his long legs stretched in front of him, powerful arms folded across his chest. A large mass of sunflower seeds bulged from his left cheek, his tongue and teeth working in tandem to separate seeds from shells.

"Like lambs to the slaughter, huh Romano?" It was the cocky Baxter kid, his voice dripping with an unmistakable note of satisfaction. He nodded in the direction of the Washington High infield, where the boys from Group B milled about in small clusters, anxiously awaiting judgment.

No one had told them to organize this way, to separate into the groups they had been assigned after the first day of junior varsity tryouts, once the opening round of cuts had been made. They had done it of their own accord, a silent nod to the now-established pecking order and their respective places within it.

Frank spit a seed into the dirt. "Not so much." He offered a lukewarm smile to Ray and the other members of Group A, who were carrying on boisterous conversations throughout the dugout, then turned his attention back to the lost souls wandering around the infield. "Because the lambs don't know what's coming."

It wasn't difficult to surmise how the groups had been formed. After Wednesday's cuts, when the field of forty-three had been whittled down to thirty, Frank and seven others had been placed into Group A, the select few who had almost certainly made the eighteen-man squad based on their reputations and first-day performance alone. Castillo and Richards were also freshmen. Frank knew them from previous Little League seasons, and both of them had played with him on last year's city-wide all-star team. Four others, sophomores who Frank didn't know, were returning players from the previous year's JV squad.

The seventh boy, this Ray Baxter kid who had moved to the city from Sacramento the previous summer, was the biggest surprise of the week. A lanky redhead with a constellation of freckles blanketing pale and skinny arms, Ray sure didn't look like much. But his narrow shoulders and slim build were deceiving—he could throw the ball harder than anyone on the field, with the possible exception of Frank.

The other twenty-two boys—some Frank knew, most he didn't—had been lumped into Group B, to compete for the final ten spots. While Frank and the boys in Group A had already developed an easy camaraderie, laughing and messing around between drills, he sensed the atmosphere in Group B was different. Tense and anxious. They had no illusions about where they stood, and they knew darn well that the majority of them would not be wearing an Eagles uniform when the season began in three weeks.

"Here they come," Ray said. He rubbed his hands together and looked to the deserted parking lot, where the team's coaches, Rogers and Baker, marched in lockstep toward the field. Rogers, the head coach, had a clipboard in one hand, while Baker carried a large mesh bag bulging with gray and scarlet jerseys and hats.

"Yep, looks like it," Frank agreed. He spit a seed at the chain-link fence that separated the first base dugout from the field. "Judgment Day is upon us."

Despite the gravity of his tone, Frank was certain his name would be amongst those called. Groupings aside, he had put on quite a clinic throughout the three-day tryout, showing off his strong arm, powerful bat, and the defensive ability to play any position on the diamond. Though running was not his strong suit, even his sixty-yard dash had been impressive, good for third place within the forty-three-man field.

"Hey, bring it in," Coach Baker boomed, instantly commanding the attention of every boy on the field. A standout player at Washington High more than a decade before, with powerful legs and arms that put even Frank to shame, the man might as well have been chiseled out of marble. Armed with a mouth like a megaphone, Coach Baker spoke, and all the boys listened. "Everybody around the mound, fellas. C'mon, let's go!"

Trotting behind Ray, Frank followed the procession out of the dugout, joining those boys who had already formed a semicircle around the mound. Frank positioned himself in the back of the group, close to the first base line, behind those who kneeled in the front. He pulled the brim of his cap lower on his forehead, shielding his eyes against the sun, which was beginning to set behind the left field fence. The temperature had dropped rapidly, and Frank regretted not slipping into his sweatshirt before leaving the dugout.

Coach Rogers arrived at the mound. He kicked deliberately at the dirt in front of the rubber and waited for Baker to put down the mesh bag before handing off his clipboard. Much older than Baker, Rogers was tall and thin, with a rounded gut that seemed out of place on his otherwise angular frame.

"Sun's getting ready to set," Rogers began, hooking his thumbs into his belt loops, then pausing to stare at the puffy bank of purple and orange clouds floating over left field.

Frank shot daggers at Ray Baxter, who was giggling under his breath. This was the way Coach Rogers always spoke. With a slow cadence and an accent no one could quite place, the man sounded like a sheriff in a bad western film, and he took a circuitous route to every point he made.

"I know you're all ready to hear the names on that list," Rogers continued, "but before Coach Baker ends your collective suffering, I want to take this opportunity to commend each and every one of you for the effort you put in this week."

Met with silence and nervous stares, the coach pressed on, gaining momentum and clearly enjoying the moment. "It takes courage to do what you young men did this week—to wager on yourselves, to risk failure in the pursuit of a personal goal. It's a mark of character that you boys showed up in the first place."

He paused again, his eyes locking and lingering on Frank, then continued.

"And for those who don't make the team, I encourage you to keep that spirit alive. Keep putting yourself out there, be willing to take some risks, and try new things."

Frank nodded, scanning the faces of the boys around him. A few, Ray Baxter in particular, looked relaxed and self-assured. But most of them looked anxious, if not downright scared.

"And on that note," Rogers concluded, gesturing to his young assistant, "over to you, Coach Baker."

Baker stepped forward, clipboard in hand, and ran his fingers through his impeccable flattop while he surveyed each face in the group. The sandy flattop, combined with the neatly trimmed mustache and navy-blue San Francisco Fire Department T-shirt, gave the man an almost military bearing.

"Like Coach Rogers," Baker said, slowly panning across the crowd, "I'm proud of all you boys. You showed a lot of guts this week, and I wish we could keep every one of you. Unfortunately, though, I only have eighteen hats and jerseys in this bag, so some of you are shit out of luck."

Frank laughed at the coach's joke. It came as no surprise that the man ran into burning buildings for a living. Baker was a hard-ass, for sure, but he understood the game on a deeper level than anyone Frank knew, and he had a wry sense of humor that all the boys enjoyed.

As the laughter subsided, Baker pressed on in a more serious tone. "I'm going to read off these eighteen names. If your name is read, you made the team, and you can meet me by the bleachers to divvy up hats and jerseys. If your name is *not read*," he continued, his voice rising while annunciating carefully, "it means you *did not* make the squad. But you have an entire year to regroup, develop your skills, and be ready for next year's tryouts. Any questions?"

Frank shook his head, hoping that no one would ask a dumb question and delay this slow-moving train from reaching the station. He was excited to receive his cap and jersey and even more excited to take them home and show his father. It was hard to keep Pop's attention for more than a few minutes at a time, but his nightly recaps of the tryouts had been all they'd talked about over dinner for the last two nights.

Baker cleared his throat and launched into the list. "Ryan, Nosse, Chamberlin," he called.

None of the first three names belonged to players assigned to Group A. Coach Baker continued reading from the sheet, listing additional names of boys who'd been assigned to Group B, while Frank counted roster spots in his head. Frank had already reached eleven by the time Baker paused, shuffled papers on the clipboard, and produced a separate sheet.

"Shit," Frank muttered, suddenly unsure of himself. He did the math again in his head. Forty-three boys had shown up on Monday, with thirty remaining after the first cut. Eight kids, essentially shoo-ins, had been placed in Group A, meaning the other twenty-two were competing for ten of the eighteen spots. Though it made no sense why eleven names had been called from Group B, he was sure his math was sound.

"Hunt, Resing, Duggan," Baker called. He nodded to each of the boys as they walked toward the gaggle of kids that formed in front of the bleachers.

All three names belonged to kids in Group A. Frank shifted his weight from one foot to the other and wiped his damp palms on the legs of his baseball pants.

Baker cleared his throat again, then read the remaining names on the list. "Castillo, Richards, Mahurien, and . . . Baxter."

Reality landed like a sucker punch to the gut. A wave of nausea swept over him, and he clenched his jaw to avoid puking in the dirt.

"All right, boys, that's the list," Coach Rogers broke in. "Thanks again to everyone who tried out, and congratulations to those who made the squad." He led a brief round of applause, in which Frank was too devastated to join.

He was frozen in disbelief. Hands hanging like bricks at his sides, Frank struggled to make sense of it all. *Had there been a mistake? Had he missed his name?*

He replayed each day of the tryouts in his mind, searching for mistakes he had made, trying to understand what he'd done to miss the cut. With the exception of a poor read on a flyball, which he'd still caught, and getting out in front of a couple of curveballs during batting practice, his performance had been flawless.

He wanted to flee, to sprint off the field and not stop until he got home, but his cleats were rooted in the dirt. The other boys streamed off the field, careful to give him a wide berth, gawking as if Frank were one of those pitiful polio patients in their textbooks and they were all terrified they'd be next.

Ray was the only one who took the risk. He placed a freckled hand on Frank's shoulder, then gave it a reassuring squeeze.

"Sorry, Romano." Ray offered that it might have been a mistake, that Frank's tryout had been the best of the week, but even he sounded unconvinced.

Frank mumbled his thanks, his eyes glued to the dirt as if a remedy for his shame and disappointment were lying somewhere at his feet, then returned to the dugout for his belongings. He shoved his mitt into the duffel bag, already bracing himself for his father's eruption and the days-long ass-chewing that would surely follow.

"Romano!"

Frank looked up, recognizing Coach Baker's voice. Standing next to the bleachers, separated from the field by the chain-link backstop, the coach had been watching him. Frank felt a hot flush engulf his cheeks; he was all the more embarrassed for having been observed in his sulking.

"Coach Rogers and I want to speak to you." Baker's tone was annoyingly light, as if the whole world hadn't just ended. "Grab your stuff and meet us in the bullpen in ten."

⋄

FRANK NERVOUSLY APPROACHED THE BULLPEN, the cramped office space that stood adjacent to the boy's locker room and served as a clubhouse for PE teachers and coaches, then peered inside the open door.

Coach Rogers was visible inside, his feet kicked up on the room's only desk, providing a bored-looking Baker a long-winded description of how to prepare the perfect steak. Frank waited to be noticed, then finally gave up and rapped loudly on the metal frame of the door to announce his presence.

"Ah, Francisco," Rogers called from behind the battered metal desk. He swung his legs off its surface and planted his feet on the floor. "C'mon in, son, take a seat."

Frank navigated around a basketball rack and dropped his duffel bag on the sticky linoleum floor. The bullpen, like the locker room, smelled of damp gym socks, disinfectant, and the type of cheap cologne pretty boys like Shane Richards bought in bulk and reapplied generously throughout the day.

"Uh, actually, it's *Francesco*, Coach. But most everybody calls me Frank."

He accepted a seat in one of the two folding metal chairs positioned in front of the desk. Coach Baker grabbed the other, dragged it noisily around the desk, and sat to Rogers's right.

"Most everybody, huh?" Coach Rogers sighed, then continued. "All right, Frank. Coach and I wanted to have a word with you. About a couple of things, actually. First, how do you think your tryout went?"

Frank froze like a deer. Mesmerized by the headlights, he stopped to consider. Had he been asked that question thirty minutes ago, his answer would have been summed up with two thumbs and a smile. Now he was unsure, his recollections tainted by failure and self-doubt.

"I thought it went okay," he began, shrugging his shoulders, "but I guess I have a lot of room to improve." He paused to compile a mental list, then began his recitation. "I misread a flyball on Thursday, had to make the throw to the cutoff man off my back foot. And I got out in front of a couple of curveballs during batting practice; hit 'em hard but pulled them both foul. And my bullpen session wasn't great, but, honestly, I'd rather catch than pitch anyway."

The coaches exchanged an odd glance, then Rogers cleared his throat. "Frank, while I appreciate your modesty and, uh, self-deprecation, 'okay' is probably the last adjective I would use to describe your tryout. Forced to narrow it down to one, I think I'd settle on 'outstanding' or something darn close."

Frank rubbed at his temple, more confused than ever, and made a mental note to look up the meaning of *self-deprecation* when he got home. He couldn't make sense of the coach's words. If his tryout had been so amazing, why had his name been left off the list?

"Thanks, coach," Frank muttered. Painfully aware of every muscle in his body, he sat up straighter in his seat and tried to erase the childish pout from his face. "That means a lot to me."

"But not as much as making the team, right?" Rogers meandered out from behind the desk, perched his lanky frame on its corner, and crossed his thin arms over his ample midsection.

"Frank, with the tryout you had this week, I'd be hard-pressed not to add you to the varsity squad. Twenty-five years I've been coaching this team, seventeen as the head coach, and eight before that as an assistant. In all those years, this was one of the top five freshman tryouts I've seen." He paused and looked to his nodding assistant for confirmation, letting his point hit home.

"The *reason*," he continued, "that you won't be an Eagle this year, varsity or otherwise, is because you're not academically eligible."

Academically eligible? Frank chewed on the words, which stuck to his teeth and gums like a mouthful of peanut butter. Delivered in the middle of the bullpen, in front of a rolling blackboard covered in a swarm of x's and o's, the coach's words might as well have been spoken in Greek.

"Simply put, son, your grades stink. In fact, they're worse than that. To *stink* would require improvement. You're failing half of your classes and barely skating by in the other half. Hell, I can't even let you come to practices on probationary status."

Frank looked from Rogers to Baker, then Baker back to Rogers. Yelling was something he was used to; this type of quiet disappointment was a whole lot worse. And while he knew his grades were bad, none of that had ever mattered before. Not when it came to baseball.

"Listen, Frank," Baker broke in, "you're a talented athlete. Maybe talented enough to play college ball in a few years. And you're smart, too. The way you understand the game, how you do all the little things that coaches love to see. All that takes intelligence. Intelligence and effort. And that's what we can't make sense of. How can a bright kid, who is so dedicated and hardworking on the field, be so goddamn lazy off of it?" Both men sat in silence, waiting for Frank's reply.

Slow seconds crawled by. Frank wanted to respond, but he

was afraid that opening his mouth would mean opening the floodgates. And he refused to cry. Not here, not anywhere.

"Okay, Frank," Rogers said, a note of compassion seeping into his voice. "We're not trying to add insult to injury. But I'll say one last thing before you go. And I want you to listen up. We've seen your potential, Frank, the type of young man you are, and we know what you can do out there on that field. Now we want to see what you can do *off the field*." He cracked his bony knuckles as Frank slowly raised his eyes.

"Now, I told you that I can't let you practice, but that doesn't mean I can prevent you from showing up at the field every once and a while. So, I'm gonna ask Coach Baker here to keep an eye on you and follow your progress as you turn those grades around."

Frank's eyes darted to Coach Baker, who seemed just as surprised as Frank by Rogers's announcement. Baker's mouth flew open to interject, then he shut it again just as quickly, his closed lips forming a straight line beneath the sandy mustache.

"We never have games on Mondays," Rogers continued, "so I want you to drop by every Monday, talk a little baseball with Coach Baker, and keep him apprised of your efforts. In fact, I think this little arrangement could be good for both of you." Rogers turned to his assistant coach, offered a subtle nod, then returned his attention to Frank. "You good with that, son?"

Frank dug deep and finally found his voice. "Yeah, Coach. I'm good with that. Every Monday."

"All right, then, Frank." Rogers stood, hiked up his pants, and returned to his seat behind the desk. "You should probably get on home then. Hit the books, huh?"

Frank grabbed his duffel and made awkwardly for the door.

"And keep practicing in the meantime," Baker added, a kind smile emerging from beneath the bristly mustache. "Tryouts are only a year away."

FRANK WAS in no hurry to get home. Far from it.

He decided to forego the city bus, walk the long way, and drown his misery in the sounds of the city. The shock of the coaches' announcement was beginning to fade, and the reality of a year without baseball was setting in.

Already, he felt an aching sense of loss. There was an emptiness inside of him now, a lonely void that threatened to swallow him whole. As much of a screw-up as he was off the field—as Pop constantly reminded him—he was a different person *on* the field. Capable and confident. The kind of kid he *wanted* to be.

But the pity party had to wait. The more pressing concern, the one that had dominated his thoughts as he made the long trek home, was how to explain this failure to his father.

Though the gulf between them was wider than ever, baseball still bridged the gap, providing their sole means of connection. Take the game away, and it was hard to imagine finding any middle ground. He could already envision the look of anger and disappointment that would soon be written across Pop's face.

Frank rounded the corner of his block, leaned forward into the gusting wind, and stuffed his hands deep into his pockets to ward off the winter chill. He stopped under the street sign and scanned the row of cars parked up and down Spruce Street, relieved to discover that the blue Cadillac was not among them.

He shuffled up the stairs in darkness, slid his key into the lock, and wondered why the porch light wasn't lit.

"Hello…" he ventured.

Though the entryway was dark, shadows flickered from the family room, accompanied by muted sounds from the television. Frank paused before crossing the threshold. He listened for sounds of his mother in the kitchen, where dinner should be almost ready by now, but the rest of the house was deathly quiet. He shut the door behind him, the familiar knot of dread forming deep in his gut.

Frank's mind returned often to that day in the shed—discovering the bottle of bourbon in its battered tin box, being interrogated by his father, then listening to his mother's frail voice, his ear pressed against her bedroom door. That was the first of many bottles he would find, concealed in the bottom of the pantry or tucked in the back of a closet. At some point, though, all pretenses were dropped. She stopped hiding her bottles, and his father stopped pretending he cared.

Frank's nostrils flared as he entered the family room, and he was overcome by the foul stench of cigarettes. That was another new development, her smoking in the house. He stood in the darkness, hands on his hips, angry that she'd chosen today of all days to hit the bottle early.

The only light came from the television, where scenes of *The Andy Griffith Show* cast an intermittent glow across the room. His mother, so small and frail, was asleep on the pea-green sofa, a half-empty glass balanced precariously on her chest and an orange-and-brown Afghan covering her lower half.

Slowly, careful not to wake her, Frank removed the glass from his mother's hand, placing it atop the end table, next to the nearly empty bottle of Old Crow. He stooped to switch off the television, silencing Barney Fife, whose limbs were flailing across the screen in a haphazard display of comedic agitation.

Frank walked to his bedroom and sat at the foot of his bed. He pressed his back against the wall and hugged his knees to his chest. He longed to talk to his mother. Not the pale ghost of his mother in the other room but the woman he'd grown up with, the one who always knew the right words to say. And who was always there when he needed her. But those opportunities were fleeting and rare, and each mess he cleaned left him feeling more like a parent than a child, more like her caretaker than her son.

Staring across the room at the wooden dresser, one knob missing from the middle of the three drawers, Frank replayed the afternoon's events in his mind's eye for the thousandth time. His brain kept returning to the same two words—*goddamn lazy*. Though Coach Baker's criticism had cut like a knife, it was hard to argue with his logic. *Failing half of your classes and barely skating by in the other half.* The coaches weren't wrong.

For as long as Frank could remember, he had always gravitated toward baseball. The game had always come so easily to him, its rhythm feeling so natural. And the more success he'd had on the diamond, the more his confidence had grown and the more he'd wanted to play.

But school had always been a battle. Every subject required reading, so nothing had *ever* come easily. And the more he struggled, the less confidence he had and the less he wanted to try. Even when he was nearly held back, it didn't really seem to matter. Not because he wanted to fail, or to be the type of person who accepted failure, but because he was not defined by what happened in the classroom. It was his life on the field that mattered. At least to Pop.

Frank crossed the room. He studied his reflection in the mirror atop the bureau. Sometimes he hated it—how much he resembled *him*. The face that stared back hardly seemed like his own, being much closer to that of a man than a boy. And with manhood came responsibilities.

His world had changed with the reading of the list. Being cut from the team had shown him that the bar of expectation had been raised. Continuing to do the thing he loved meant finding a way to succeed at something he didn't. Those were the new rules of the game, rules he would have to play by.

Frank leaned closer, his hot breath fogging the mirror. He nodded solemnly and stared into deep blue eyes; an unspoken promise was made. He would change. He would be better. Not for Pop—or even to save himself *from* Pop—but for himself.

Frank hurried back to the family room. He emptied the ashtray, then removed the glass and bottle from the end table. Bending down, he shook his mother's shoulder, gently at first, then harder when she didn't respond.

She awoke with a start and stared up with wild, red-rimmed eyes. "Jesus Christ, you scared me! What is it? What's wrong?"

Frank swallowed his anger. *What was wrong?* He didn't know where to begin.

"Nothing, Ma," he lied, trying not to resent her for all that she wasn't. Or Pop for making her this way. "But you need to wake up. It's almost six o'clock. He'll be home soon."

Chapter 4

Age 17

April 24, 1970

*A*rrogant prick. The words exploded into Frank's mind unbidden, spoken in his father's voice and sounding as clear and distinct as if they'd been whispered in his ear by the man himself.

He shot an angry look to second base, where the runner was toying with him, standing at least ten feet off the bag, rubbing a handful of dirt between his palms. Frank glanced over his shoulder, raised his right hand, and asked the home plate umpire for a timeout.

"Time!" the umpire barked, eliciting a chorus of boos from the healthy contingent of Lincoln fans who had made the trip from the Sunset District and clustered in the third base bleachers behind the visiting team's dugout.

Frank leapt out of his squat from behind home plate, removed his mask, and trotted toward the mound. Ray Baxter stared quizzically back from his perch atop the rubber, then advanced to meet his catcher at the edge of the mound. Castillo, Richards, and Mahurien jogged in from their respective positions at second base, shortstop, and third.

"He's going to take third base," Frank warned, concealing his mouth behind his mitt so his lips could not be read by opposing coaches and players.

"Ah, shit, Frank. Now why the hell would he do that?" Baxter spoke into a cupped hand, looking to his infielders for support. "There's only one out, he's already in scoring position, and their best hitter is at the plate. He's just trying to get under your skin, man."

"Trust me on this. This guy's as cocky as they come. Even with a lefty in the box, he's going to make a break for it. Ray, I want a fastball on the outside corner on the first pitch, then a pitchout on the next one." He cut his eyes to his infielders. "Richards, try to hold him close to the bag at second. Mahurien, stay close enough to the bag that you're ready to take the throw on either pitch if he's running. Understand?"

All four nodded in agreement, knowing better than to question their star catcher's intuition. Frank returned to his position behind the plate. He signaled to the umpire that they were ready to resume, then eyed the runner at second base, who was already strutting off the bag to reclaim his generous lead.

The runner on second base was Leon Jefferson, Lincoln's star center fielder and leadoff man, and his blazing speed was already the stuff of urban legends. He'd reached first base on a bunt single, narrowly beating Frank's throw, then exploited Ray's high leg kick to steal second uncontested. Crouching in a wide stance, a hand on each knee, he swung his hips slowly back and forth over well-muscled thighs; the effect was simultaneously menacing and nonchalant.

Frank glanced at the scoreboard over the left field fence, below the bright bank of metal halide lamps, confirming what he already knew. It was the top of the seventh and final inning, and Washington was clinging to a tenuous 2-1 lead. The Eagles' only runs of the game had come on Frank's first-inning home run, while the Mustangs had trimmed the lead to one when Jefferson had walked to lead off the fifth inning, then scored all the way from first on a double down the right field line.

Baxter glanced back at Jefferson, came set, and dealt a knee-high fastball that grazed the outside corner of the plate for a called strike. Jimmy Davis, the Mustangs' first baseman and number three hitter, shot a quick look at the umpire, delivering the message that he did not agree with the call. Jefferson, not even feigning on the first pitch, trotted back to second base.

Flashing the pitchout sign again, on the off chance that Ray had forgotten the strategy, Frank readied himself to jump out of his crouch, receive the pitchout, and make the throw to third base.

The righty came set. He prepared to deliver, and Jefferson was digging for third base before the ball even left Baxter's hand. Frank leapt from behind home plate, caught the pitch, and in one fluid motion transferred the ball from his glove to his bare hand and rifled a strike down the baseline into Matt Mahurien's waiting mitt.

Jefferson barreled down the baseline, powerful legs pumping like pistons on a locomotive, then dove into a headfirst slide, his arms outstretched, fingers searching for purchase aboard the base. Mahurien applied the tag, sweeping his glove across Jefferson's outstretched fingers milliseconds before they came to rest on the base.

"Out!" The umpire's call was eclipsed by the roar of the home crowd and a renewed chorus of boos from the visiting fans.

Jefferson stared long and hard across the field at Frank. He shook his head, then brushed the dirt off the front of his red and gold uniform and jogged slowly back to the dugout.

Frank smiled beneath his mask. He winked at Ray, then sneaked a quick peek into the stands, where Pop was seated in the bottom row. His father's face was a blank slate, expressionless under the bright artificial lights; if he was impressed by Frank's perfect throw, or by anything else he'd done on the field, he certainly didn't show it.

Ray speared the return throw from Matt Mahurien and returned to the mound. He needed only two more pitches, successive curveballs, to strike out Davis, record the final out, and bring the game to a close.

Frank whooped loudly as he secured the final pitch in his mitt. He pumped his fist, then gathered with the rest of the team on the infield grass, exchanging handshakes and congratulatory slaps on the back. It was moments like these, when the rest of the world melted away and only the team remained, that made him feel truly alive.

◇

"Francesco!"

Frank flinched at the sound of his father's voice, a commanding baritone that cracked like a whip from the far end of the dugout. He dropped his duffel on the ground, discarded his shin guards and mask, and fought through a cluster of bodies to reach the opposite side of the fenced enclosure.

"Hey, Pop. Helluva game, huh?" Frank eyed his father warily through the chain-link fence. He ran dirt-stained fingers through his black mane, sweeping the damp hair back and away from his face.

"That Jefferson kid is a real piece of work," his father replied, discarding with pleasantries and going straight for the jugular. "I thought he was going to embarrass you—again—but you made a decent throw when you needed to."

Frank felt the bile rising in his throat. He'd heard every possible form of this lecture before, and it always ended the same: *Do better next time.*

He stole a glance behind him, checking to see if anyone was within earshot. Most of his teammates were busy packing up their gear or excitedly recapping the final plays of the game. Only Coach Baker, who was standing at the opposite end of the dugout, arms folded across his broad chest, seemed to be taking an interest in their conversation.

"Of course, the game wouldn't have been as close," his father continued predictably, ignoring Frank's growing discomfort, "if you hadn't stranded two men in the third."

"It was a ball, Pop," Frank protested. "There's not much I can do about a missed call."

"A ball, maybe, but too close to take with two strikes. You know better than that."

Frank's hackles rose. He sniffed the bait but refused to bite, knowing the wiser play was to turn the other cheek. "I'm going out with some of the guys tonight," he offered instead. "Don't worry; I'll be home by curfew."

"Out with the guys, huh?" His father's eyes narrowed. Long seconds ticked by as he deliberated. "It's fine, I guess, but your mother expected you home for dinner tonight. She's feeling well today, or was, when I left. Well enough to put a meal on the table, anyway."

Frank nodded, easily decoding his father's not-so-subtle message. *Feeling well* meant his mother was sober, which was a rare occasion indeed. Frank felt a stab of guilt for squandering the opportunity, but he quickly set his guilt aside. If she really cared, she would have joined Pop for the game, something she hadn't done in ages. Say what you want about his father—and Frank had plenty to say, though never to Pop's face—but at least his old man showed up.

"I got it, Pop." Frank retreated to the other end of the dugout and sat at the end of the bench to pack his gear.

"Don't let him get under your skin, Frank." It was Coach Baker. Standing beside him now, he watched Frank intently, the strong muscles of his jaw working furiously to grind a piece of gum into submission. "I'm serious, kid. Shake it off and move on. You played a great game. We both know that. Just because you don't hear it from your old man doesn't mean it's not true."

Frank nodded slowly, knowing that Baker was right. Baker

made a habit of being right. Though Frank had dreaded their weekly chats in the beginning, feeling like he and his academics were under a microscope, he'd soon found himself looking forward to the visits.

In the three years since his ill-fated freshman tryout, Frank had formed a relationship with Baker that extended well beyond the boundaries of the baseball diamond. Eventually, after a year of listening to Frank recount his troubles at home, Baker even opened up about his own life—about his time in the Air Force, spent mostly on some dusty airstrip in the middle of Oklahoma, manning a firetruck on the edge of a taxiway. And about the woman he'd met there, then married when he was only twenty-two. Even about the son he'd been forced to leave behind when his contract was up, and their marriage went down in flames.

Baker listened to Frank in a way Pop never did, and he was always good for a pep talk. Sometimes in the bullpen after practice, other times down at Mel's Drive-in over a burger and a strawberry shake. It was Baker who had helped Frank find the confidence he needed to succeed in the classroom. And it was also Baker who had pushed, poked, and prodded until he'd finally submitted those college applications the previous fall.

"Yeah, I know, I know," Frank acknowledged, grateful, as always, for Baker's kindness. "I promise, I do." He rose from the bench and grabbed his duffel. "Doesn't mean I can't be a bit pissed off, though, right?"

"No, it doesn't," Baker conceded. He reached up and rested a meaty hand on Frank's shoulder. "And speaking of pissed off, that's what I'm going to be on Monday afternoon if I find out you boys got into any trouble tonight." He chewed his gum slowly, his eyes locked with Frank's. "I mean it, kid. This was a huge win, and you boys deserve to celebrate. But I know how Big Ray gets, especially when he has a couple of beers in him."

The "Big Ray" nickname was no joke. Always tall for his age, the once skinny kid from Sacramento had filled out substantially since freshman year. Though not as muscular as Frank, he was an inch taller and at least twenty pounds heavier. And he'd never met a beer he didn't like.

"Gotcha, Coach," Frank said, shirking off Baker's hand and flashing his most reassuring smile. "We'll be on our best behavior. Scout's honor." Frank slung his duffel over his shoulder and darted out of the dugout, knowing, as did Baker, that he'd never been a Boy Scout.

⚾

WHILE FRANK WAS the team's undisputed leader when they were *on the field*, everyone knew that "Big Ray" Baxter was calling the shots *off the field*, particularly on Friday nights, when spirits were high, and the boys were ready to cut loose. Despite Frank's assurances, Baker had ample cause for concern.

Parading around the locker room after the game—with one towel wrapped around his waist and another coiled tightly in his hands, ready to snap at teammates' backsides as they walked by—Ray had rushed the team through the showers, shouting out strings of obscenities that were often punctuated by the vicious snap of wet terrycloth on bare ass. Though Frank practiced a different style of leadership, Ray's special brand of encouragement had achieved its desired effect, and the boys were showered, dressed in their Friday night best, and crammed into booths at Mel's Drive-in on Geary within an hour of the final pitch.

"You planning to party tonight?" Matt Mahurien shouted from across the booth. He inspected Frank's attire with a raised eyebrow and more than a hint of pretty boy contempt.

While most of his teammates were wearing bell-bottom pants and colorful patterned shirts unbuttoned to the sternum to expose mostly bare chests, Frank stuck with his usual: a faded pair of blue jeans and a gray GW Baseball T-shirt, a scarlet eagle soaring across his chest.

"We'll see," Frank said. He shrugged his shoulders and

pretended to give it serious consideration, though both he and Matt already knew the answer was no.

For all his panache on the field, Frank was still painfully shy when he was off of it, and he felt like a fish out of water around *the capital G's*—Gatherings and Girls. Stuffed in the middle seat of a red, vinyl, semi-circular booth at the back of the diner, he was more than content to let his teammates carry the conversation, or what he could hear of it over the loud music and general hubbub from surrounding tables.

"Oh, shit," Mahurien said, giving Frank a pass and directing everyone's attention to the scene outside. "There goes our boy!"

Parked in front of the diner, separated from their booth by only a thin pane of glass, was a cherry-red Camaro with its stereo blasting. A tight-skirted blonde, with a voice that played second fiddle to her figure, was perched on the hood, shouting out the lyrics to Neil Diamond's "Sweet Caroline." Watching through the glass, Frank was relieved when Ray Baxter joined the group around the Camaro, signaled for the car's owner to turn down the volume, and struck up a conversation that marked the end of the girl's ill-fated solo.

Ray knew his role and played it well. As the team's designated point-man for extracurricular activities, he took it upon himself to make the rounds, slapping backs and shaking hands, and ultimately finding out where the party would be later that night. Ray returned quickly from outside. He called for the group's attention, then stood importantly in front of their cluster of tables and booths, waiting for conversations to be silenced.

"Spit it out, you freckled freak," yelled Jorge Castillo. He tossed a French fry in Ray's direction but missed badly, hitting a girl at a neighboring table instead.

Frank cringed and mouthed an apology to the girl on Jorge's behalf. Castillo, an even bigger booze hound than Ray, had been sipping cheap whiskey from a silver flask since they'd left the locker room, and he was already slurring his words.

"First off," Ray said, "piss off, Jorge. Next, and more importantly... I've got a line on a keg party."

The news was met with a round of applause from the team, with the exception of Frank, who was less than enthused. The last time he'd agreed to join them at a party, he'd been unable to get a ride home in time for his eleven o'clock curfew, and his father's justice had been swift.

"Plenty of beer and plenty of girls," Ray continued, flashing his palms to quiet the cheers, "but it's not kicking off until ten, which means there's no point in showing up until eleven. Until then, beers at my place!"

◆

FRANK STOOD ON THE SIDEWALK, fiddling with the band of his watch, fighting the urge to check it again. Though it was barely past nine o'clock when the gaggle of boys arrived at the peeling front door to Ray's dilapidated three-story apartment building on Clay Street, his guilt about missing dinner at home was getting the better of him, and he was already anxious about making it back in time for curfew. His last *infraction*—a favorite term of his father's—had clipped his wings for a month. It was a mistake he wasn't planning to repeat.

Frank reluctantly agreed to come inside and followed Ray up the narrow flight of stairs and into the second-story apartment. While other kids his age might have been self-conscious about living in squalor, Ray took it all in stride. Hell, he practically embraced it.

His mom worked two jobs, one of which kept her out past midnight on a regular basis, and his father had been "out of the picture" since he and his two younger brothers moved from Sacramento before freshman year. The few times Frank had been there, the crowded two-bedroom apartment had been littered with trash and smelled more like a locker room than a family dwelling.

Frank followed Ray into the entry hall, waded through piles

of dirty clothes, and stepped over a kid-size bicycle that had been dumped unceremoniously in front of the coffee table. Ray's younger brothers were nowhere to be seen, but empty fast-food bags and French fries scattered across the cushions of the sagging couch indicated the kids weren't long gone.

"Take a seat," Ray said, gesturing to the couch and tearing into one of the cases of Coors that he'd finagled from "his connection" at the corner liquor store.

Frank cleared a spot on the fry-laden couch, took a seat, and watched as the rest of the boys stormed through the door, most with open beers in their hands and laughter on their lips. He was already plotting his escape, hopefully one that didn't lead to a long round of ball-busting from his teammates.

"Brewski?" Ray offered. He was clutching an unopened beer, his arm cocked back, ready to toss it underhand in Frank's direction.

Frank steered clear of alcohol in the same way he avoided large gatherings and pretty girls. He'd witnessed its effects on both of his parents—the fits and the fights, the heated late-night arguments followed by icy next-day stalemates—and he had no interest in following them down that path. He shook his head, this time not even pretending to deliberate, then made room on the couch for Matt Mahurien and Tommy Grzelak, a lanky blond who seemed to persist entirely on a steady diet of Dr. Pepper and menthol cigarettes.

Frank spent much of the next hour and a half drifting in and out of various competing conversations, glancing covertly at his watch, and trying to decipher the fast-paced banter of Johnny Carson and his *Tonight Show* guest, Tony Curtis. He felt a slight headache forming behind his eyes, likely a product of the stifling heat in Ray's apartment, combined with the noise made by his increasingly drunk teammates. Most of them were huddled around Ray's second-hand kitchen table, competing to bounce quarters off its surface and into a glass, hooting and hollering in unison every time a coin rattled noisily home.

"Okay, fellas," Ray announced finally, "it's time to finish the beers and head out."

Frank knew this was his moment. With only twenty minutes to get home, he rose from the couch and edged his way toward the door. He was hoping for an opportunity to slip quietly into the hall, which was presented by Jorge Castillo when he staggered to the bathroom, one hand covering his mouth, to relieve his stomach of its flask of cheap whiskey.

Frank watched as the rest of the team cheered him on and trailed him to the commode, then eased open the front door and slipped into the rundown hallway, escaping from the party like a thief in the night.

◇

Frank was relieved to be back on the street in front of Ray's building. He filled his lungs with the damp night air, the cool breeze presenting a welcome contrast to the oppressive heat of Ray's crowded apartment. With his mind still focused on the time—and his dad's stiff penalties for breaking curfew—Frank bent to tighten the laces on his Converse, then slowly trotted in the direction of home.

Clay Street was nearly deserted, and Frank picked up his pace as he crossed Presidio Avenue, darting through the intersection without waiting for the signal to turn. He breezed through the next four sleepy blocks, then accelerated as he made the turn onto Spruce, flying past empty storefronts and falling into a steady rhythm, his sneakers skipping effortlessly over the pavement below.

He had just crossed busy California Street, only minutes from home, when he stopped dead in his tracks, clutching at a pain in his stomach. It was a familiar pain—the knot of fear that he'd come to think of as a sixth sense. That wrenching in his gut, a sickening twist of the intestines that he experienced when something was about to go horribly wrong. He hesitated for a split second, then set the pain in his abdomen aside and broke into a sprint. He covered a full block in the span of seconds, almost skidding into a parked delivery truck as he rounded the curve in the road that marked the intersection of Spruce and Mayfair.

Frank didn't break stride but scanned the two blocks in front of him, where two red-and-white fire engines were parked in the middle of his street, facing the row of houses and forming a "V" that blocked approaching traffic from either side. He could hear it now, the distant wailing of the sirens, and he could see the glow of the flames coming from a house near the end of his block. He said a silent prayer, hoping he was wrong and that it was someone else's house—anyone's but his.

Frank ignored the screaming in his legs. He devoured the remaining blocks in a dead sprint, his heavy footfalls and ragged breaths nearly drowning out the blaring of the sirens. He arrived at a makeshift cordon, yellow tape and red cones that were meant to separate the transfixed onlookers from the team of firefighters that swarmed in front of the house.

Inside the cordon, the firefighters wrestled with thick hoses, blasting heavy jets of water high above the street into the pockets of flames that had already engulfed the entirety of the house. *His* house. *Their home.*

The scope of destruction sickened him.

He gasped for air, sucked in a lungful of the acrid fumes, then doubled over and gagged, expelling the remnants of his burger and fries onto the black patch of asphalt at his feet. He wiped his mouth with the back of his hand and tried to duck under the tape, but strong arms wrapped around his waist, arresting his motion from behind.

"You can't go in there," a man warned, his tone assertive but calm. He pinned Frank's arms at his sides and tried to drag him away from the tape.

"I live there!" Frank pleaded. "*We* live there!" He twisted and writhed, but strong as he was, he couldn't break the man's grip.

A second set of arms—belonging to an Asian man Frank

vaguely recognized as a neighbor—joined the cause, pulling Frank away from the chaos and forcing him roughly to the curb, across the street from the fire. He opened his mouth to speak, but nothing came out.

"This is the son," the neighbor said, pointing at Frank but addressing his words to the helmet-clad fireman. "This is him, the Romano boy."

The firefighter removed his helmet, revealing a reddened face, his cheeks stained by streaks of soot and sweat. He stared down at Frank, his eyes coming to rest on Frank's GW Baseball T-shirt.

"You play ball for Washington." It was a pronouncement, not a question, but Frank responded anyway.

"Yes, sir. Catcher." Frank's ears burned at the absurdity of his statement. The firefighter kneeled to look him in the eye, seeming not to notice.

"Okay, kid, my name's Martinez. We're trying to get things under control over there. But to do that, I need you to sit here, *right here*, and promise me you're not going to move." He waited for Frank to nod, to acknowledge his command, then continued. "I'll be back to check on you soon."

Frank nodded again. He watched Martinez pull the neighbor aside. The firefighter whispered some instructions that Frank couldn't hear over the sound of the sirens, then he waved him away, urging him to "make it quick."

The neighbor scrambled back to his house, leaving Frank alone on the curb, scanning the crowd frantically for any sign of his parents and watching the firefighters tend to what remained of their home. The crews had nearly extinguished the blaze, one team preparing to enter the house while the other continued to spray a long arc of water over the charred façade and into the smoldering back of the house.

Frank stayed put, did as Martinez had asked, then felt the irresistible tug of impatience as the minutes ticked by and his parents did not appear. He felt a door begin to swing open in his mind, but he slammed it shut, unwilling to confront the possibilities that were hidden behind it.

Frank rose from the curb.

He walked back to the edge of the cordon, where Martinez and another fireman were speaking to a gray-haired mountain of a man who had just arrived on the scene and was clearly in charge.

"Looks like it started in the front, in the family room," Martinez told the mountain, pointing upward to the skeletal frame of the bay windows.

The gray-haired man only nodded in response, his face grim, then turned to the second firefighter, a smaller man who couldn't be much older than Frank.

Frank advanced as far as the tape would allow. He strained to hear the men's words over the constant rumble of the fire engines and the overlapping conversations of the gawkers.

"Two souls on deck, Sir," the firefighter said, a nervous tremor in his voice. He inspected the asphalt at the foot of the gray mountain, then continued in a more even tone. "One in the front, what used to be the living room, and one in the bedroom at the back."

Two souls?

Frank's head swam. He was broadsided by another wave of nausea as the implications of the man's words hit home. His legs wobbled beneath him. He almost collapsed as he stumbled back to his place on the curb, then let his head fall between his knees.

Someone draped a blanket around his shoulders, but Frank didn't look up. He just stared at the flooded gutter, trying to organize the jumble of thoughts crashing through his mind. He struggled to contain his emotions. Anger, despair, and guilt all simmered inside of him, threatening to bubble over.

Was this his fault? Did he do this?

His mother had wanted him home. Could this have been prevented if he'd just done as she'd asked?

"Hey, kid. Can I sit?"

Frank jumped, startled by the familiar voice and its intrusion upon his dark thoughts. He looked up, saw Coach Baker standing above him, then nodded, unwilling to speak for fear of bursting into tears.

"Martinez saw your T-shirt, Frank. He figured it was best to give me a call."

Baker had clearly rushed right over. His eyes were puffy from sleep, lines from the pillow ran down the side of his face, and he was wearing only jeans and a T-shirt despite the chill of the night.

"There are some things we need to talk about," he said, helping Frank to his feet. "But not here, and not right now."

Frank lifted his head, his eyes meeting those of his coach.

"You're coming home with me, kid. At least for tonight, until we can get this thing sorted out."

Frank battled the insane urge to laugh, wondering just how *this thing* could ever be sorted out. His life wasn't a car or a clock. Some things, once broken, can never be fixed.

He trailed Baker down the sidewalk, then stopped and turned. He cast a long glance back at the house. For the first time in years, he thought of the statue—Benjamin Franklin, the one in the park—and the time capsule buried beneath. They had sworn an oath that day, he and his mother, to return together for its opening.

Memories of Ma overwhelmed him. Old memories. Memories of a time and a person that were no more and never would be again.

Frank stifled a sob as a dam inside him broke, allowing cold torrents of truth to come rushing in. She was really gone, and their oath was just one more in a long line of promises she would never be able to keep.

And only he was left to blame.

Chapter 5

Age 18

January 15, 1971

Frank peered anxiously from behind the curtain, wishing he'd called in sick and avoided the entire spectacle.

His gaze drifted beyond the rows of folding chairs positioned neatly across the stage, scanning the sea of faces in the fast-growing audience. A steady stream of spectators filed in from the back of the brightly lit auditorium, and many more were already seated, but Coach Baker was nowhere to be seen.

"Have you seen Coach Baker yet?" Frank asked. He didn't need to check his watch to know that time was running short. "Showtime is in five minutes."

He turned to Sammy Long, who stood on tiptoes behind him. He was angling to get a better view of the crowd, waving to his large contingent of friends and family who had come to watch the graduation ceremony.

"How would I," Sammy replied, unleashing the sly smile that always preceded a punchline, "with that fat dome of yours in the way?" He landed a playful punch to Frank's shoulder, then retreated to avoid the backward swat of Frank's outstretched arm.

"And I think it's time you start calling him 'Chief' anyway. He's your boss now; and this isn't Little League, slugger."

Frank let the curtain fall and poked a thick finger into the gold lettering on his friend's chest. "Yeah, and maybe it's time folks stop calling you 'Schlong,' too, but I doubt that's going to happen."

All the students in the Santa Rosa Junior College Fire Sciences Program wore name tapes, sewn above the left breast pocket of their navy-blue shirts, which identified them by first initial and last name. It hadn't taken long for their instructors to turn "S. Long" into "Schlong." Despite Sammy's objections, the name had stuck.

Before Sammy could respond, Chief Gombocz, one of the three battalion chiefs from across the county who served as instructors at the academy, called for the group's attention.

"All right, ladies. Let's get lined up in alphabetical order. In a couple of minutes, we'll take the stage, just like we rehearsed." Gombocz watched with shark-like blue eyes as the men formed the line, then inspected their placement to make sure they had, in fact, mastered the intricacies of the alphabet. "And watch your footing when you're on the stage," he cautioned. "These people didn't come all this way to watch you morons trip over your dicks."

Frank chuckled into the back of the head in front of him—the man certainly had a way with words. Fifth from the rear in the line of twenty-four young men, all of them dressed in matching navy-blue trousers and short-sleeve button-down shirts, Frank walked stiffly onto the stage, cognizant of his dick and all other tripping hazards. He stood to the left of his assigned chair, then took his seat when instructed.

The place was packed. He finally caught sight of Baker, who had arrived just in time—wearing a fancy suit and tie, no less—and taken a seat toward the rear of the auditorium. Frank exhaled deeply, releasing some small measure of the morning's tension, and felt the muscles in his neck relax as he sank into the cushioned backrest of the folding chair.

In the months following the fire, Frank and Coach Baker, who he still couldn't force himself to call "Hal," had grown closer than ever. Baker's presence had become the one constant in Frank's life, keeping him anchored, even when the swift currents of grief, guilt, and resentment threatened to send him adrift.

That first sleepless night on Baker's couch had turned into two, and before Frank knew it, a week had passed. With no family to speak of, Frank had nowhere else to go. He knew it, and so did Baker. But Frank was never made to feel unwelcome, never treated as a burden. And so, he stayed put, becoming a permanent fixture on the sofa in Baker's small one-bedroom apartment off Geary.

The first few weeks were the worst. There were occasional moments of intense grief, moments when he couldn't catch his breath and it felt like his heart would burst inside his chest, but the prevailing sense was one of emptiness, like a fundamental part of his being had been consumed in the fire, leaving a gaping void in its place.

Frank spent most of his waking moments wandering in a heavy fog, still trying to make sense of the tragedy that had upended his life, leaving him an orphan on the precipice of his eighteenth birthday. He continued to attend classes—Coach Baker made sure of that—but he didn't swing a bat or catch a ball for the rest of his senior year.

Though he hated his father's postgame critiques, the endless barrage of criticisms and slights, the idea of playing the game they both loved without Pop in the stands was more than his conscience could bear. As hard as he tried in the beginning, he just couldn't separate the two—his passion for baseball and his guilt over Pop's death—so he turned in his uniform instead, quitting the team and leaving the game behind.

Though Frank hoped the fire inspector's investigation would bring some sort of closure, the lengthy report, which was filled with a host of five-dollar words he'd relied on Baker to explain, had been *inconclusive*. While it was clear that the fire had started in the family room where his mother's body was later found, the inspector could not say with certainty how it had begun. While it was suspected that an unattended cigarette was the culprit, this point could not be proved definitively, which was made clear in the inspector's final conclusion. Frank had read the report, cover-to-cover, more times than he could count, always looking for some new piece of information. And always trying to answer the same questions.

What could he have done differently? Would it have made a difference?

Through it all, Coach Baker had been his rock. He helped Frank navigate the legal process, made more complicated by his parents' failure to leave a last will and testament. And he'd broken the news to Frank when the bank foreclosed on the charred remnants of their home, taking ownership of the valuable lot where it once stood. His parents had accumulated a mountain of debt, and his mother had stopped making insurance payments many years before.

Baker handled the lion's share of the funeral planning, coordinating with his father's precinct for the rendering of police honors. And he helped pick out the black suit that Frank wore to the funeral, laying a steadying hand on Frank's shoulder as he stammered his way through a hand-written eulogy, delivered at their small grave-side service on a rainy Saturday morning in early May.

So, when Baker sat him down in front of a giant stack of pancakes on a Sunday morning in July and told him that he'd been hired for a new job, as a battalion chief for the city of Santa Rosa, it seemed only natural to both of them that Frank would move, too. With no intention of playing baseball again and no money to pay for tuition anyway, Frank's motivation to go to college had faded fast. What he needed was a fresh start, and Santa Rosa—only an hour north of the Golden Gate, but seemingly light-years from 680 Spruce—seemed as good a place as any to begin anew.

Frank jumped at the sound of his name. Spurred by a modest round of applause, he walked gingerly across the stage, still afraid he might trip and humiliate himself, and received his diploma in one hand while shaking Chief Benjamin's hand with the other. He reclaimed his seat, then looked to Coach Baker, who was still standing and applauding, a broad smile lifting the edges of his considerable mustache.

Frank laughed with the rest of the crowd during Chief Benjamin's closing remarks, a hodgepodge of firefighting anecdotes and well-wishes for the graduating class, then exited the stage, zig-zagged through a crush of bodies, and met Baker in the carpeted side aisle that ran the length of the auditorium. Frank reached out for a handshake, but Baker reeled him in for a hug instead.

"Congratulations, kid." He released Frank from the bearhug and held him at arm's length, one hand resting on each shoulder. "I'm proud of you. And I know your folks would be proud of you, too."

"Thanks, Coach." The weight of Baker's remark dragged him back to Earth, highlighting the stark reality of another graduation without his parents.

Frank swallowed the hard lump in the back of his throat and forced a thin smile. Seeing the look of pride written across Baker's face was bittersweet. The closer they'd become, the more Frank had to remind himself of a simple truth: Coach Baker was not his father, and he never would be. Just like Frank would never replace the son Baker had left behind in Oklahoma, Baker would never supplant the father he'd lost. No matter how much he wished otherwise.

"But you know my Pop would give me a rash of shit for becoming a 'hose jockey' and not a cop, right?"

Baker laughed a little too hard. He pointed to the rolled

diploma in Frank's hand and smiled. "Time to retire that term, buddy. You're one of us now."

Baker looked to Sammy, who stood in front of the stage, surrounded by a large congregation of family and friends, demonstrating a fireman's carry on a giggling younger cousin. "Go grab your fellow graduate for me. I have some errands to run, but I want to talk to both of you before I go."

Their graduation was the culmination of eighteen weeks of introductory fire prevention and firefighting training. Their class met only once a week, for three-hour sessions, with the remainder of the week dedicated to reading thick manuals and memorizing nit-noid details that would later be evaluated through written tests and practical applications. Frank dreaded the written tests (and loathed the hours of reading required to pass them), but he hit his stride with the practical applications, where he'd established himself as one of the top performers in the class.

Of the twenty-four men in the graduating class, nine already had jobs lined up with the Santa Rosa Fire Department. Most of the others would be starting their firefighting careers in neighboring towns like Sebastopol, Healdsburg, and Cloverdale. Only Frank and Sammy, no doubt through the pulling of various strings, had been assigned to Baker's new firehouse, Station 6, on Calistoga Road.

Frank returned with Sammy, who had deposited his unruly cousin next to the stage and was combing his fingers through his sandy hair, trying to restore it to its usual glory. Sammy flashed his movie-star-quality smile, his perpetually tan skin only accentuating the whiteness of his teeth, bringing a taste of August to the dreary January morning.

"Hey, guys," Baker began, welcoming Sammy with a slap on the back. "Congratulations again. This is the start of something great for both of you, and you should be very proud of yourselves. Now, I told you fellas that tomorrow is your first day, and that's technically true, but there's some paperwork that you need to complete *today* to be squared away for tomorrow."

Frank nodded and looked to Sammy, whose dazzling teeth were now hidden behind taut lips. Sammy always enjoyed being the center of attention, but they'd both been warned about life at the bottom of the totem pole, so he offered no argument in return.

"So, I need you guys to hustle over to the station," Baker continued, glancing at his watch, seemingly unaware of the shift in Sammy's mood. "I spoke to Stitch Alvestal this morning and told him you'd be there by noon, so you'd better get a move on."

◇

"You can always walk, you know," Frank told Sammy, taunting his friend as they passed under a dense canopy of trees in the crowded parking lot of the JC.

Sammy had been busting Frank's balls about his driving *again*, which meant little to Frank, coming from a guy with a glovebox full of unpaid tickets, who treated the speed limit as more of a suggestion than a rule.

Frank stopped, a hand on his hip, before unlocking the door of the black Chevy C10. "It'll only take you an hour, and I'll let them know you're on the way once I get there."

Sammy kept his mouth shut. He waited for Frank to unlock his door, then slid into the passenger seat. Despite the chill of the morning, he rolled down the window, then messed with the dials of the radio as Frank merged into traffic.

"Who's manning the shop today?" Frank asked, pointing across the cab and out the window at the two-story brick building on the opposite side of Mendocino Avenue, the name "Long & Sons Construction" carved in large, stylized lettering on the massive wooden sign out front.

"Nobody," Sammy replied sorely, a pinched expression contorting his face. "My Dad shut it down for the morning—said everyone wanted to be there for the graduation." He pointed to the empty parking lot as confirmation.

It was Baker who had first suggested the job at Long & Sons, telling Frank it would be wise to acquire some "practical skills," particularly if he were truly interested in following Baker into the fire department, where a man's ability to fix a sink or patch some drywall was nearly as important as driving an engine or extinguishing a blaze.

Frank's first week on the job had been anything but promising. He'd lost a thumbnail to a hammer, nearly dropped a beam on the foreman's head, and been told by any number of people that he was "slower than molasses in January." Were it not for Sammy, and his willingness to show Frank the ropes of his family's business, Frank would have been out on his ear after that first week, probably bagging groceries at the supermarket or bussing tables at The Pizza Shack.

Though Frank was a quick study, and he enjoyed working outdoors with his hands, he became convinced as the summer wore on that his future was in firefighting, not construction. Firefighting was a job with purpose, where you made a difference and were part of a team. Almost like a family. Those ideas appealed to Frank, and apparently to Sammy too. With three summers' worth of construction work under his belt already, Sammy had made it clear to his father and grandfather that the building gene had skipped a generation and that that summer would be his last. So, when registration for the Fire Sciences Program opened in the last week of August, Frank and Sammy had hopped in the truck, made their way down to the Junior College, and happily signed on the dotted line.

"Smells like bullshit to me," Sammy complained, shouting over the noise of the radio. "Asking us to show up a day early just to sign some stupid paperwork."

"Yeah, I guess," Frank agreed. He silenced the radio, then slowed the truck and made the turn off of Calistoga Road and into the parking lot of Station 6. "But you remember what Chief Gombocz said, right?"

"Don't trip over your dick?" Sammy erupted in a fit of high-pitched laughter, as he often did at his own jokes.

"I don't think you need to worry about that," Frank countered, glancing at Sammy's crotch and squinting his eyes for effect. "No, I'm talking about his number one rule for rookies."

"Ah, yes." He reorganized his face into a serious expression and pointed an index finger straight into the air, just like Chief Gombocz. "Rule number one, morons: Shut the hell up and do what you're told!"

◇

"You know why they call him 'Stitch,' don't you?" Sammy asked, his brown eyes cutting to Frank as they darted across the two-lane street and up the concrete driveway of Station 6.

Ahead of them was the station's maintenance bay, a slanted brown-shingle roof perched atop twin retractable bay doors. One of the doors was open, the cab of a red-and-white engine barely visible inside the bay.

"From what Chief Benjamin told me," Sammy continued, "he had a bit of a screw-up when he was a rookie—cleaned his own clock sliding under the engine to change the oil. Opened up a big gash on his forehead." Sammy lowered his voice to a whisper as they approached the open bay door. "He was embarrassed, ya know, so he didn't want to tell anybody. Instead, the tough son of a bitch grabbed a sewing kit, went to the bathroom, and stitched the thing up all by himself. Then he sauntered out a few minutes later, acting like nothing had happened."

Frank sized him up, his bullshit detector fully engaged. He was always on his toes around Sammy, who never let the truth get in the way of a good story.

Startled by a loud whistle and a call of "Hey, fellas," Frank whirled to face the lobby of the administrative wing, where the outline of a thin man was barely visible in the shade of the covered walkway that connected the low-lying building with the adjacent maintenance bays.

"I'm Stitch Alvestal," he offered, advancing into the light to shake their hands. He swept a lock of tawny hair away from his craggy face, exposing a jagged purple scar that started above his right eyebrow and ran diagonally up and across his forehead. "And you must be our rookies. C'mon inside, boys; I'll give you the grand tour."

Frank ignored Sammy's *I told you so* smirk and trailed Stitch through the double doors, trying to keep pace as he sped past the lobby and through the main hallway of the station, pointing out different features of the building as they flew by.

"The dorm is back that way," Stitch called. "Hopefully, your mamas taught you how to make a rack; we're sticklers for that shit around here."

Frank flinched at the mention of his mother. He bit the inside of his cheek but didn't break stride. He'd become more and more accustomed to these acute flashes of grief, and he'd learned to steel himself against the occasional jolts of guilt and resentment. Most days he wasn't sure who he blamed more for the fire—his drunken, careless mother or himself. But he knew it wasn't worth dwelling on; she was gone. And no amount of bitterness or remorse would bring her back.

"Chief Baker said there was some paperwork we needed to fill out," Sammy prompted, with all the subtlety of a wrecking ball, as he and Frank followed Stitch into the station's recreation room.

Frank admired the wood-paneled walls, which were covered with honorary plaques, awards, and framed photographs, tributes to the men who had come before. Besides a television set, the room was furnished with a pool table and an ancient pinball machine that looked like something out of a 1950s arcade. A matching leather sofa and recliner sat in front of the television. Both were empty; both had seen better days.

"Paperwork, huh?" Stitch's face went blank for an instant, then lit up with recognition. "Yeah, of course. There's a whole stack of ID-10-Tango forms you'll need to fill out before you can officially start. Unfortunately, they're all locked up in a file cabinet, you see, and Captain Lewis took the keys with him. We had a bit of a . . . plumbing issue this morning, so he and the other guys went to the hardware store to pick up some parts."

Frank suppressed a smile as he watched Sammy spiral into a slow burn, annoyed to have been summoned to the station to complete a set of forms that were conveniently locked inside a cabinet.

"The guys should be back soon," Stitch said, shrugging his shoulders. "In the meantime, I was just about to make some lunch—I'll whip you fellas up a couple of sandwiches and bring 'em on in. You can take a seat in the meantime; flip on the TV and relax."

Frank claimed a spot on the bowed sofa and flipped on the television. He and Sammy were nearly done with their sandwiches, and two-thirds of the way through an episode of *The Beverly Hillbillies*, when a voice exploded from the back of the room.

"Well, isn't this cute."

Frank spun in his seat, spilling potato chips into his lap and across the worn leather cushion of the couch. The owner of the voice, a barrel-chested man with a neatly trimmed mustache and a hooked nose that dominated the rest of his face, was bearing down hard from across the room, a small posse in tow.

"I'm Captain Lewis," he announced. He watched with beefy arms folded across his chest as Frank and Sammy scrambled up from the couch. "And you two must be our rookies. I was told you two graduated from the JC this morning, but that can't be true. I worked with Chief Gombocz for damn near ten years, and I know that any men he trained wouldn't have the balls to show up at the station on their first day, park their assess on the couch, and watch *The Beverly-fucking-Hillbillies!*"

The irate captain turned and looked to the quartet behind

him for affirmation. All of them, Stitch Alvestal included, nodded their heads in unison.

Frank tried to explain the mix-up, but the captain cut him short.

"Listen, shit stain," Lewis interjected, blanketing Frank in a fine spray of spittle. "When I want to hear your lame-ass excuses, you can be damn sure I'll ask for them."

Frank looked over Lewis's shoulder, eyes pleading, expecting Stitch to come to their rescue and explain that he and Sammy had only done what they'd been told to do. But Stitch, and all the others for that matter, were either looking away or covering their mouths, trying not to laugh. Frank gritted his teeth and shook his head, angry to have been played like a fiddle.

Stitch stepped around Captain Lewis and joined Frank next to the couch. "Well, hold on now, Cap," he began, his voice slathered in bullshit. "I know these two clowns aren't off to a great start," he continued, placing a calloused hand on Frank's shoulder, "but I think I know how to get 'em back on track. You just let me take it from here, huh?"

◆

"THAT ASSHOLE," Sammy complained through clenched teeth as the glass doors of the lobby swung shut behind them, "is a real son of a bitch, isn't he?"

Frank only nodded in response. He ran a hand through his still-damp hair, then wrinkled his nose at the persistent smell of bleach that clung to his hands. After an exhausting four hours—during which time he and Sammy had scrubbed every toilet, cleaned every shower, mopped every floor, and cleared every gutter in Station 6—he was ready to close the book on their disastrous first day.

"Hold up!" Stitch called from the doors, freezing them both in place. He walked out to the driveway to meet them, gripping a ballpoint pen in each hand.

"We almost forgot about the forms," he said, smiling pleasantly as if the events of the last four hours had not taken place. "You remember the name I told you earlier? Well, it's one you should definitely remember." He handed them each a pen. "So, jot it down on your hand for later, dummies."

Frank stepped forward, about to pop off, but Sammy shook his head and tugged lightly on his arm.

"Okay, it's *I*, then *D*," Stitch began. He stared at their hands until the pens stopped moving. "Then a dash and the number ten, followed by a second dash and the letter T, as in tango. ID-10-T."

Frank's body was ablaze. He clenched the pen, nearly snapping it in two. "Idiot," he read off his hand, aware of the hard edge to his voice but not in the least bit sorry. "That's a real knee-slapper, Stitch."

"Oh, you may not think so today," Stitch told them, a smile playing at the corners of his mouth, "but someday you will. What you all went through today, if you haven't figured it out already, was something of an initiation. You'll still be rookies when you come in tomorrow, but you'll be rookies on the best damn team you'll ever join. The kind of team where men look after one another, where they *have each other's backs*. So, welcome to Station 6, fellas. I'll see your asses at 8 a.m. sharp." Stitch winked and collected his pens, then sauntered back toward the doors of the lobby.

Frank and Sammy watched him go, then turned and walked back to the truck in silence. Frank considered Stitch's parting words, and the hard mass of anger in his chest melted into shame, like it always did when he lost himself in the moment and behaved like his father's son.

"It could have been worse," Sammy said finally, resting a muscular forearm on the tailgate of the truck. He flashed a sly smile, his first since they'd left the graduation ceremony. "We could have tripped over our dicks."

Chapter 6

Age 23

April 9, 1976

"Something's up," Sammy declared, bursting into the rec room with wild eyes and an air of mischief. "You'd better come quick."

His entrance startled Frank, who nearly spilled his mug of steaming coffee into his lap. Frank eyed his friend through narrowed lids but made no move to get up from his post in the recliner. He'd been on the receiving end of Sammy's pranks before, more times than he cared to admit, and experience had taught him to look before he leaped.

"Ahh, c'mon," Sammy complained. He threw his hands in the air, waited for Frank to change his mind, then turned for the door. "Okay ... but it's your loss."

Frank sipped his coffee, debated, then threw caution to the wind. He heaved his body out of the recliner, followed the squeaking of Sammy's boots down the freshly-waxed hallway floor, and arrived at the open door to Captain Lewis's office just as he hung up the phone.

"Well?" Sammy asked breathlessly, hands gripping the top of the doorway as he leaned into the captain's cramped office.

Lewis stared up at them from behind his cluttered desk. He didn't speak, just blew a thick cloud of smoke toward the door, then motioned for them to come in. True to form, he took his sweet time extinguishing his cigarette in the overflowing ashtray next to the phone, letting long seconds tick by, basking in their suffering.

"You're always cracking jokes, Schlong; you ever hear the one about the horse in the pool?"

Frank and Sammy exchanged wary glances, waiting for the punchline, hoping they weren't the butt of the joke.

"No? Well, me either." Lewis rolled back in his chair, slapped his thick thighs with both hands, then broke into a shit-eating grin. "So, let's pack up the LARK and go take a look."

◇

"Drop me off there," Lewis demanded. He extended a furmatted hand and wrist through the open window of the fire engine and pointed to the mouth of a tree-lined driveway with a sprawling ranch-style house hunkered at the other end. "Then grab the kit and meet me up there."

Frank parked the engine on the gravel shoulder, behind a rusty horse trailer that was the last in a procession of vehicles that included two police cruisers and an ambulance. He joined Sammy at the engine's open side-storage compartment, grabbed one end of the bulky black duffel bag, and helped Sammy extract it from the compartment.

A kaleidoscope of butterflies fluttered in Frank's gut. He'd worked with the large animal rescue kit before, but his LARK experience was limited to closely controlled training events; he'd never worked with a real animal before. Let alone one that was injured and anxious.

They walked side by side up the shaded drive, the LARK suspended between them, then dropped it onto the asphalt next to Captain Lewis, who was engaged in an animated one-way conversation with a uniformed police officer. The officer, who couldn't have been older than fifteen by Frank's estimation, shifted his weight uncomfortably from one foot to the other, looking like he was about to radio for backup.

"I'm not even sure why we were called," Lewis barked at the kid, one thick arm flailing in the direction of the house. "I mean, this is clearly police business. The horse is trespassing, is it not?"

The wide-eyed officer, identified as Marks by the embroidered name above his uniform pocket, looked from Lewis to Sammy, then over to Frank, unsure if the captain was serious or just pulling his leg. Frank only shrugged in response; he and Sammy had seen a variation of this bit before and Sammy had said it best: It's like watching your dog hump a friend's leg—though embarrassing and painful to watch, it's better to just let him finish.

Marks opened his mouth to respond, then snapped it shut when Lewis erupted in a throaty laugh, which was joined first by Sammy, then halfheartedly by Marks himself.

"I'm just screwing with you, Marks," Lewis clarified, sending the officer stumbling with a hearty slap to the back. "This is definitely our lane. Is the veterinarian here yet? From what I was told, we're going to need him."

Frank and Sammy hoisted the LARK off the ground and followed the captain and Officer Marks through a side gate and into the home's spacious backyard. The boundaries of the lot were protected by well-hewn cedar fences, but a large swinging gate in the back of the property stood open, providing easy access to the oak grove and rolling hills beyond.

Frank stopped to watch the unfolding spectacle. A plump middle-aged woman—presumably the owner of the home—was having a grand old time holding court on the patio, clutching a pitcher of lemonade, a tray of glasses sitting atop the wrought iron table next to her. She welcomed the newcomers, then continued pouring glasses for the growing crowd of neighbors and responders, all the while wowing them with the story of how she'd heard the commotion in her backyard, recognized the neighbor's horse —"Snickers," she called him—then rushed inside to call 9-1-1.

Their theatrical hostess offered Frank a glass of lemonade, which he politely declined. He weaved through the throng of people instead, wishing there were fewer of them to contend with, then knelt at the edge of the hourglass-shaped pool.

The star of the show was an adult Arabian horse. He stood in the shallow end of the pool, flicking a thick black tail that was mostly submerged in the water. Chestnut in color, with a swath of white that started between his ears and formed a nearly symmetrical stripe down to his nose, he was anxious and alert, pacing to and fro like a caged lion, and moving with a pronounced limp.

Frank had little experience with horses, but five years in the department—and nearly eighteen years under Salvatore Romano's roof before that—had taught him a thing or two about fear and remorse. And judging by the horse's wide-eyed terror, he suspected old Snickers was regretting the series of decisions that had landed him in this pickle.

Captain Lewis and Sammy joined him at the edge of the pool. "I spoke to Smithers, the veterinarian," Lewis shared, gesturing across the patio to a bespectacled man in a beige cardigan. "The horse hurt his leg during his little romp, and they can't coax him to walk up the steps and out of the pool."

Lewis walked them through the broad strokes of the plan—which included the captain "supervising" their efforts while he and Sammy took an icy plunge in the unheated pool—then glowered down his substantial beak as they unzipped the black duffel bag and assembled the sling.

Frank chewed at the remains of a fingernail and watched in nervous anticipation. The horse's owner, an elderly man with leathery skin, wearing a sweat-stained cowboy hat older than Officer Marks, coaxed Snickers to the side of the pool with a cube of sugar. He stroked him behind the ears, calming the horse as the cardigan-clad veterinarian injected a mild tranquilizer into the taut muscles of his neck.

"Quietly," Frank cautioned Sammy. Careful not to startle the horse, who remained standing at the edge, Frank eased into the pool. He stifled a gasp as the frigid water ran up the inner sides of his thighs, then waded slowly toward the edge, Sammy trailing close in his wake.

Communicating more through gestures than words, they ran the nylon sling under the full length of the horse's torso, then paused for a moment, letting the owner settle the horse before attaching a series of straps to the sides of the sling. Frank slowly exited the water, clenched his jaws to still his chattering teeth, and stood by the side of the pool.

After Smithers had carefully positioned the horse with its body parallel to the side of the pool, Frank—joined by Sammy, Lewis, and a few of the uniformed police officers—grabbed the straps and heaved in unison.

Straining to free the horse from the water's grip, they lifted Snickers over the lip of the pool and onto the patio. They paused for a few seconds, panting and catching their breath, then dragged him across the slick concrete surface, coming to rest a few feet from the edge of the pool.

Sedated but still anxious, Snickers unsteadily regained his feet, eliciting a round of cheers from the first responders, his owner, and the gaggle of neighbors who had thankfully retreated to the far edge of the patio, giving Frank and the team enough room to work.

Frank looked to Sammy, who sat beside him in a puddle of their own making. Still breathing heavily, Sammy's teeth chattered. His purplish lips curled to form a boyish smile.

"You don't see that every day, now do you?" He stood, then offered an outstretched hand to Frank.

Frank saw it first, a chestnut flash exploding in the far edge of his vision. Resisting his owner's attempts to walk him away from the edge of the pool, Snickers bucked strongly, shooting two well-muscled legs back into the air behind him.

Frank tried to shout a warning. He reached for Sammy's arm, but it was too late. He watched helplessly instead, cringing as one shoed hoof connected squarely with Sammy's thigh.

Sammy yelped like an injured pup, then tumbled backward and across the concrete deck, landing in the icy pool with a resounding splash.

◇

FRANK HUSTLED through the shaded parking lot, toward the entrance to Memorial Hospital's emergency room, then changed his mind and opted for the main lobby instead. *Sammy can hold his horses.* He snorted at his own joke, wished that someone was there to appreciate his humor, and made a mental note to use the line later, should an opportunity arise.

He passed beneath a large semicircular overhang, supported on each side by thick cylindrical stone columns, then stepped through the glass doors of the four-story hospital and into the chill of the air-conditioned lobby. The small gift shop was nestled in the corner, to the right of the main information desk, and Frank ducked inside to assess the inventory.

He blew past the colorful floral arrangements, which didn't strike the particular chord he was aiming for, then paused to read the host of inspirational messages embossed on the front of the shiny helium-filled mylar balloons. Not surprisingly, none of them seemed to match the occasion. Bypassing the row of postcards, snow globes, and assorted knickknacks, he searched up and down the shelves lined with stuffed animals. Opting for a large chocolate-brown teddy bear, a crimson heart clutched lovingly to its chest, he moved toward the cash register and reached for his wallet. If this gift didn't capture his sentiment—equal parts sympathy and mockery—then surely nothing would.

Frank tucked the oversized bear under his arm. He backtracked to the emergency room and eyeballed the assembly of people sitting in rows of identical patterned chairs or milling slowly about its white-walled lobby. For a weekday afternoon, the ER was surprisingly packed, the prevailing mood one of boredom and frustration.

Frank had been there many times before. He knew his way around, and he had no interest in sitting in the cramped waiting room. He ducked past the nurses' station, making a beeline for the closed double doors and the row of examination rooms concealed behind them.

"Hold up!" a young nurse called. She craned her neck to see over the counter, then rose from her post behind the reception desk.

Frank watched her lower the volume on a hand-held radio, then smooth the hem of her starched white uniform and tuck a loose strand of strawberry blonde hair back into her matching cap as she walked out from behind the counter.

"Where's the fire?" she asked stiffly, both hands planted on shapely hips.

She stared at Frank, who stared right back, confused by her question and more than a little embarrassed about being publicly reprimanded.

She was tall, with a supple build. And even her uninspiring nurse's uniform did little to disguise the attractive frame beneath.

"That was a joke," she explained at last. "You know, because of your shirt..."

A hot flush ignited the base of Frank's neck, then spread up and across his cheeks. He'd changed out of his wet uniform when he'd left the station; now he was wearing faded blue jeans and a red Santa Rosa Fire Department T-shirt.

"If you're here to visit someone, you need to check in first. Rules are rules, even for firemen." She flashed an electric smile, the kind that could light up a room, or an entire hospital wing for that matter, then sauntered back to her seat behind the counter.

Frank swallowed hard and cleared his throat. "Sorry about that, miss. I'm here to pick up one of our guys. Samuel Long."

Frank raised off his heels, leaning over the counter to study her features as she ran a red, manicured fingernail down a list of hand-written names on a clipboard. She had a smattering of tiny freckles on her small button nose and hazel eyes that sparkled like jewels when she smiled.

"Ah, yes, Mr. Long." She pursed her glossy lips and rolled her eyes. "We met earlier . . . but I didn't take him for the stuffed animal type." She nodded at the bear under Frank's arm and flashed that smile again. Frank returned it sheepishly as he ventured a glance at her name tag. "You can find him in room 113—through those swinging double doors and around the corner to the right."

"Thanks, Elizabeth," Frank replied, repositioning the cumbersome bear under his arm. He blushed again, embarrassed by the stupid bear but more so by the intimate act of forming her name with his lips.

"Not a problem, Mr. Fireman. But I go by Ellie."

Frank rewarded her confession with an awkward nod. He repeated her name in his mind, again and again, committing it to memory as he and the bear retreated down the hall toward the double doors. Behind him, he heard the radio return to its previous volume. It had been blaring an auto parts commercial when he arrived. Now he realized she was listening to the baseball game.

Frank hadn't watched or listened to a baseball game in years. Not since that night in April, when his entire world burned. But he knew from the morning news that it was opening day and the Giants were playing their archrivals, the Dodgers, in San Francisco.

His body humming with the same nervous energy he used to feel behind the plate, Frank stole a quick glance back as he passed through the doors, intrigued by her, by *Ellie*. Pretty girls were a dime a dozen. Spend an evening out with Sammy, and you'd certainly get your fill. But how many of them liked baseball and even enjoyed the game enough to listen on the radio at work? Now, *that* had to be a much shorter list.

Frank pushed his new acquaintance from his mind and paused outside room 113. He pressed his ear against the closed door and listened to the voices emanating from within. After eavesdropping for long enough to decide it was playful banter he heard and not serious medical discussion, he eased the door open, letting the head and arms of the comically large bear lead the way.

"That's the thing most people don't understand," Sammy was saying, his tone suddenly grave, oblivious to the bear's intrusion. "When you put on that uniform and go to work each day, you have to have the mindset that this might be your last day on Earth. Anything could happen, ya know? Those are the risks, babe."

Sammy was addressing a shapely nurse, reciting a tired collection of lines Frank had heard more times than he could count. She was standing close to his bedside, equally unaware of Frank's entrance, seemingly hanging on Sammy's every word.

"Or it could be a day like any other day," Frank interjected, pushing farther into the room, startling the raven-haired nurse. "Except for the part where a horse punts you into a swimming pool."

Frank grinned at his friend. He held the bear at arm's length in front of him, pleased with his theatric entrance and presentation. Sammy was usually the star of the show; it was rare for Frank to even land a speaking role and almost unheard of for him to steal his friend's spotlight.

"Thanks," Sammy said, the word sliding through clenched teeth, his handsome face frozen somewhere between a grimace and a smile. "That's really great. Just super." Sammy shook his head and mouthed the word *asshole* as the nurse made a hasty exit, leaving them alone in the windowless examination room.

Frank had been rooming with Sammy for more than four years, splitting a small two-bedroom apartment on Armory Drive. In those four years, Frank had learned one undeniable truth:

Sammy had an unquenchable appetite for the ladies. He wasn't envious, though, as Sammy's relationships were like hand grenades: short-fused, explosive, and fated to end in disaster.

"Can you believe the nurses around here?" Sammy asked, the sting of Frank's entrance already forgotten. "I need to get hurt more often." He snatched the teddy bear from Frank's hands and sat it upright on the bed next to him. "And the one at the desk? Even hotter. Damn near a fire hazard . . . in my professional opinion." He grinned like a moron at his joke.

Frank recalled her expression when he'd mentioned Sammy's name at the front desk. The pursed lips and rolled eyes. The not-so-subtle look of disapproval.

"You mean Ellie?" Frank asked, trying to keep his tone light. He walked across the room and squeezed his large frame into a small, padded chair. "Yeah, I met her coming in."

"Nah, I think her name's Elizabeth," Sammy said. "Or Liz, maybe?"

Frank relaxed into the back of the chair, somehow pleased that she hadn't shared that little piece of herself with Sammy.

"Anyway, looks like only a sprained knee," Sammy continued, patting his heavily wrapped right leg. "Four weeks on crutches, then I should be right as rain." He picked up the bear, held it at arm's length, and addressed it with mock seriousness. "And next time, I'll know not to stand so close to a horse's ass."

"That's funny," Frank remarked, watching the pitch sail toward home plate and preparing to knock it into the stands. "Because Snickers told me the same thing."

⚜

FRANK PROMISED to meet Sammy out front, left him in the examination room to complete his discharge forms, and went to retrieve his truck from the distant lot. He passed through the same set of double doors through which he'd entered, cast his most purposefully nonchalant glance behind the counter, and spied Nurse Ellie. She sat at the desk, unaware of his presence, scribbling on a notepad.

Frank steeled his nerves, approached the desk, and cleared his throat. "Is it okay if I park my truck in front?" he asked. "Just while I load up my friend?"

"Sure is, Mr. Fireman. Just don't leave it there for long." She smiled expectantly, paused as if waiting for him to respond, then lowered her gaze back to the stack of files on the desk in front of her.

"It's Frank, actually. Frank Romano."

She looked up and addressed him in a conspiratorial whisper. "You know, I figured it might be something more ordinary. It would have been a terrific coincidence: if your last name was actually *Fireman*."

Frank laughed a little too loudly. He rocked back and forth on the soles of his shoes, then searched the immediate area for something—*for anything*—to keep the conversation moving. His eyes settled on the radio, which played quietly in the background.

"How's the game going?" he asked. "It's opening day, right?"

"It is!" she replied, her delicate features animated with excitement. "The Giants are up 3-1 in the sixth inning." She launched into an inning-by-inning recap of the game, including a breathless description of the solo home runs by Gary Matthews and Bobby Murcer.

Frank nodded and smiled throughout her summary, impressed by her knowledge of the game. "Sounds like you're a big baseball fan," he remarked lamely, sneaking a quick peek at the bare ring finger of her left hand.

"Three older brothers, all of them baseball players." She shrugged and wrinkled her cute little nose in a way that made Frank's knees buckle. "Kinda hard not to be, right? What about you?"

Frank faltered for a moment, left off balance and exposed. It was a simple question but one with a complex answer. Chief Baker had tried to pin him down on a couple of occasions, wanting to understand why Frank had turned his back on the game, but the truth was indescribable. He didn't possess the words to explain the swirl of guilt and remorse that clouded his memory of both his father and the game they'd loved. He just knew that it hurt. And like everything else related to Pop, it was complicated.

"I was," he finally managed. "I mean, I am. Just not the way I used to be." Frank kicked himself for his stupid response, then inspected a mangled paperclip on the counter as the conversation lapsed into uncomfortable silence.

"Listen, Frank," she said gently, breaking the quiet and fixing him with her hazel eyes. "I get the impression that you don't do this very often, unlike your friend back there, so I'm going to make this easy on both of us."

Frank wondered at the meaning of "this" and watched her as she reached for the stationary pad she'd been scribbling on when he spied her from the doorway.

"*This*," she said, as she ripped off the top sheet, "is my name and my telephone number. Below is my address. The address is for you to pick me up tonight at eight o'clock. Sharp. And the phone number is in case something comes up and you have to reschedule." She smiled alluringly as she handed him the sheet.

Frank took the paper from her hand and gave his best approximation of a confident smile. At a loss for words, he just repeated hers. "Eight o'clock. Sharp."

"That's right, Mr. Fireman," she teased. "I'll see you then."

Frank left the emergency room in a delighted daze, arriving at his truck with no recollection of how he'd gotten there. He started the Chevy's engine, eased out of his parking spot, and had nearly pulled onto Montgomery Road before he remembered he still needed to collect Sammy before heading home.

Not wanting to break the spell by reappearing inside, Frank sat outside the ER, engine idling, waiting for Sammy to emerge. He relived each detail of the encounter in his mind, thrilled by her boldness, kicking himself for his own clumsiness, and wondering again and again if he was even worthy of her affections. He turned on the radio to silence the shrieks of doubt, scanning through one AM station after another until he finally landed on KSFO.

Frank leaned back in his seat and closed his eyes. He listened to Lon Simmons's voice and let the familiar sounds of the ballpark wash over him, carrying him back to an earlier time. To his bedroom in the house on Spruce Street. To his mother's portable radio and a trove of baseball cards splayed across his bed.

Opening Day had always been magical when he was a kid. It was a day brimming with hope and promise, when every team was undefeated, dreams of October glory were renewed, and anything seemed possible.

Frank took a deep breath and pictured the Washington High School baseball field in his mind. The dark clouds of guilt and remorse evaporated, leaving only the emerald field, the rich brown earth, and the flawless, blue sky behind.

Frank reached for the radio and raised the volume. It was the bottom of the seventh inning, and the Giants led the Dodgers 4-1.

Chapter 7

Age 25

December 31, 1977

Frank sat at the far end of the table, his face concealed behind the sports section of *The Press Democrat*, trying desperately to think of something, anything, other than that goddamn box. At this point, even thoughts of the dreaded gala seemed like a pleasant distraction.

He'd been awakened early by the duty cook's alarm, then tossed and turned in his rack, growing more annoyed with each snore, grunt, and fart that reverberated in the tomb-like stillness of the dorm. He'd *wanted* to go back to sleep, to savor that last hour of rest before the crew was scheduled to rise, but his mind was singularly focused on the tiny black box, stuffed inside a steel-toed boot, hidden in the darkness at the bottom of his locker.

Eventually, he'd given up on sleep. He'd quietly stripped his linens, then moved to the kitchen to help Fred Wilson prepare breakfast. It was probably a good thing he had; Wilson was a liability in the kitchen. A well-intentioned but hapless nineteen-year-old, he was the newest addition to their crew, and he was already making a run for Sammy's title as the station's worst cook. He'd been there for less than a month, but Wilson had already set off the smoke alarm twice, earning the nickname "Four-Alarm Freddy," a moniker he wasn't likely to shake.

Frank knew he was bad company. Anxious and irritable, he was trying his best not to dampen the collective mood. The rest of the men were annoyingly upbeat, as the scheduling gods had smiled upon them, and they were the off-going crew on the last day of the year.

While the other three men discussed their plans for the evening, Frank feigned distraction with the sporting news, trying to ignore the sickening knot in his gut that had nothing to do with Freddy Wilson's runny eggs.

"Hey, Romano! You with us or what?" The words were accompanied by a burnt corner of toast, which sailed over the top of the newspaper and tumbled into his lap. He could tell by the hard edge of Lewis's voice that it was not the first time his name had been called.

"Yeah, I'm with you, Cap." Frank deposited the newspaper on the edge of the long oak table, offering Captain Lewis his full attention.

"All right, gents, we've got about forty-five minutes before our relief crew shows. You know those poor bastards are going to be in for a helluva night, so let's make sure we're setting them up for success. I want the kitchen and the dorm looking tip-top before they get here, so we can roll right into equipment checks and crew change when they arrive."

Frank nodded to Vic Sosa, the fourth member of their crew. They rose from their seats and gathered mugs and dishes from the table. Captain Lewis remained seated in his customary place at the head of the table, slurping loudly from his second cup of coffee, then gestured for Frank to pass him the sports section of the newspaper. In the fire department, like in the military, rank afforded certain privileges.

"Is there any coffee left?"

The tired voice came from the doorway, startling Sosa and nearly causing him to drop an empty mug that was balanced precariously atop two plates and a handful of silverware as he walked toward Freddy Wilson and the stainless-steel sink.

Frank greeted Baker with a sympathetic smile. He noted the dark circles under the chief's eyes, the unmistakable remnants of another sleepless night, then grabbed a fresh mug and poured him a cup from the gurgling Coffee Master on the counter.

He wasn't surprised to see their battalion chief up and around this early on a Saturday morning, even on New Year's Eve. Baker's days of maintaining equipment and responding to calls were long behind him; now his hours were occupied with training plans, shift schedules, and more reports than Frank could keep track of, the product of overseeing a handful of firefighting companies spread over three different stations. Baker was burning the candle at both ends, and it showed. Seeing the monotonous nature of the job—and the chief's struggle to balance his work life with the demands of marriage and a six-month-old kid who had yet to master sleeping through the night—made Frank question whether he ever wanted to rise that high within the department.

"I've got some reports to knock out," Baker muttered, speaking to no one in particular. He shuffled down the hallway, coffee mug in hand. "I'll be in my office for the next few hours if anyone needs me."

◇

FRANK MADE quick work of the dishes, loaded the linens into the washing machine, and moved to the engine bay to prepare for shift change. He took pride in the thoroughness of his equipment checks, knowing that this was a business where attention to detail could mean the difference between life and death. Regardless of how he was feeling, or how deep that little black box burrowed into his brain, no corners would be cut on his watch.

"Y'all ready to get the heck outta here, or what?"

Frank looked up from the maintenance log he'd been studying and rose from the rolling stool to greet Jimbo Maddox.

A Georgia-born mountain of a man, even compared to Frank, Jimbo had moved to California at the age of twelve but never shed the tell-tale drawl.

"Sorry you got stuck with the New Year's shift, big fella."

"Hell, not a big deal," Jimbo replied. He shrugged his massive shoulders out of his quilted winter coat and broke into a gap-toothed smile. "I had Christmas off already. And who wants to spend that much time with his old lady anyway, right?"

Frank and Jimbo worked their way from one end of the fire engine to the other, verifying the functionality of all the engine's systems and ensuring that all onboard equipment, from hoses and nozzles all the way down to traffic vests and cones, was present and serviceable. After reviewing the maintenance logs and discussing planned tasks for the day, Frank said his goodbyes.

He exited through the small side door of the bay and trudged halfway to his truck before changing his mind and returning to the dormitory instead. He retrieved his baseball mitt from his locker—while willfully avoiding the steel-toed boot and the knowledge of what was hidden inside—then made his way back down the hall to Baker's office.

"Knock-knock," Frank called, rapping his heavy knuckles against the wooden frame of Baker's partially open office door. "You have a few minutes, Coach?" Frank leaned his thick torso through the door, clutching the mitt to his chest.

Baker's gaze drifted up from his work. He saw the mitt in Frank's hand, raised one questioning eyebrow, then exchanged his tired frown for a kindly smile.

"Sure do," he said. "Just give me a minute to finish up."

Frank surveyed the line of framed photos on the walls of the sparsely furnished office as he waited for Baker to complete whatever mind-numbing task had brought him to the station on his day off. He'd seen them all before, this small but important collection of moments in Baker's life. The people and events that mattered most. Frank sometimes wondered about the boy, Gabriel, whose picture was conspicuously absent from the walls.

It had been years since Baker had mentioned his estranged son, and though curious, Frank knew some questions were better left unasked.

He skirted the chairs and drifted across the small office. On the far wall, framed alongside Baker's wedding photo and a picture from baby Sarah's baptism, was the team photo from Frank's senior year. Occupying the central position in the back of the two rows, Big Ray Baxter had his hat pulled so low that all you could see of his face was his shit-eating grin.

Ray remained in the city after high school and enrolled in community college. He played half a season of baseball but quickly drank his way off the team and out of school. Last Frank heard, Ray had moved back to Sacramento, taken up with a dancer—not of the "classically trained" variety—and gone to work as a mechanic in his dad's auto garage.

"All right, Frank; I'm all set here," Baker said, thumb and index finger massaging the bridge of his nose. He pushed back his rolling chair and stepped away from the desk, its surface barely visible under all the stacks of paper.

"It's like the world's most depressing game of solitaire," Frank observed, eyeing the desk warily and nodding to its fastidiously aligned and carefully overlapping paper columns.

"You being clever?" Baker asked. He issued a wry laugh as he reached into his bottom desk drawer to remove his mitt. "I'll have to remember that line years from now when *you're* the one behind the desk on a Saturday morning and I'm happily retired."

⬩

THE AIR OUTSIDE was bitingly cold, tinged with the musky-sweet smell of damp rot and fallen leaves. Frank exhaled forcefully, his breath forming a cloud in front of his face, as he and Baker made the short walk from the station's lobby to the ribbon of grass on the far side of the engine bay.

Years before, when Frank had first started working there, that area had been home to a row of scraggly bushes and a narrow dirt path that turned to mud with the first winter rains. It hadn't been tough to convince Baker to let him rip up the bushes, level the earth, and install the long strip of grass that now ran parallel to the engine bay, all the way to the chain-link fence that separated the back of the property from the dense woods beyond.

He and Baker had dubbed the area "the bullpen," paying homage to the cramped coaches' office back at Washington High. In the years since, the bullpen had become an extension of the recreation room, complete with a Weber grill, horseshoe pits, and a picnic table that was popular with the smokers in the group.

"Jesus Christ, it's cold," Baker complained, blowing noisily into his clenched throwing hand. He raised his glove, signaling to Frank that he was ready to receive the ball.

"Sure is," Frank agreed. He tossed the ball on a high arc into Baker's waiting mitt. "Should warm up in a few minutes, though, once the sun gets up and over the ridge."

Frank nodded to the east, where the sky was slowly transitioning from gray to blue, and the first rays of golden sunshine were leaking over the tops of the rolling green hills.

They tossed the ball back and forth in silence, one or the other periodically taking a step back to increase the distance between them. As their arms warmed up, the velocity of their throws increased, and the corresponding *pop* of the ball impacting their mitts grew louder in the otherwise silent morning.

Without warning, Baker dipped his shoulder and slung the ball side-arm into the ground in front of Frank's feet. The ball hit a bump on the grass and took a high and nasty bounce.

Calm and collected, Frank speared the ball with his bare right hand, adjusted his grip on the seams, and rifled a strike into Baker's outstretched glove. Both men smiled.

"You're still quick," Baker observed, pausing the game to remove his mitt and massage the reddened heel of his palm. He replaced the glove on his left hand but made no move to throw the ball back. "You called me 'Coach' back there in the office. You don't do that very often anymore. Kinda made me think you had something on your mind other than playing catch." He blew into his hand again, flexed his fingers, and threw the ball back to Frank.

"I bought a ring," Frank said, the words catching on a hard mass in his trachea. He cleared his throat and spit into the grass at his feet. "I bought a ring," he repeated, louder this time, "that has been hidden in my locker for almost a month, doing nothing but making me miserable."

He removed his glove, walked to the picnic table, and planted his ass on its frigid surface, his feet resting on the bench below. Baker hesitated, then joined him on the cold table.

"I was excited when I bought it. But then the days kept passing, and I just couldn't get the damn words out. And now, honestly, I'm not even sure if I should." He looked up from the grass and locked eyes with Baker, who watched from beneath furrowed brows.

"Go on," Baker prompted.

"Ellie's wonderful, you know?" Frank bit the inside of his cheek, groping in the darkness for the right words. "I've never met anyone like her. She's smart and self-assured. Loyal and sweet . . . but doesn't put up with anyone's shit."

He laughed lightly, then paused again, fingering the seams of the baseball.

"And the way she makes me feel—it's like she brings out the very best in me. That confidence—the way I used to feel on the baseball diamond, like I'm actually *good enough*—that's how I feel when I'm with her."

Baker smiled knowingly. He blew into his bare hand, then snagged the ball from Frank. "Well, from what I've seen, and what you're telling me, it sounds like she's perfect for you. So, what's the problem, kid?"

"The problem," Frank said, his frustration rising, "isn't whether she's right for *me*—because I know she is—but more a question of whether I'm right for her. Whether I'm *enough* for her. Sometimes, I just don't know."

Baker cocked his head. He raised the ball to his face and used it to scratch the salt-and-pepper stubble on his cheek.

"Frank, I think you know by now that I have no shortage of good things to say about you. And if you need to hear them, line for line, I can do that—though I might need to go inside and grab a jacket first." He smiled and continued. "You know, I remember your freshmen year. You were so goddamn unsure of yourself, everywhere but on the baseball field. You were absolutely convinced that you were dumb, and that you didn't have what it took to make the grades. And even when you decided to turn things around, you weren't able to *really* believe in yourself until others believed in you first."

Frank nodded, conceding the point. "But this is different," he argued.

He wanted to tell Baker *how* it was different, to explain what had really been keeping him up at night, but his words and his courage failed him, so he just stared at his feet instead.

"Is it? Oh, I don't know." Baker hesitated, taking his turn now to search for the right words. He sighed and ran his palm over the front ridge of his flattop, which was badly in need of a trim. "Ellie sees something special in you, kid. Of that, I'm sure. If you don't see those qualities in yourself, maybe you just need to look harder. And maybe, with a little faith, you'll start to believe in *yourself* the way that she believes in you. The way *I* believe in you."

Baker stood, patted Frank's shoulder, and began walking back to the station. "And one more thing," he added, turning to toss the ball underhand back to Frank. "You're not *him*." He repeated the words, emphasizing each syllable as if Frank hadn't heard him the first time. "And Ellie isn't your mother, either. So whatever other garbage you've got floating around up there, it's time to bag it up and take it to the curb."

Frank sighed, wondering when he'd become such an open book yet grateful that Baker had the ability to read it. To read him. A soft glow warmed him from the inside out despite the chill of the morning.

He smiled as the chief walked briskly back to the station. Even when stressed, sleep-deprived, and an hour's drive from Mel's Diner, the man still gave one hell of a pep talk.

◊

FRANK ANGRILY CRANKED the key in the ignition, barely waiting for her door to slam shut before throwing the truck in gear and speeding away from the parking lot.

"I looked like an asshole," he said, speaking through clenched teeth. His knuckles were white, hands wrapped around the steering wheel. "I'm serious, Ellie, if *I* saw *me* walking into that gala, I'd think... now there's a guy who got lost on his way to the asshole convention."

He cringed at the stupidity of his remark. His mind turned to mush whenever he was angry, which was why he hated to argue. Especially with her.

"No, you only *sound* like an asshole," she corrected, her bare arms folded across her chest. She turned to face the window. "You *looked* very handsome."

The two settled into an uncomfortable silence as Frank wondered for the hundredth time how he'd let Ellie convince him to attend the hospital's New Year's Eve Gala, a fundraiser to support the construction of a new surgical wing. Usually, the price tag alone, an ungodly $100 a plate, would have been enough to discourage him from going. But Ellie, and many other nurses at the hospital, had been gifted the tickets by one of the doctors. Left without a leg to stand on, Frank had buckled. He didn't have the heart to deprive her of a glamorous evening, no matter how much he loathed those stuffy events.

Frank had been told little about the gala ahead of time, other than the basics—cocktail hour, followed by dinner and dancing—but had learned all he really needed to know before they even stepped through the door to the event center. Every man standing in line, without exception, was wearing either a dark suit or a full-blown tuxedo, while Frank had clearly missed the memo regarding proper men's attire for the evening.

Frank's off-white three-piece suit, the only suit that he owned, had been purchased two years before for Chief Baker's wedding. The burgundy satin shirt he wore underneath the jacket and vest, which Ellie had given him the previous week as a gift, matched her elegant floor-length gown perfectly. While she looked stunning, he knew from the host of muffled giggles and slew of sidelong glances that he stuck out like a sore thumb.

Despite looking and feeling out of place—and standing as the lone bastion of sobriety in the entire building—Frank had done his best to roll with the punches. He'd trailed Ellie from one inebriated cluster of people to the next, weaving between the circular tables that formed a tight perimeter around the glossy dance floor. He made small talk the best he could, laughing at presumed jokes he could barely hear over the rising din of cocktail hour while complimenting women whose names he would never remember on the beauty and sophistication of their *ensembles* (a word he'd learned from an issue of *Cosmo* he'd paged through at the dentist's office but never imagined he would utter aloud). He even managed to force a tight-lipped grin when Ellie's attending physician, a red-faced Steve McQueen lookalike with slurred speech and 80-proof breath, grabbed him by the arm and asked him in all seriousness if he needed "to be seen in the ER—for a case of *Saturday Night Fever*."

In spite of his best efforts, the night had taken an irreparable turn for the worse after dinner. The band was in full swing, and Ellie, having had one cocktail too many, again, tried to drag him against his will onto the crowded dance floor. He finally lost it. And when he jerked his hand free and demanded that she "stop goddamn touching him," a loud argument ensued. In the messy aftermath, she grabbed her purse and teetered for the door as fast as her four-inch heels would allow, leaving Frank holding the bag, forced to issue a quick round of embarrassed apologies to a group of people he hardly knew.

"We could have stayed, you know," Frank said finally, shattering the barrier of silence that separated her side of the truck from his.

"No. You didn't want to be there in the first place. You made that pretty *goddamn* clear."

She wasn't wrong; he *didn't* want to be there. He'd only gone for her, to make her happy. But he'd tried to make the best of it, to be the man she wanted him to be. Instead, he'd acted like the man he always feared he'd be. Like Pop.

Deflated by his realization and already regretting his part in the argument, Frank fiddled with the radio, eager to turn the page and move on.

"Turn it off," she said flatly, still staring out the window. "I'm not in the mood." She paused for a beat as he silenced the radio. "And take me back to my place. I want to sleep in my own bed tonight."

Frank leaned forward to catch her eyes, trying to confirm the meaning behind her words. Though Ellie was still technically living in her cramped one-bedroom apartment off Montgomery Drive, she only spent the night there when Frank was on duty at the station. This was her making a point.

The last vestiges of anger drained from his body as they drove on in silence. Though they didn't argue often, this was the way it usually went: Ellie's anger continued to burn bright long after Frank's was extinguished.

He slid his hand into his jacket pocket, searching for the ring box, checking to ensure it was still there. Had he known their night was going to devolve into an unmitigated disaster, he wouldn't have brought it with him in the first place.

Frank eased the Chevy off Montgomery Drive, into the parking lot of Ellie's apartment complex, and brought it to rest under the carport, in one of the two numbered spots assigned to her unit. They sat for a moment in the quiet of the cab. The only noise came from the truck's engine, which he made no move to silence.

"I'm sorry," Frank said finally. "About everything." Though he meant the apology, the words sounded phony and forced, even to his own ears. Another Sal Romano specialty.

"Yeah, me too," she said, clutching her purse and opening the door. "I guess you better get going before you miss the rest of the *asshole convention*." She slammed the door of the truck with window-rattling force and marched up the sidewalk toward her apartment.

Frank chuckled wryly under his breath. She was always good at that: getting the last word. He stewed in the silence of the cab—remembering Baker's assurances and trying to convince himself he was right—then shut off the engine and jogged up the sidewalk after her. He caught her as she reached the apartment, its door painted forest green to accent the brown exterior of the two-story building.

"Ellie, wait. There's something I need to say."

Atop the brown welcome mat, she froze, an elegant statue in a floor-length gown, her keys suspended halfway between her hip and the door. When she turned, he could see that she was crying. She wiped away the tears, smearing her mascara in the process.

"Just find the nerve to say it then, *Frank*. You've been somewhere else, been *someone* else, for the last couple of weeks. If you have something to say, if you're going to end this, just be a man and spit it out."

Startled by her ridiculous assumption—and by the way she'd spit his name into the night, like an insult or a curse—the words died on his lips. He watched her turn and fumble with the lock, her hand shaking so badly she couldn't get the key into the slot.

"Ellie, listen to me." He closed the distance between them, simultaneously reaching for her right hand, then falling to one knee.

She turned and fixed him with mascara-marred hazel eyes.

"I'm not good at this," Frank confessed, still holding her hand as he reached into his jacket pocket for the ring box. "Frankly, I'm not good at a lot of things . . . dancing and small talk with strangers being two of them." He had hoped to coax a smile, but her face remained impassive. "But I feel like I'm better at everything, like I'm the best version of myself, when I'm with you. So, what I'm saying is, what I'm asking is . . . will you marry me?"

He released her hand, fumbled to open the box, then held it and the ring up to the light. The diamond looked smaller and less impressive than it had in the store, but that was the least of his worries.

The seconds stretched agonizingly into hours as her expressionless eyes shifted from his face to the ring, then back again.

She turned wordlessly, finally managed to unlock the door, and crossed the threshold into her apartment, leaving Frank baffled and still bent on one knee, anchored to the earth.

"You coming in, or what?" she asked from the doorway, a slight smile lifting the contours of her tear-streaked cheeks. She sniffed loudly, kicked off her shoes, then disappeared into the darkness of the apartment. "Somebody needs to help me out of this dress."

Chapter 8

Age 27

September 17, 1979

"Get your hotdogs!" Frank barked to the rows below, his shamelessly corny imitation of a ballpark vendor.

He gripped the cardboard tray with both hands, carefully balancing its weight as he descended the last broad concrete step, then pivoted to face the long row of orange plastic seats. "We've got two hot dogs, two Cokes, and one basket of fries drizzled with ketchup, per the lady's request."

Ellie sat up straighter in her seat and craned her neck to inspect the preparation of the French fries. Pleased with his work, she smiled from under the brim of her ballcap, nodding her approval as she held down the folding seat of Frank's chair.

In the year since the two had married, Frank had become something of an expert regarding Ellie's little quirks, such as the way she cut her sandwiches diagonally, or how she liked to drizzle thin ropes of ketchup across the surface of her French fries, favoring this method over the standard dipping technique that Frank employed.

Frank handed off the cardboard tray, slid into the aisle seat next to her, and surveyed the field from their seats behind first base. The evening was unusually calm, a rarity at Candlestick Park, and the last remnants of daylight were quickly fading over the western rim of the stadium.

Though he and Ellie had watched plenty of games on television throughout the year, this was the first time they'd visited the ballpark since the season began in the spring. And it was Frank's first time in San Francisco since that rainy day in April, when he'd secretly taken a vacation day and driven to Washington Square alone without announcing his trip to Ellie or anyone else.

He'd huddled under a black umbrella, shivering at the edge of the crowd as Mayor Feinstein opened the time capsule that had been painstakingly removed from the base of the park's Benjamin Franklin statue. While the capsule's treasures were remarkably unremarkable—an issue of *Harper's Magazine* from 1872, a small tin of mints, and other assorted knickknacks common to the era—its contents were irrelevant. What mattered was his promise to his mother, which he had finally kept. His end of the bargain had been upheld, and the ledger was now closed. A small penance, it was both the least and the most he could do.

"Frank, let me introduce you to our neighbors for the evening, Mr. and Mrs. . . ." Ellie let the sentence dangle, providing the elderly gentleman seated next to her with the window to make his own introduction.

"Rob Cook's the name," he announced, the vigor in his voice at odds with the deeply etched lines in his face. "And this beautiful lady is my bride, Claribel." Mr. Cook reached around Ellie, clenched Frank's hand in an iron vise, and pumped it up and down with the enthusiasm of a seasoned car salesman who'd just closed "the deal of a lifetime."

Frank eventually reclaimed his hand and cast a loving glance at Ellie. He wasn't surprised that she'd made new friends during his brief trip to the concession stand. Chatty and inquisitive, she had a charisma that Frank admired, a gravitational pull that drew people inevitably into her orbit. To Ellie, a stranger was just a friend she had yet to meet.

"It's great to meet you both," Frank said, taking in their matching Giants hats, both adorned with so many commemorative pins that the faded black bills were the only surface left uncovered. Frank even spied the famous Croix de Candlestick pin, awarded exclusively to those diehard fans who stayed for the full duration of extra-inning games, even on the coldest and windiest Candlestick nights.

"Bad news, honey," Ellie said to Frank. "They introduced the players while you were gone—looks like he's not playing tonight."

Frank's eyes darted to first base. His heart sank as he confirmed it was Mike Ivie positioned next to the bag and not the great Willie McCovey.

"That's too bad," Frank said, slowly shaking his head. "I was really hoping to see old 'Stretch' play one more time." The longtime Giants slugger had been hampered for years by a slew of injuries—feet, hips, and knees, to name a few—and Frank had heard rumors that this season might be his last hurrah. With Mays and Marichal already retired, McCovey was the last of a dying breed, the only colossus of Frank's boyhood left standing.

Frank reached into the box in Ellie's lap, retrieved his Polish sausage, and savored the first bite as pregame warmups continued on the field below. On the mound, Vida Blue was completing his warmup, recognizable as the only player on either team with his first name emblazoned on the back of his jersey instead of his last. Mike Ivie threw groundballs to each of the other infielders, who took turns fielding the ball and zipping it back to his outstretched glove at first base. And Dave Collins, the leadoff man for the Cincinnati Reds, was taking practice cuts in the on-deck circle, watching Vida warm up and trying to gauge the speed and break of his pitches.

"You know, it's amazing," Frank remarked. He was speaking to Ellie but staring out into center field, then up to the concrete rim of the stadium and the banks of powerful lights that illuminated the diamond below. "No matter how many years pass, no matter how many games I've been to, there's always a moment, just as I'm walking out of the concourse and looking down onto the field, when it just hits me—the wonder of it all. It's like I'm a kid again, you know, seeing the field for the very first time. Sharp white lines drawn on reddish-brown dirt, the green of the grass—the checkered pattern that the groundskeepers mow into the outfield. It just blows me away. Every time."

He looked over to Ellie, who smiled her agreement, watching him with sparkling hazel eyes as he watched the field below.

"How old were you?" she asked. "When you went to your first game, I mean."

Frank leaned back in his seat and tilted his chin skyward as he plowed through the fields of time. "That would have been '62 or '63, I think. So, I was ten or eleven at the time. The Giants were playing the Mets; I remember that."

He sat up straighter in his seat, a jolt of electricity surging through his body as the memories flooded back.

"And get this," he continued, smiling now, "it was one of those miserable windy nights at the 'Stick—the kind where you spend the whole game with your hand clutched to your head, so your hat doesn't go flying—and a gust of wind comes during the Mets' batting practice, right? Now, this gust, I shit you not, was *so strong* that it lifted the batting cage up and off the ground, flung it into the air like it weighed nothing at all, and carried it all the way to the pitcher's mound—sixty feet away!"

Ellie opened her mouth to comment, an impressed look on her face, then shut it just as quickly as Mr. Cook chimed in from the seat next to her.

"It was definitely '63, son, not '62." He nudged his preoccupied wife with his elbow. "You remember that game, Clarie? The wind was so bad that we almost pulled up stakes and hit the road?"

His wife nodded in agreement but didn't look up. "Sure do," she confirmed, her sharp eyes trained on the field. She had a scorebook in her lap, and she was watching every warm-up pitch with the intensity of a professional scout. "Casey Stengel was managing the Mets at the time, and he threw a goddamn hissy fit when the cage blew away. He canceled the rest of batting practice and made his boys field pop-ups instead."

Ellie leaned in toward Frank, offering a smile and a conspiratorial wink as she whispered, "He has very sharp ears, that Mr. Cook. And his wife has the mouth of a sailor." Then in her normal voice, "Who did you go to the game with? The game that was definitely in '63, not '62."

Before Frank could answer, the crowd broke into a modest round of applause as Dave Collins squared up in the batter's box and Vida Blue threw the first pitch of the game, a called strike. Frank could tell from the sharp pop of the ball into the catcher's mitt that Vida was throwing hard—mid-90s at least. It sounded louder than normal in the sparsely populated stadium.

Frank waited for the applause to die down, then cleared his throat, which was suddenly tight. "With my father, actually. We sat over on the third base side. And I remember, like I was saying, the feeling of coming out of the tunnel, looking down, and seeing a big-league field for the first time." His eyes drifted across the field, trying to pick out the exact tunnel his father had led him down as a boy. "You know, Pop actually made me cover my eyes, then he led me by the hand as we walked out of the concourse. And then we stood there for a minute, just me and him together, his hand on my shoulder, staring down at the field."

Ellie turned in her chair, smiled sweetly, and reached for Frank's hand. She intertwined her fingers with his and offered a reassuring squeeze.

"I never saw it coming," Frank continued, his mind sifting through long-dormant memories. "I'd been bugging him for a long time to take me to a Giants game, but he always refused. He took it pretty hard when I picked the Giants over his beloved Yankees, you know?"

Ellie nodded. "He was from New York, right?"

"Right. And if I'm being honest, I think it was his love for the Yankees—Mickey Mantle in particular—not my constant haranguing, that finally got him to give in. That was about the time that the whole *Mays vs Mantle* debate was really heating up. I think the old man just needed to see Mays in the flesh, to confirm with his own eyes what he already believed in his heart." Frank smiled at the memory. "Mays could have hit four home runs that game, and I don't think Pop would have left here feeling any differently."

"And if he'd gone 0-for-5? Would that have changed your opinion one iota?"

Frank laughed and wagged his head emphatically from side to side. One time, as a boy, he'd rounded up all the neighborhood kids on Spruce Street, formed a bicycle-mounted search party, and spent the better part of an afternoon going door to door, hunting in vain for the apartment building on their street where Willie Mays was *rumored* to live. So, no, one poor night at the dish wasn't going to change his mind.

"No, ma'am, I suppose not," Frank answered, his voice rising in pitch and volume as he jumped excitedly to his feet.

On the field below, Dennis Littlejohn, the Giants' catcher, received the pitch from Vida Blue and threw a frozen rope to second base to throw out Dave Concepcion, who was trying to steal second. The small crowd, fewer than five thousand, by Frank's estimation—but full of diehard fans who came to support the team regardless of its place in the standings—erupted as the umpire signaled the runner out, marking the end of the top of the first inning.

"We might actually have a shot at this," Frank said, a reference to the respective records of the two teams. The Giants were winding down another lackluster season while Cincinnati's Big Red Machine seemed as well-oiled at the end of the decade as it had been at the beginning.

"So was the issue ever resolved?" Ellie asked, settling back into her seat.

"Mays vs Mantle? Nah, not really. Mays obviously had the edge defensively, but there will always be an argument over who was the better man at the plate." Frank reached into the box in Ellie's lap and searched for the perfect fry, wishing again that he had a reservoir of ketchup to dip it in.

Ellie cleared her throat, her eyes searching his face as she spun her wedding ring back and forth around her ring finger. This was another of her little quirks that Frank had grown to love. This one, in his experience, meant that she had something on her mind and was debating whether or not to share.

"That's not what I meant," she said finally, leaning into the bulk of Frank's shoulder and keeping her voice low, safeguarding their conversation from prying ears. "I meant the one between you and your father. You almost never speak about him, or your mother for that matter, and I think this is the first time you've *ever* mentioned his name with anything but a grimace on your face." She pursed her lips and stopped fiddling with her ring. "I just wonder sometimes, you know?"

Of course, he knew. Ellie came from a close-knit family—the kind that gathered at holidays, had hosts of treasured traditions, and even seemed to genuinely enjoy each other's company—and she sometimes seemed incapable of imagining an upbringing any less storybook than her own.

That said, Frank had always played his cards close to his vest, leaving the trove of unhappy family artifacts hidden away in the Romano family time capsule, where they belonged. Though Ellie wasn't one to push, she wasn't afraid to occasionally poke, and her curiosity was always lurking, hidden just below the surface.

Frank shrugged and offered a halfhearted smile. "He was a hard man to know, Ellie. And even harder to please." It was an understatement, he knew. Even now, a decade after the man's death, Frank was still trying to impress his father, still trying to prove that he was *good enough*. And still coming up short.

He reached for another fry and chased it with a long swig of Coke, but the bad taste in his mouth remained. "Now let's see if we can put some runs on the board," he said. He clapped loudly, closing the book on their conversation as he turned his body and attention back to the field.

◆

LOYALTY TO THE TEAM, and not wanting to be admonished by the likes of Claribel and Robert Cook, kept Frank and Ellie rooted to their seats until the final out of the game.

After scoring five runs in the bottom of the first inning, the Giants' bats remained mostly quiet for the next eight frames. But they managed to withstand a late push by the Reds and held on for a 7-4 victory. Seeing a win always put a smile on Frank's face, serving as a happy reminder of the joy Ellie had brought into his life. It was no small feat, separating his feelings about his father from his love for the game. And he never could have done it without Ellie there beside him, helping him sift through the ashes to unearth and revive the passion he was certain the fire had claimed.

Frank reached for the dashboard of the Chevy and adjusted the heat. It was nearing midnight, and the temperature outside had continued to drop during the drive home from the city. After sitting in stadium gridlock for nearly an hour trying to leave the congested parking lot, he was thankful to find only a smattering of cars on the stretch of Highway 101 that ran north from the Golden Gate Bridge, past San Rafael and Novato, and through the center of Santa Rosa.

Frank looked across the cab as they passed the lonely sign on the shoulder of the highway, marking Santa Rosa's city limits. Ellie had folded his thick winter coat to make a pillow, which was now providing a layer of insulation between her head and the truck's door. He was always impressed by her effortless ability to sleep in a car. It was a talent he both lacked and envied.

"Ugggh," Ellie moaned. She sat up abruptly, crinkled her button nose, and reached for the volume knob to silence "Desperado," which was playing quietly on the radio. While she loved The

Eagles—"Witchy Woman" was a frequent selection for the one-woman concerts she performed in the shower—she absolutely despised this particular song. She'd been outspoken about her dislike in the past but cagey about the reasons. Frank had his suspicions, but he never pressed her for answers; they were both entitled to a secret or two.

She turned to face him, adjusting her seatbelt to accommodate her movements. Feeling her eyes roving over him, Frank turned to meet her gaze. He reached across the cab of the truck and brushed aside a strawberry blonde lock of hair that had come loose from her ponytail, tucking it securely behind her ear.

"Good nap?" he asked, a note of envy seeping into his voice. "You've been out for most of the trip."

"Some napping," she replied, staring out the window into the black curtains of night. "Some thinking, too."

She was twirling her wedding band around her ring finger again, rotating it back and forth over her pale skin.

"Frank, there's something I need to tell you. I've been trying to find the right moment for a week now, but I'm starting to think that moment doesn't exist."

He nodded but remained silent.

"I'm pregnant," she said, her tone flat and even. Despite the weight of her announcement, the words seemed to float in the space between them, lingering like fog over the bay.

Frank could feel Ellie's eyes boring into him, probing and searching, watching him while waiting for a response. His heart galloped in his chest, audible, at least to him, over the steady rumble of the truck barreling down the highway.

"Are you sure?" Frank finally asked, his eyes still fastened to the road. "This isn't supposed to happen with the pill . . . right?"

"Are you kidding me?" She scoffed. "You remember I'm a nurse, right?"

Her voice was saturated with exasperation, and he could feel her defenses rising, making him regret his pitch selection, wishing he'd gone with the soft stuff instead of the heater.

"You remember that one time," she continued mockingly, "when I showed up to a burning building, pulled you away from the fire engine, and asked you if you were *sure* that the building was on fire?" She paused, took a deep breath, then continued in a more controlled tone. "Yes, Frank, I'm 100 percent and unequivocally sure that I'm pregnant."

"Well, then . . ." he said, pausing midsentence to navigate the freeway offramp and pilot the truck onto Bicentennial Road, "I am 100 percent and unequivocally thrilled by the news."

"Really?" Her voice was etched with skepticism. "Are you sure? Or are you just telling me what you think I want to hear?"

"I'm sure," he managed, his eyes finally leaving the road. He manufactured a smile, piece by piece, and assembled it on his face. "Unequivocally sure."

She undid her seatbelt, scooted across the bench seat, and nestled her head into the nook between his shoulder and neck. He forced a breath into his constricted lungs, taking in the floral fragrance of her shampoo, and held it for a count of five. He released the breath slowly, loosened his death grip on the steering wheel, and felt his heart begin to slow within his chest.

"I love you, Ellie," he breathed, this time not having to force the words. He raised his right arm and drew her in beneath it. "You know that, right?"

"I do. And I love you, too, Mr. Fireman."

⬦

FRANK HAD BEEN LYING awake for the better part of an hour, watching a slideshow of unhappy childhood memories playing on an endless loop, projected by his anxious mind onto the darkened ceiling above their bed. The drinking and the fighting, the loneliness and neglect, these were the memories that clung to his psyche like a drenched shirt in a downpour. And try as he might, they were all but impossible to strip away.

He lifted the covers and crept from bed, careful not to wake

Ellie. His precautions were unnecessary; she slept as soundly in their bed at home as she did in the cab of his truck.

He was still getting used to the idea of *their bed* in the master bedroom of *their home*. They had felt so very adult during the whole process—touring different houses in different neighborhoods, listening to the realtor rattle off various information and statistics, then securing the loan and signing a seemingly endless stack of paperwork. It had been an exhilarating experience for both of them and one that had finally cemented the reality of their marriage in his mind.

Frank turned on the overhead light in the kitchen and eased open the sliding door to the pantry. He didn't have much of a sweet tooth, but there was something comforting about a plate of Oreos and a glass of milk when he couldn't sleep. Taking six cookies from the package, he placed them on a plate—neatly aligned in two columns of three—poured a glass of milk, then sat at the walnut butterfly-leaf table in the dining room.

The table was a wedding gift from Ellie's parents, and it was easily the nicest piece of furniture they owned. Everything else in the home was either carried over from their respective apartments or purchased from the Goodwill store downtown. They had planned to upgrade the furniture over time, piece by piece, but that plan might need to be put on hold for now, with a new arrival on the horizon.

New arrival. The words sounded ominous in Frank's mind. He was no expert on apples, but he'd been told they rarely fell far from the tree. Despite Baker's assurances—that Frank wasn't like Pop and never would be—the prospect of fatherhood had tapped into the swift current of doubt that flowed just beneath the frozen surface.

Frank looked at the empty chair beside him and remembered the long hours spent at the kitchen table in their old house, a book in front of him, and his mother sitting patiently beside him. He wondered what she would tell him now, what the moral of *this* story would be.

Frank cocked his head, listening to slipper-clad feet padding down the hallway.

"Penny for your thoughts?" Ellie rested one hand lightly on his shoulder and reached for his plate, snatching an Oreo before taking a seat across from him.

"Plural?" he asked, arching an eyebrow. "You should know by now that I only have one thought at a time. Usually with long gaps in between." He rearranged his remaining cookies, forming a two-by-two square, with the fifth cookie centered on top, like a belltower above a church.

"Why do you do that?" she asked, eyeing his plate as she chewed her cookie.

"What, make jokes? Besides bringing you flowers, it seems to be the best way to make you smile."

"Not the jokes . . . though they do make me smile." She flashed a goofy grin, seemingly unaware of the black cookie remnants lodged between her front teeth, then gestured to his plate. "The thing with the cookies . . . and everything else. You're always reordering things, making them symmetrical. Why?"

He stared at the plate and the cookies arranged so precisely across its surface, then shrugged. "Honestly, I don't know. Old habits, I guess. From when I was a kid. I just appreciate a certain order sometimes, knowing that everything is in its place."

He plucked the belltower from atop the church, submerged it in milk for a four-count, then ate it in one bite.

"Fair enough," she replied, taking another cookie from his plate. She repositioned the three remaining cookies in a closely grouped triangle, then looked pleased when he nodded his approval. "So, are you going to tell me what's on your mind?"

"Would you believe me," Frank began, rubbing one ear as he felt them both turn hot, "if I told you that it was an alligator?"

She eyed him skeptically from across the table, trying to ascertain if he was kidding or not.

Frank sighed, debated whether or not to continue, then made

up his mind and pressed onward, his words pouring out faster than usual.

"It was a book I read with my mother, as a child. A young alligator has a toothache, and there's nothing the zookeeper can do to help, so Alli—that was the alligator's name—has to take a bus to go see the dentist. Unfortunately, he's *terrified* of the dentist."

"Okay, I'm with you so far."

"So, he ends up getting on the wrong bus, but it turns out to be a good thing because he meets a boy—who happens to be the son of the same dentist he's going to see. The boy listens to Alli's fears, convinces him that his father is a good man, and swears that he will stay by Alli's side through the whole operation."

"Okaaaay..."

"But here's the twist: when they finally arrive at the office, the dentist takes one look in Alli's mouth and discovers the pain Alli is feeling is only a wisdom tooth growing in. No procedure is required, and in a day or two it will be fine."

Frank shrugged, then folded his hands on the table, waiting as Ellie digested the finer points of the story.

"That's a lovely plot," she said sweetly. "And you told it so well." She took a long sip of his milk and swished it around in her mouth, perhaps aware of the crumbs in her teeth after all. "But I'm afraid I've missed the point."

"The *point*," he said, his inflection rising as he handed her another Oreo and grabbed one for himself, "is that sometimes the thing we're most afraid of, the thing that keeps us up at night, exists only within our own mind. So, really, when you think about it, there's nothing to fear at all."

"Hmm, I see." She searched his face from across the table. "And I'm guessing this epiphany pertains to the news I gave you on the way home?"

Frank nodded, slowly chewing on both his cookie and her word—*epiphany*. He'd come to accept that he would never be a reader, but he appreciated that she was. And he'd even come to enjoy the fancy words that leaped from the pages of her books and landed in the middle of their discussions.

"I know that this is a lot to wrap your mind around, Frank. And that it probably stirs up a lot of old feelings for you. Maybe you want to talk about it?"

Frank looked up from his plate, confused by her question. "I thought we just did."

Ellie sighed long and hard and walked around the edge of the table, again reaching for his shoulder. "For what it's worth, Frank Romano, your father wasn't the only man who is hard to know." She let her hand linger, then brushed his cheek with her lips. "Come to bed when you're ready, huh?"

He watched her shuffle down the darkened hallway, then stared down at the remaining cookie on his plate. His thoughts returned to the night's game and the saddening absence of Willie McCovey. Hopefully, old Stretch would have one more season left in the tank.

"Last man standing," Frank whispered to the cookie, his mind back in his bedroom on Spruce Street, laying face up on his bed, the sounds of the game squawking from his mother's portable radio.

He picked up the cookie from the plate, felt the weight of it in his hand, then walked to the pantry and returned it to the package. He left his plate and glass in the sink, then turned off the kitchen light before following Ellie back to bed.

Chapter 9

Age 27

May 13, 1980

"If you want to watch something else," Ellie said, offering a hard smile in response to Frank's most recent in a long series of sighs, "we can change the channel. It's okay, really."

She made a dramatic show of putting down her book and locating the television remote, then extended her arm in the general direction of his uncomfortable wood-framed chair, which he'd positioned in the small aisle next to her bed.

"No, no, let's leave it here," Frank mumbled, resigned to his fate. He waved her hand away, reaching again for the issue of *Sports Illustrated* he'd snagged from the waiting room on their way in. "I don't think I could live with myself," he continued, cutting his eyes to the portable television set that sat atop a wheeled cart across the room, "if I left this hospital not knowing what happened next to Erica Kane and the other sad saps of Pine Valley."

They were midway through their third consecutive soap opera. Though the shows served as a mindless distraction for Ellie, Frank had received more than his daily fill of sex, scheming, and over-the-top sentimentality. The cramped two-patient room was at least ten degrees warmer than the hallway outside and felt like a prison from which they'd never escape. Thankfully, the room's second bed—which had a stunning view of the parking lot below—was unoccupied, offering them some small measure of privacy.

Despite Stitch Alvestal's warning as Frank sprinted from the station, he had found the "ride" thus far to be anything but "fuckin' wild." In fact, if pressed for an adjective, he'd probably settle on something like "routine." Maybe even *boring*.

Though she'd been breathless and anxious when they'd spoken on the phone, the Ellie he'd found waiting for him at home—reading patiently on the porch in her antique rocking chair, her tattered copy of *Little Women* resting atop the broad curvature of belly, her pea-green vinyl overnight bag packed and sitting at her feet—was the picture of composure. Whatever panic she'd experienced when her water broke in the kitchen that morning had evidently passed, replaced with an eerie calm that challenged Frank's preconceived notions of labor.

In truth, Frank had little in the way of real-life experience to base these notions upon. As an only child, with no extended family to speak of, his experience with children—and the process through which they came into the world—was extremely limited. Even in the course of his firefighting duties, most calls involving pregnant women were quickly handed off to the paramedics, forcing him to draw from his imagination instead—fueled by the sweat-filled and scream-riddled versions of childbirth he'd seen in movies and on television. So far, the slow-paced reality of labor had failed to measure up to his action-filled expectations.

After three sharp raps that startled them both, the door to the room opened wide, allowing passage for Ellie's white-coated doctor, led by a pear-shaped nurse whom they'd yet to meet. The nurse scrutinized the front of Frank's magazine, its cover adorned by Lakers star Kareem Abdul-Jabbar, then nodded her approval and made way for the doctor to approach.

At least seventy years old, with a bulbous rosy nose, a mane of white hair, and a flowing white beard to match, Dr. Desautels' resemblance to Father Christmas was unmistakable. It took every ounce of resistance Frank could muster not to offer the kindly doctor cookies and milk when he visited their room every half hour, spreading good cheer and monitoring the vital signs of both mother and child.

"How are we doing?" he asked Ellie, his vibrant voice reverberating off the room's yellow and white striped walls. "You think we're ready to get this show on the road?"

Without waiting for an answer, the doctor perched on a rolling stool and positioned himself at the foot of the bed. Despite being five centimeters dilated when they'd arrived, Ellie progressed slowly in the hours since.

"Well, I've got some good news for you," the doctor confided, depositing his latex gloves in the trash can before jotting some notes in her chart. "You, my dear, have now reached the magical number of nine centimeters, which means we're ready to move you into the delivery room. Ready or not . . . you're about to have a baby!"

Frank and Ellie exchanged nervous smiles. Rising from his seat next to the bed, Frank reached over the top of the guard rail and gave Ellie's hand a reassuring squeeze. Her skin was unusually cold to the touch.

Toppled by a wave of emotion, Frank fought to find his voice and searched for the words of encouragement he knew she needed to hear. "You've got this, honey," he offered lamely, his voice coming out choked. "You're going to do great, and I'm going to be with you every step of the way. I promise."

She nodded rapidly and clamped down harder on his hand. For the first time since he'd picked her up at the house, he saw a small crack in her brave façade.

"Please go call my parents," she said. Her breath came in shallow gasps, her voice anxious and strained. "They've been waiting at home for hours now. I want to give them plenty of time to make their way over here."

"I will," Frank assured her, breaking into an ironic grin.

"Assuming they haven't formed the troops and set up camp in the waiting room already."

◇

Minutes later, after a frantic search for a phonebook and a hurried discussion with Ellie's parents—Bob was holding the receiver, but Ruth was firing questions over his shoulder, doing the lion's share of the talking—Frank trailed the pear-shaped nurse down the well-lit corridor of the maternity ward. Despite the considerable difference in their heights, he struggled to match her brisk pace.

"Okay, Dad," she said firmly, slamming on the brakes outside the windowless stainless-steel door of the delivery room. Her skin, a brown so dark it was almost black, had a youthful quality that made it almost impossible to discern her real age. But her authoritative tone spoke volumes, and Frank guessed she was older, maybe fifty, and had been fighting in the trenches of the maternity ward for a long time.

"My name's Nurse Jackson," she continued, stating her name with conviction, as if Frank had disputed her identity, "and I'm going to go over some ground rules with you before we go in there."

She placed a hand on her well-padded hip, then looked him up and down before continuing. "Follow the rules, and everything will be peachy." She raised and waggled one plump finger in front of his face. "Break the rules, honey, and you and I will have to talk."

It was all the warning Frank needed. He nodded vigorously in response.

"Rule number one—when you're in that room, you're there for your wife. Do what she needs when she needs it." She searched his face for comprehension, waiting until he nodded again to continue. "Rule number two—you are not to interfere with the delivery or get in the way. If I, or the doctor, or another nurse, or even Otto the janitor, asks you to do something, you do it right away. Understand?"

Frank understood. Blown away by Nurse Jackson's brusque delivery, he was sure she could give Captain Lewis—or even Pop, for that matter—a run for his money. "Got it," he responded, focusing on her instructions and pushing those thoughts aside. "Do what Ellie needs, and don't get in the way."

"And rule number three, perhaps the most important of the rules, is this—if you feel, *at any time*, like you are going to pass out, *you need to let someone know!* The last thing we need is a second patient in the room. Got it?"

Small feet rooted to the floor, both hands now clamped to her hips, she waited for his response.

"Yes, ma'am," Frank stammered, more nervous now than he had been before her impromptu speech. He'd never even *considered* the possibility of passing out. Now his chest grew tight as he pictured himself facedown and unconscious, his limbs splayed across the delivery room floor. "You won't have any problems from me, I promise."

"Oh, you'd be surprised," Nurse Jackson said, her expression softening. "But stick to the rules, sugar, and you're gonna do great, just like your friend Kareem." She looked him over one last time, flashed a reassuring smile, then pulled the door wide. "Okay, Dad, *it's showtime.*"

◇

"Holy shit," Frank muttered, his voice echoing in the stillness of the deserted hallway. He pushed the heavy door of the delivery room closed behind him, then steadied his shaking hands long enough to consult his watch. More than three hours had passed since Nurse Jackson's reading of the rules and the beginning of his *wild fucking ride.*

Even television and movies couldn't fully prepare him for the staggering barrage of sights and sounds he experienced in that room. Or the worries and fears that had been jarred loose inside of him. He'd spent months convincing himself he was ready for this, *ready for fatherhood*, only to see that confidence melt into a puddle of self-doubt as Ellie writhed in agony on the table and he watched helplessly from her side, powerless to help.

Frank's mind raced as he walked the length of the hallway, hardly feeling the linoleum squares passing beneath his feet. He stopped a few feet shy of the swinging double doors that led to the crowded waiting room and unfurled the sleeves of his shirt, which had been rolled to the elbow.

The skin of his right hand was angry and red, marred by deep crescent-shaped gouges Ellie's fingernails had left during the final push. He used one sleeve to wipe his forehead, which was still beaded with sweat, then ran his fingers through waves of damp hair, sweeping stray locks away from his face before wiping his hand on the thigh of his trousers.

Peering through the rectangular window in the center of the door, he could see Ellie's family congregated on one side of the large waiting room. He took stock of the packed house, noting Bob and Ruth, both sets of Ellie's grandparents, her three brothers, and what appeared from a quick glance to be all of their wives and children. They had seemingly piled into their cars and made the short drive from Petaluma to the hospital as soon as he'd placed the call.

The once-neat arrangements of tables and chairs had been reconfigured to support the sprawl of the entire Snyder clan, to include the far corner of the room, which had been commandeered by the gaggle of children and transformed into a formidable blanket fort. The few surfaces not being used for seating were littered with cardboard trays, food wrappers, and all the other telltale remnants of a cafeteria-style meal.

Frank retreated from the window. He sucked in a deep breath, held it for a count of five, then let it out slowly before repeating the process two more times. The tightness in his neck and shoulders eased, though the persistent tremor in his hands remained. He smoothed the front of his damp shirt, then propelled himself through the swinging doors and into the noisy lobby.

The energy in the room morphed as he entered the lobby, and conversations ceased. Bob and Ruth rose from their seats and crossed the waiting room, arm in arm, to meet him next to the nurses' station. Seeing the pair together, it was impossible not to recognize Ellie's features in those of her parents. From Ruth, the wavy strawberry blonde hair, button nose, and inquisitive hazel eyes. From Bob—a baseball player in his youth and a farmer all his life—came the tall stature and athletic build. Ellie seemed to have won the genetic lottery, walking away with the best each parent had to offer.

Frank noted the worried expression on their faces, felt a pang of guilt for not sending word sooner, and broke into a forced smile while delivering the news. "It's a boy!" he called, his words directed at Bob and Ruth but projected loud enough for the rest of the family to hear. "His name is Daniel Victor, and I personally counted two arms, two legs, and ten each of the smallest fingers and toes I've ever seen."

At the sound of Frank's announcement, the entire Snyder family—adults first, followed closely by the raucous mob of children—rose to their feet and erupted in a sustained round of applause.

Tired and anxious as he was, Frank couldn't help but laugh. As a child, he'd never contemplated the loneliness of their small family's existence, never wondered what joys an extended family might bring. Only later, by becoming a part of Ellie's family, did he realize what had been missing from his life all along.

"And Ellie?" Ruth asked, her voice rising sharply to be heard over the commotion. "How's our little girl?" She reached for Frank's hand and clasped it between both of hers.

Frank's heart swelled with pride. "She was amazing, Ruth: incredible from start to finish. She's exhausted, though, so the nurses are moving her into a private room and giving her a few minutes to rest while they bathe the baby and run a few more tests."

Ruth's worries melted away from her features, replaced with relief and then unbridled happiness. She wiped joyous tears from her eyes and wrapped her arms around her husband's waist.

"I'm going to go check on the baby," Frank said. "Then I'll pop in on Ellie, see how she's doing, and ask her if she's ready for visitors."

Frank looked to Ruth, who still had one arm wrapped around Bob's waist, while the other rummaged in her enormous purse for a tissue. She hesitated for a moment, then reluctantly agreed. Ellie was the youngest of Bob and Ruth's four children, and she would always be considered the baby of the family. Whether Ellie was ready or not, Frank doubted Ruth would be held at bay for long.

"That sounds good, Frank," Bob said, gently disengaging himself from Ruth's grasp. He shook Frank's hand and looked him solemnly in the eye. "Congratulations, son. Whether you fully appreciate it or not, your world changed forever today. And on behalf of me, and the five other fathers behind me, let me be the first to welcome you to the club."

He released Frank's hand, offered a sly wink, and playfully muffled his wife's ears. "We'll teach you the secret handshake later."

◇

FRANK RETRACED his steps and disappeared behind the double doors of the maternity ward. The noise level dropped as the doors swung shut behind him, offering a welcome respite from the sustained ruckus of the waiting room.

He wandered uncertainly into the deeper recesses of the ward, thankful for the series of directional signs, which were posted at regular intervals on the otherwise bare cream-colored walls. All of the hallways looked alike, and it was easy to become lost inside the labyrinth of windowless corridors.

Frank passed the central nurses' station, a busy hub of activity, then made a series of turns, continuing to follow the "newborn nursery" signs until he arrived at a bank of windows comprised of reinforced glass. Behind the glass, like a museum exhibit for the wonders of human reproduction, were a series of blanket-lined bassinets, neatly aligned in rows of five. Frank counted twenty bassinets, with only nine tiny occupants, all grouped on the right side of the room, and all sleeping soundly despite the harsh fluorescent lights that shone from above.

A young nurse sat on a chair in the corner, immersed in what appeared to be a romance novel, biting her lower lip as she flipped to the next page. Frank tapped lightly on the glass, careful not to wake the sleeping babies.

The startled nurse looked up sharply, saw Frank standing at the window, and hurried to the closed door that separated the nursery from the corridor.

"Mr. Romano?" she whispered, opening the door just enough to permit her willowy shoulders passage into the hallway.

Frank answered with a wry smile. Twenty-seven years old, but he still looked for his father every time someone threw the word *"mister"* in front of his last name. That, like fatherhood itself, would require some getting used to.

"Your son is in the back room with Nurse Jackson," she continued. "She's going to finish his bath, get him nice and clean, then bring him out in a few minutes." She gestured to an empty bassinet in the row closest to the window. "That will be his right there." She smiled shyly, closed the door behind her, then returned to her novel.

Alone in the hallway, Frank stared down at his hands, which had finally stopped shaking. He closed his eyes, summoning a mental image of the precious cargo they'd held only minutes before, and remembering the sensation—equal parts apprehension and wonder—when Nurse Jackson placed his son into his arms.

He'd been embarrassed to admit it to the nurse, but he'd

never held a baby before today. Clutching Daniel's tiny body in the delivery room, afraid the child would slip from his grasp, had lain bare Frank's fears and dragged his self-doubt to the forefront.

Life with his folks had been no picnic. The product of a disastrous marriage and two deeply-flawed parents, what business did Frank have raising a kid of his own? Hell, even Baker—the best man Frank knew and the closest thing he ever had to a *real* father—had screwed things up the first time around. Didn't this kid deserve better?

"Excuse me, Frank."

The words, though spoken softly, ripped him from his trance. He turned to greet Bob, who stood behind him in the otherwise deserted hallway.

"I'm sorry to intrude. One of the nurses came and grabbed Ruth; she said Ellie was asking for her. I thought this might be a good time for us to talk."

"Of course," Frank said, welcoming the distraction. "The nurse said he's back in the locker room, taking a postgame shower."

Perhaps a bigger baseball fan than Frank, Bob laughed loudly at the joke and joined him in front of the windows.

"You know," Bob began in his low gentle voice, his eyes trained on the glass window and the room full of babies that lay beyond, "I was only twenty-two when Carl was born, Frank. Quite a bit younger than you are now. Then Pete came next, two years later. Then Jimmy two years after that. After Jim, we almost gave up on the idea of a girl. But Ruth insisted, so we gave it one last go. And that's when God gave us our Ellie."

Bob removed his glasses. He held them up to the bank of overhead lights, inspecting the cleanliness of the lenses before folding the arms and slipping them into the pocket of his flannel shirt.

"It's been a long time now, Frank, but I can still remember what it felt like—bringing that first one into the world, I mean. And I suspect, though you've never been the easiest man to read, that you're feeling the weight of the world on your shoulders right now."

Frank avoided Bob's eyes and continued staring through the spotless glass to the nursery on the other side. Pop's ghost had haunted Frank's thoughts for much of the past nine months, and he couldn't help wondering now what it would feel like to have this conversation with his own father. What wisdom, if any, would his old man have to offer? And given Pop's track record—enough failures and mistakes to cram every page of a twenty-six-volume encyclopedia set—would Frank even be wise to listen? He felt an insane urge to share these thoughts with Bob, then quickly abandoned the notion, swallowing his tongue instead.

"Yep, I figured as much," Bob said, his words followed by a long sigh. "Well, I have one piece of advice for you, Frank, so here goes: You're probably feeling like it's the bottom of the ninth inning, the bases are jammed, and you're down by three. But the truth is, it's not. Instead, it's the first game of your rookie year, and you have a long season and an even longer career in front of you."

Frank formed a tender smile. This was Bob's way: imparting life lessons through sports analogies. He'd raised all his children this way, Ellie included. It was a trait that reminded Frank of Coach Baker, and one he hoped to emulate with Daniel.

"And though you need to take things a day and a game at a time," Bob continued, his voice rising as he gained steam, "you also need to understand that the old adage is true: You can't win 'em all, son."

He turned to face Frank, rested a calloused palm on his shoulder, and carried on, his volume increasing commensurately with his passion.

"And as good as those wins are going to feel, some of the losses are going to hurt even more. And some days, you're going to question whether you even belong out on that field at all. But win or lose, you still need to show up every day, *every damn day*, ready to play."

Frank looked up sharply. He'd never heard Bob Snyder raise his voice, let alone curse.

"And never feel like you have to do it alone," Bob added, his voice returning to its normal range. "That's what a team is for, Frank. And you have a darn good one behind you. You know that, right?"

Frank's eyes burned as he blinked back twenty years' worth of unshed tears. He faced Bob, their eyes locking for the first time. "Thank you, Bob." His words traveled on a choked whisper. "You're a good father."

Behind the glass, Nurse Jackson shuffled into view. Daniel, swaddled in a white blanket with blue and red stripes, rested comfortably in the soft crook of her arm. Spying Frank through the glass, she smiled warmly and gestured for them to join her in the nursery.

"I hope you're warmed up," Bob said, gripping Frank's right bicep. "The pitcher's out of gas, and your number's been called. Let's go say hi to your son."

Chapter 10

Age 31

December 23, 1983

"God, I needed that," Ellie purred, grazing Frank's neck with soft lips before rolling off of him and curling her body next to his on the bed.

"Me, too." Frank's breath came in uneven gasps. He pulled her closer, basking in the warmth of her flesh and the soft glow of reconciliation. Sleep had been elusive—his conscience made sure of that—so he'd already been wide awake this morning when she'd pressed up behind him and whispered sweetly into his ear.

He reached toward the ceiling, straining to grasp the corner of the beige pillow that was wedged strategically between the wall and the oak headboard, dampening the sounds of their morning pursuits. He jerked the pillow free, motioned with his other hand for Ellie to lift her head, and slid it between her damp hair and the rumpled sheets below.

"Shhhh," Frank said, his mind registering the sound of a dull *thud* from elsewhere in the house. He raised an index finger to his lips, listening intently for signs of movement outside their locked bedroom door. "Did you hear that?"

"Sounded like it came from the kitchen. I'm pretty sure he's up." She squinted at the digital alarm clock on the nightstand. "I mean, it's 7:28 on a morning that you and I both have off. Of course, he's up."

They laughed lightly, trying to be quiet, trying to delay Danny's chaotic entrance into their morning. Though impossible to rouse on workdays—when Frank and Ellie needed to rush him through the morning routine and drop him off at daycare—he was up at the crack of dawn on those rare occasions when both his parents had the day off. It was only a matter of time before he'd come barreling down the hallway, knocking at their door.

"You can sleep some more, honey," Ellie offered, the previous day's tension seemingly erased by their spontaneous lovemaking. "I've got him this morning."

Frank admired her form as she rose from the bed and crossed the room to the mirrored dresser that ran perpendicular to the bedroom window. His eyes gravitated to their new addition, which was becoming more prominent with each passing week. Though hardly visible when she was fully clothed, the gentle curve of her abdomen was accentuated by the pale winter rays streaming in from the window behind her.

As if reading his mind, she turned, cocked her hip, and presented her profile. "It's getting bigger," she observed, placing a protective hand over the top of the bulge and the new life growing inside her. "Look out—it won't be long now before I'm going to have to break out the sexy maternity pants."

"Or . . ." Frank said with a smile, watching her fasten the belt of her threadbare terry cloth robe, "you can just wear that robe to work. I'm sure Dr. Lomax and the other nurses wouldn't object."

Frank fished under the covers at the foot of the bed, located his sweatpants in the tangle of sheets, and hoisted them to his waist. "I'll tell you what—you make a pot of coffee, and I'll go sit with the kid."

He opened the bedroom door and was immediately greeted by the racket of little feet—ten of them in all—sprinting out of the kitchen and down the tiled hallway toward the master bedroom. Danny, hotly pursued by their two Siamese cats, charged around the corner and wrapped his arms around Frank's thigh.

"You're a mess, little man," Frank observed, reaching down to smooth Danny's tangled mop of wavy black hair. His dinosaur-patterned pajamas were at least two sizes too small, exposing wide swaths of olive skin on his forearms and calves. Despite Frank's best efforts to coax his son into accepting his new pajamas, these remained the boy's absolute favorite, and he stubbornly refused to wear anything else.

"C'mon, Dad. You have to hurry," Danny said, his words painted with that particular shade of urgency that only a three-year-old can muster. "He's already changing his sweater, and I don't have my cereal yet!" *He*, of course, referred to Mr. Rogers, whose show had become a staple of the Romanos' morning routine.

"You go watch." Frank shuffled awkwardly down the hall with Danny still anchoring his leg. "I'll get the cereal and meet you on the couch."

Danny released his grip and turned tail. He sprinted in the direction of the family room, the two felines hot on his trail. The cats, Willow and Basil, were generally wary of the raucous child but shadowed him closely in the morning when they knew milk would be close at hand.

Carrying a bowl in each hand—Crispix for himself and Frosted Flakes for Danny—Frank joined his son in the carpeted living room. Danny perched on the edge of the brown-striped sofa, a knitted blanket wrapped around his shoulders to ward off the morning chill. His hazel eyes, one of the few physical features he'd inherited from his mother, were glued to the television set.

Frank placed Danny's bowl on the glass surface of the coffee table and looked to the television, where Mr. Rogers had already swapped out his sweater and shoes and was now commiserating in soft tones with some of his friends from the neighborhood.

"Move down to the floor, buddy. No eating on the couch."

Frank braced himself for an argument, but Danny obeyed

wordlessly, his attention still focused on the television set. It was a rare concession from the obstinate child; even at three years old, it was obvious he'd inherited his mother's stubborn temperament, approaching meals and bedtime like a tiny business tycoon, knives sharpened for a high-stakes negotiation.

"He's going to eat it," Danny said with certainty. He nodded to the screen, where Mr. Rogers was showing his friends a chocolate ice cream bar that was molded in the shape of a gorilla. The station played reruns in the months between seasons, and they had seen this episode at least twice before. "But when he was a kid," Danny explained seriously, "he didn't like eating foods that looked like animals. He thought they had feelings and would get mad at him. But that's silly, right?" He raised a loaded spoon to eye level, inspecting each flake to ensure none of them had been crafted in the shape of animals.

"Maybe silly," Frank conceded, "but considerate, too. How would you feel if he had a Danny-shaped ice cream bar?"

Danny nodded gravely as if overwhelmed by the idea of Mr. Rogers devouring a frozen treat that was minted in his likeness.

Frank finished his cereal, then followed the rich aroma of coffee beans into the kitchen, where Ellie was standing in front of the sink, scrubbing a casserole dish she'd left to soak the night before. Her royal-blue robe, worn thin from years of steady wear, had seen better days. He'd gifted her a new one for her birthday in October, but she clung to that robe with the same obstinacy with which Danny clung to his pajamas.

"You two planning to head out soon?" She let the dish clatter noisily in the sink and wheeled to face Frank in the dimly lit kitchen. "I need some time to wrap presents before I head out to the grocery store."

"Sure, babe," Frank soothed. He could hear the renewed tension in her voice and knew she was annoyed by more than tough baked-on grease. He also knew he was mostly to blame.

This was the first year they would be hosting Christmas dinner, perhaps the biggest event on the Snyder family's long list of annual holiday gatherings, and the enormity of the evening had been weighing heavily on her mind for the past week. She'd planned to do the grocery shopping the previous afternoon, but Frank had insisted she join him and Danny at the ice arena instead.

Life with the Snyders had taught him the value of traditions, and he was determined Christmas on the ice would be one of theirs. But she'd refused to skate with them, concerned she might slip on the ice and endanger the baby, and spent the entire two-hour session reading in the café, building up a head of steam that she unleashed as soon as they arrived home and put the kid down for a nap.

Frank tried to take the high road. He really did. But he eventually succumbed to his anger and belted out a few choice expletives of his own. It was a regrettable outburst—reminiscent of his father in a way that made his skin burn with shame—and one he wished to take back almost immediately.

"I'll get him ready after he's done with breakfast, and then we'll head down to the station to help with set-up for the potluck." He moved to the row of cupboards that lined the wall above the counter, watching her profile and hoping she would not breathe fresh life into the previous night's argument.

He removed two coffee mugs, handed her one, and kissed her gently on the cheek. "And don't forget," he added, lowering his voice so as not to be heard from the living room, "to bring the gift from S-A-N-T-A when you join us later. I will not be held responsible for ruining that little boy's Christmas."

"Whoa, hold on little man," Frank cautioned, watching Danny unbuckle his seatbelt and leverage his foot to fling open the passenger door of the truck. "Let me walk around and give you a hand."

Frank stepped down from the cab of the truck and into the

crisp December morning. Though it was cool in the shade of the massive elm under which he'd parked, the sun shined brightly, offering the promise of a fine winter's day. He jogged around to the front of the vehicle and found Danny already standing on the sidewalk, his hands on his hips and a triumphant grin plastered across his face.

"Uh-oh," Danny began in a sing-song voice, "you're too slow." He clutched the edge of the door with both hands and gave it a sharp tug, barely clearing his fingers from its path before it slammed shut.

Frank winced at the near miss and stifled the urge to shout at the boy. He didn't have many hard and fast rules in his parenting playbook, but keeping his cool and not belittling his well-intentioned child were two of them. That said, Danny had no shortage of destructive impulses, and Frank had no doubt he'd be nearing his quota of patient parental lectures before the day was done.

Walking hand in hand, Frank and Danny stepped into the sunlight, darted across Calistoga Road, and approached the broad driveway of Station 6. Set-up for the station's annual Christmas potluck was already well underway, led by Stitch Alvestal, who, together with his wife and four kids, were decorating a massive noble fir that had been erected in the driveway in front of the nearest of the two closed maintenance bay doors. Standing at least fifteen feet high, the enormous Christmas tree cast a long shadow that was nearly the length of the driveway.

"Hey, Frank!" Stitch called from above. Standing near the top of a ladder that leaned against the retractable door of the bay, he was in the process of attaching a large golden star to the crown of the tree. His eldest two children, anchoring the ladder at its base, shouted contradictory instructions from below. "How's it look?" he asked, annoyed with his children's antics. "Nice and straight?"

Frank eyed the star from below. Though he took some small measure of joy in watching Stitch on the receiving end of someone else's shenanigans, he resisted the urge to join in and gave the thumbs-up sign instead. "Looks good, Stitch. Santa himself couldn't have done it better."

Frank eyeballed Danny, whose ears perked up at the mention of Father Christmas. For the children attending the potluck, the highlight of the event was an opportunity to sit on Santa's lap and receive a special gift. Danny's gift, as special as they come, would be his first baseball mitt, which Ellie was wrapping and bringing with her to the potluck.

"You mind keeping an eye on this guy?" Frank asked Annie, Stitch's eldest child and the de facto head of the tree-decorating committee.

Annie, tall and lanky like her dad—but without the jagged scar across her forehead—grabbed Danny by the hand and led him to a bulging cardboard box, which was brimming with tinsel and ribbon and an assortment of brightly colored baubles. Danny's eyes lit up in anticipation.

After warning Annie to keep Danny on a short leash, Frank spent the next couple of hours working with the crew to set up tables, finish decorating, and prepare the station for the arrival of guests. And with Sammy Long carefully guiding him from the front of the vehicle, Frank moved the fire engine out of its bay and onto the far side of the driveway, where he would be giving a demonstration later and—to the delight of the children—firing the engine's water cannon down the side of the maintenance bay, over the chain-link fence, and into the woods behind the station.

◆

"You think we'll have enough food?" Baker asked for the third time. He paced at the edge of the lawn, worriedly pinching the skin of his throat as he watched the procession of guests filter through the buffet line.

In his first year as battalion chief, Baker had initiated the Christmas potluck tradition in all three of his stations. He took great pride in the annual events, seeing them as a way for the fire departments to connect with the communities they served, and he agonized over each and every detail.

"I didn't expect this many people," he explained again, gesturing to the lawn, where all the tables were full and at least a hundred people were seated or waiting in line for food. "Probably could have used a few more hams."

Originally, the event had been scheduled for the previous Saturday but was postponed due to rain. This was the first time they'd held it on a Friday afternoon, or this close to Christmas, and Baker had been concerned that attendance would be low.

"Yeah, it's a helluva turnout," Frank replied with a distracted nod, not giving two shits about the dwindling supply of ham.

He looked around for Danny, a jolt of fear running down his spine as he realized that the elusive boy had disappeared, again, out from under his nose. He rapidly scanned the crowd, then breathed a sigh of relief when he located him on the far side of the driveway, sitting atop Sammy's shoulders as the two inspected the pump panel of the fire engine.

"Look at those two," Frank said. "You know why they get along so well, right? It's because they have roughly the same maturity level." Both men laughed. Despite his jokes, Frank appreciated the bond his best friend had forged with his son.

"Ahh, c'mon. He'll be a good dad, someday," Baker said, his eyes still trained on Sammy and Danny. "Once he finds *Ms. Right*, that is."

Frank rolled his eyes. Sammy's long-time pursuit of *Ms. Right* had become legendary within the department. And after years of high-volume catch-and-release, Frank doubted there were many fish left in the proverbial sea.

"Speaking of Ms. Right," Baker said, "what time is Ellie getting here? We're expecting Santa Claus within the hour."

Frank glowered at his watch and shook his head. It was half past one, and he'd been waiting on her for the last hour. Though irritated, he was hardly surprised. Ellie was a woman of many virtues, but punctuality wasn't one of them. And with Sunday's

Christmas dinner looming, he had no doubt that her grocery list was longer than his arm.

"Oh, she'll—" Frank cut his explanation midsentence and listened. Barely audible at first, the wailing of competing sirens grew progressively louder, seemingly headed in their direction. An ambulance roared by a few moments later, followed closely by a fire engine, both of them turning heads as they went. From the numbers painted in elaborate red script on the stainless-steel bumper of the engine, Frank could tell it belonged to Station 4, one of the two other stations under Baker's charge.

"And that," Baker said, shaking his head and pinching the bridge of his nose, "is why we coordinate in advance."

Holding an all-hands event like the potluck—and taking the station offline for a few hours to do so—required coordinating ahead of time with his other stations, and the department's central dispatch office, to ensure that crews were available to answer a call from within their zone.

"I'm going to call over to Station 4 and see what's going on," Baker said. He shot another nervous glance at the line for the buffet, which finally seemed to be dying down. "Just make sure Sammy doesn't eat all the ham, huh?"

◊

SEATED at a round folding table with Sammy and the entire Alvestal family, Frank shifted Danny's weight from his left knee to his right. He'd given up on trying to coerce the child to eat any of the ham, mashed potatoes, or green bean casserole that was sitting untouched on his plate. Instead, he watched him devour what was likely his hundredth chocolate chip cookie of the afternoon.

Frank consulted his watch again and felt the bile rising in his throat. It was nearly 2 p.m., Ellie was *still* a no-show, and the stage had already been set inside the empty engine bay for Santa's imminent arrival. In a few minutes, Santa—played for years by retired Battalion Chief Ralph Halverson—would appear magically behind the double doors of the lobby, then burst from the building, a massive red velour bag slung over his shoulder, and make his way across the driveway and into the engine bay, a gaggle of boisterous children trailing in his wake. Within Santa's bag would be gifts that had been collected from the children's parents in the hours and days before the potluck. But with Ellie still absent, Danny's present had not yet been added to Santa's trove of gifts.

"Hey, bud," Frank said, hoisting Danny out of his lap and depositing him onto the vacant seat next to him. "I'm going to run inside for a minute. You stay with Uncle Sammy while I'm gone."

Frank exchanged nods with Sammy, who pulled Danny's chair closer and slipped the kid another cookie, then weaved impatiently through a sea of tables and partygoers to cross the short distance from the station's front lawn to its lobby. With any luck, he could reach Ellie at home. And maybe, if she left *right goddamn now*, she would still arrive in time to slip Danny's gift into Santa's bag.

Frank flung open the door and marched across the expanse of the festively decorated lobby. He reached down to unlatch the swinging gate at the end of the reception counter, then stopped short when he saw Baker, a pale apparition looming in the near darkness, standing outside the door to his office.

"Jesus, Chief," Frank said, startled as much by Baker's vacant stare as his presence at the end of the hall. In the dim light of the windowless hallway, Baker's countenance was ashen and wan. "Were you able to get in touch with Station 4?"

Baker took two unsteady steps toward Frank, then halted and placed his hand against the wall. "Frank..."

Baker coughed, choking on his words. Still leaning heavily against the wall, he continued in a strangled whisper. "The call, the one that Station 4 responded to . . . it was a car accident. About a mile from here. A truck veered over the center line and forced the oncoming driver off the road. She—the driver of the other car—lost control and ran into a telephone pole."

"Shit," Frank muttered. He shook his head and emitted a low whistle. "Right before Christmas, too. She gonna be okay?"

Baker's hand dropped from the wall and came to rest at his side. He closed the distance between them, his steps labored and uncertain. "Frank, I don't know how to tell you this. The other driver, the woman who hit the pole, it was Ellie. They identified her at the scene and one of the guys from Station 4 recognized her name and called it in."

Frank's blood ran cold.

He froze outside the gate, his feet rooted to the floor. All vestiges of anger drained from his body.

Long seconds ticked by as he stared at Baker's slack mouth, trying to comprehend the words it had spoken.

"And?" Frank asked finally, choking on the bitterness of the question. He gripped the top of the gate with both hands, leaning against it for support. Bracing himself.

Baker hesitated again, the edges of his gray mustache twitching as he stared past Frank, his nostrils flaring, blinking back tears.

"*And?*" Frank demanded. He slammed his palms against the top of the latched gate as he fired the question into the void between them.

"And . . ." Baker began softly, the truth Frank already knew etched in the deep lines of grief on his face, "she's gone, Frank. They tried to resuscitate her on-site, but it was too late. Nothing could be done."

Frank reeled. His vision blurred as the room and his world spun out of control. Not this. Please, not this. *Not Ellie, too.*

His mind flashed to her precious cargo. Their baby. A primal howl erupted from deep inside, and his misery turned to molten rage as he remembered what he'd done. The ice arena and their argument from the night before. His stubborn selfishness—the reason she was driving alone on that road in the first place.

Frank's legs failed him. He reached for the surface of the counter, trying to steady himself, then collapsed heavily to the ground in front of it.

From underneath his arms, Baker's strong hands grasped him, lifted his torso off the floor, and brought him to a seated position.

His back was pressed against the counter while his legs sprawled limply in front of him. He stared down at his feet, just as he had years before. His mind was transported back to the chaotic scene on Spruce Street, when he sat alone on the curb, holding his head in his hands as he watched his world burn. This time he didn't need to wonder. He knew he was to blame.

Baker dropped to the floor beside him. He wrapped his arm around Frank's shoulders and pulled him close. Tears streamed down the chief's face, amplifying Frank's guilt as he couldn't shed any of his own.

"You're not alone," Baker promised, his arm still wrapped around Frank's shoulders. "No matter how you feel in this moment, no matter what happens next, I want you to know that. You *are not* alone."

Frank struggled to force air into his lungs. To control his breathing. And to slow his heart, which threatened to explode inside his chest.

"I know that," Frank replied automatically, not even considering Baker's words.

His mind conjured an image of his parents' funeral—two open graves, two mounds of damp and freshly churned earth. But it wasn't him standing in front of the yawning pits, dressed in an ill-fitting black suit, shivering uncontrollably in the cold drizzle of the morning. It was his son. It was Danny.

"I need to go," Frank said, more to himself than to Baker. He removed Baker's arm and hoisted himself off the floor.

"Hold on a minute," Baker called. He rose to his feet, wiped his tears, and reached for Frank's arm.

Frank brushed aside his hand and turned toward the door. An image of Ellie, standing next to the dresser, the sunlight accentuating the curve of her womb, flashed through his mind. The guilt was more than he could bear.

He forced his eyes shut and shook his head violently from side to side, refusing to let the image take hold. Refusing to yield to his grief and his shame and despair.

"I need to go," Frank said again, more forcefully this time. He expelled all thoughts of Ellie and their unborn child from his mind, crossed the lobby, and reached for the door. "I need to find my son."

Chapter 11

Age 35

May 6, 1988

"Hey, wake up," Frank said, his voice reverberating off the concrete walls of the empty dormitory. He leaned over the rack, grasped the corner of the heavy down comforter, and pulled it down to expose the impossibly long body stretched below.

It seemed to have happened overnight, this prolonged growth spurt that had Danny cycling through shoes and clothing at breakneck speed. He'd been smack dab in the middle of the growth chart, average in both height and weight, until just before his sixth birthday. In the two years since then, the kid had been off to the races.

"I'm serious," Frank warned, his early morning frustration mounting. He shook Danny's bare shoulder, gently at first, then more insistently when the child emitted a sharp groan and pulled the blanket back up and over his head. "I let you sleep in, but now you need to hurry. Get dressed, then cereal and teeth. We're out the door in twenty minutes."

Frank paced in front of the wall lockers as Danny wiped the

sleep from his eyes, then lingered in the doorway of the dormitory until the boy's feet hit the polished linoleum floor.

It was still exhausting, getting Danny ready for school in the morning, while also trying to perform his duties at the station and get his day underway. But it had grown slightly easier with time and repetition, especially as the boy grew older and the tantrums were fewer and less severe.

Frank retraced his steps down the long hallway that connected the dormitory of Station 3 with its maintenance bay, still trying to shake the echo of Ruth's voice, which had been ringing annoyingly in his ears since long before the sun came up. *It's time to move on, Frank.*

Her words, delivered the week prior when he'd arrived at the farm to pick up Danny, had landed with the eye-watering impact of a sharp jab to the nose. He'd been stunned at first, hardly able to absorb the rest of her well-rehearsed speech or comprehend her lengthy list of recommendations for how to *finally move forward*. His shock had faded during the drive home, replaced with simmering anger, as if the guilt and the grief—as if *loving Ellie*—were all controlled by some magical switch in his mind, one that he could access and flip at will. He'd been licking his wounds ever since.

"All good?" asked Gary Garcia, his green eyes darting up from his clipboard as Frank hustled back into the brightly-lit maintenance bay. He stepped forward from the back of the fire engine and nodded toward the hallway, his flat oval face breaking into a knowing smile.

Garcia, like all the men in Station 3, had been understanding of Frank's situation when he transferred from Station 6, needing to be closer to home and to Danny's school. They had all gone out of their way to welcome him and Danny to the family. And in the years since, Danny had become an honorary member of the crew, a fireman in spirit, and a near-constant presence around the station.

"Same shit . . ." Frank began, shaking his head as he reached for the clipboard. Garcia had three young kids of his own, so he understood what life was like in the trenches.

"Different day," Garcia finished. He clapped Frank on the shoulder and chuckled at what had become their shared mantra.

Frank worked quickly through the standard series of equipment checks, completed his crew change checklist with Garcia, then went hunting for Danny. He found him sitting on his unmade rack, his face buried in one of those *Narnia* books Dorothy Baker had bought him for Christmas. Frank had never read the series, but he got the gist. And with all the time Danny spent curled up on his bed with a book, lost in his own little world, the kid might as well have a magical wardrobe of his own.

"Teeth brushed?" Frank asked skeptically from the doorway. He calculated the odds, knowing they were not in his favor.

Danny lowered the book, broke into a ridiculous caricature of a smile, and pushed his tongue through the gaping hole left by the front tooth he'd lost the previous week. "Wanna smell my breath?" he offered, not waiting for a response before blowing out a long gust of air in Frank's general direction.

"No. That's gross. But I do want you to make that bed. Now." Frank glanced at the clock mounted above the exit sign over the doorway, confirming that the trains were still running on time. "And hurry up," he added, nibbling at a fingernail that was already chewed down to a jagged nub. "I have somewhere to be this morning after I drop you off."

⚾

"I SAID I DON'T KNOW," Frank repeated, sinking deeper into the plush cushions of the wingback chair, compelled by a force greater than gravity. "It's like a weight, I guess." He shrugged and stared down at the expensive-looking rug, studying a patch located halfway between their respective seats. "I don't know how else to describe it."

He stole another glance at his watch, counting down the

remaining minutes, still kicking himself for allowing Ruth to strong-arm him into scheduling this appointment. She had been adamant, though—this being one of her many *recommendations*—and Frank found his mother-in-law's particular brand of coercion almost impossible to resist. And besides, with everything he asked of her, everything she and Bob did for him and Danny, it seemed unfair to deny her one small concession in return.

"That's interesting," Doctor Moreland replied, a thoughtful frown casting a shadow across his boyish features. He leaned forward in his matching leather wingback, closing the distance between them. "I want to revisit that word you used. Tell me more about this *weight*. When do you feel it, and what exactly does it feel like?"

"I don't know," Frank lied, his tongue feeling clumsy and thick in the dryness of his mouth. He knew exactly how it felt: like waking up each day to a baby elephant squatting on his chest, crushing his ribcage, squeezing the air from his lungs as soon as he opened his eyes.

"I'm sure you have *some* idea . . ." the doctor prompted, casting his line into the stream, then slowly reeling it back in, enticing Frank to bite. He leaned back in his chair, waiting patiently, watching Frank through kind brown eyes.

"I used to go to the lumberyard when I was a kid," Frank said finally. He stared over Moreland's head and counted each of the six framed diplomas and certificates that lined the wall behind him. "You know, with my father? He would pick out the boards, and I would trail behind him, like this." He demonstrated, reaching out with bent arms, palms facing upwards, elbows hugged close to his sides. "And he'd just keep stacking 'em up, board after board, higher and higher, until my biceps started to shake, and I felt like my forearms would snap under the weight."

"That's a great description," Moreland encouraged, scribbling in the leather-bound journal that sat in his lap. "But can you tell me what these boards represent now, Frank? What do they mean to you today, as an adult?"

Frank kneaded the back of his neck, desperate to be somewhere else. *Anywhere else.* "Things, I guess."

"What kinds of things?"

"Things I have to do. Things I'm *responsible* for. It's a long list, you know? Laundry, cooking, dishes, all the yard work . . . homework with the kid. All of that on top of my job."

Moreland nodded, issued an extended *hmmm* that was annoyingly similar to the purring of a cat, then scribbled some more in his journal.

"It's a constant uphill battle," Frank continued, spurred by a hot flash of frustration, his words spilling out faster than before. "I'll get ten things done one day, only to have fifteen more pile up the next day. The more I get done, the more there is *to get done.* And the pile just gets higher and higher. It never ends." He looked down at his hands, which were balled in his lap. He relaxed his grip, slowly flexed his fingers, and wiped his damp palms on the thighs of his jeans.

"And these boards, Frank, the ones that represent the *things* you're responsible for, they weigh on you the most in the morning? As soon as you wake up?"

Frank nodded. He licked his lips, which grated like sandpaper against his tongue. He regretted not accepting the glass of water the doctor offered at the beginning of their session.

"There's a word for what you're experiencing, Frank. It's called *anxiety*, and it's incredibly common. Especially for people in your . . . situation."

Frank nodded again, slower this time, watching Moreland through narrowed lids and wondering exactly what he meant by that word. *Situation.*

The doctor had been relentless, spending most of the session poking and prodding, constantly trying to bring the conversation around to her. To Ellie. He'd shared only the barest facts, steering clear of the most painful details, like the baby she'd carried inside of her. Or the fact that it was his fault she'd been on that damn road in the first place. That was a secret he'd never shared. Not with Chief Baker or with Sammy, and certainly not with Bob and Ruth. The shame he carried inside of him, and the thought of exposing that ugliness to another living soul, was more than he could bear.

"What I mean," Moreland continued hurriedly, seeming to read Frank's mind and mood, "is that I see this with single parents. I see it much more frequently with women—because there aren't that many single fathers out there—but the causal elements remain the same. You're overworked, overwhelmed, and just trying to keep your head above water. It's natural, Frank. And it's okay to feel this way." He smiled, his expressive eyes conveying a measure of sympathy that almost seemed genuine.

Frank sighed and drummed his fingers against his thigh, trying to digest the doctor's words. He peered through the wooden slats in the horizontal blinds, out the window, and into the central courtyard of the downtown office building. A little boy a couple of years younger than Danny stood on the stone ledge of the multi-tiered granite fountain, his eyes closed tightly, flicking a coin into the water below. If only it were that easy—toss a coin, make a wish.

"So, what do I do?" Frank asked, tearing his gaze away from the boy and centering it back on the doctor.

"Well, let me ask you something, Frank. At the fire station, you have schedules, right? Plans that dictate when and how you do certain things?" He waited for Frank's confirmatory grunt, then continued. "So why shouldn't your life at home be the same way? Take the time to map out your activities and chores. Formulate a plan—a recurring schedule, so to speak—and try to stick to it. By building in structure, for both you and Danny, everything will seem that much more manageable."

"I guess that could work," Frank acknowledged, thankful for a morsel of practical advice and not some more garbage about *confronting his feelings*. He paused, shifted uncomfortably in his chair, then took the plunge. "And what about the other thing?"

he asked, returning to their earlier line of conversation, the growing distance between him and Danny.

"Your son, you mean?" Moreland flipped back through his notes, purred again, then lifted the notebook off his lap long enough to cross one corduroy-clad leg over the other. "I think that's an even easier fix," he said. "It's okay that you two are different people, Frank, that you're cut from a different cloth. He doesn't have to enjoy building models and you don't have to love reading books. You just need to love each other. Find something you *both* enjoy. Create a world you can inhabit together, then use that shared world to help you connect."

Frank chewed on his lower lip, processing Moreland's words, then followed the doctor's gaze to the wall clock, which had finally completed its slow march to the top of the hour.

"It was a pleasure meeting you," Moreland said, rising from his chair and tugging at the sleeves of his tweed jacket. He offered his hand. "And I'm looking forward to our next session, Frank. I feel like we have so much more to discuss."

Frank shook the doctor's hand—small and soft, and nothing like his own—and formed a noncommittal smile, knowing for a fact there would never be a *next session*. "Yeah, take care, doc."

Frank bolted through the door, still mulling over the doctor's suggestions and making a mental list of things he needed to accomplish. At the top of the list, written in red pen and capital letters in his mind, was task number one—*LEARN TO SAY "NO" TO RUTH.*

◇

FRANK EASED the truck into the driveway. He let his gaze linger on the faded exterior of the ranch-style house and noted the laundry list of tasks left undone. It needed more than a coat of paint: there were weeds to be pulled and hedges to be trimmed, and theirs, regrettably, had become the lawn that the other neighbors scoffed at, making snarky remarks about "declining property values" when they strolled by.

He reached for the plastic shopping bag on the passenger seat —grabbing the wall calendar and small chalkboard he'd purchased on the way home—then stopped short of the front door. Parked on the street, nestled against the curb in the gap between his driveway and the one adjacent, was Chief Baker's tan Volvo station wagon. From his vantage point on the front porch, he peered through the side window, confirming there was no one behind the wheel.

"Hello?" Frank called loudly. He stepped through the unlocked door of the house, seeing his own worried reflection in the mirror on the wall of the entryway.

"We're in here," came Baker's reply, shouted from the direction of the dining room.

Frank kicked off his shoes, adding them to the haphazard pile next to the front door, and made his way to the dining room, wondering who had accompanied Baker into his home unannounced. It was unusual for the chief to drop by without giving notice, downright odd for him to let himself in with the key Frank had provided in case of emergencies.

"Sorry to have let myself in," Baker apologized, meeting him at the doorway to the dining room and lodging his broad frame between Frank and the room beyond. He shrugged his shoulders, then nodded, angling his strong jaw in the direction of the dining room. "I just wasn't sure what to do."

Frank followed him across the threshold and saw Danny seated at the far end of the table. Clutching a McDonald's milkshake in his right hand, his left hand sat atop the table, buried under a large bag of frozen peas. Though his face was expressionless, the skin around his eyes was red and puffy, a tell-tale sign that tears had recently been shed.

"The school tried to reach you here first, then at Station 3," Baker explained, shifting his weight from one steel-toed boot to the other. "When they called the station a second time, the boys over there thought it was best to give me a ring." He shot a pointed glance across the table. "Danny Boy got himself into a bit of a scrape at school, so the principal, Mr. *Yama-something*, sent him home."

"Is that right?" Frank asked. He folded his arms across his broad chest and glared down the length of the oval table to the stone-faced child on the other end. "So, you bought him a milkshake?"

"Easy, there," Baker replied, not unkindly. "You should wait until the facts are in before you pass judgment." He walked to the far end of the table and ruffled Danny's wavy black mane. "Hang in there, huh, kiddo?"

"Thanks, Uncle Hal," Danny mumbled. He offered a half-smile in return but didn't look up from the McDonald's cup, which he was watching intently, as if afraid it might sprout legs and walk away.

"And if memory serves," Baker added, offering a wink and a pat on the shoulder as he made his way past Frank and through the doorway, "there was a time in *your* life when there was nothing in the world that a strawberry shake couldn't fix."

Frank suppressed a smile. He summoned his game face instead, then waited for the front door to close before pulling out a chair at the end of the table and sitting down next to his son. Disciplining Danny was his least favorite part of the job, made all the more difficult because he was in it alone and therefore always the bad guy. There's no "good cop, bad cop" when you're a one-man department.

"All right, let's hear it," Frank said, lifting the bag of peas to examine the knuckles below. Though vaguely purple, there was minimal swelling. Whatever, *or whoever*, Danny had hit seemed to have gotten off easy.

"It wasn't my fault," Danny said, refusing to make eye contact, then slurping his milkshake loudly.

Frank snorted and shook his head in frustration. He'd been expecting this line, which was Danny's standard opener. He snatched the milkshake, slid it out of Danny's reach, and stared down expectantly.

Danny pulled his hands, and the bag of peas, into his lap, then mumbled something—likely a smart-ass remark—unintelligibly under his breath.

"What was that?" Frank thundered, his voice and his hackles rising in tandem. He checked himself, sucked in a deep breath, and let it escape slowly through his nose. Moments like these required caution, lest he open his mouth and hear Pop's voice emerge instead of his own.

Danny looked up sharply from the table. Though tears had begun to well in his eyes, his voice carried a defiant edge. "I *said*, 'Little Orphan Danny.' That's what Ricky Tolliver called me. And that's why I slugged him."

Frank tugged at his ear, mouthing the name, *Little Orphan Danny*, trying to make sense of the ridiculously outdated insult.

"The class was making cards," Danny continued, "you know, for Mother's Day. And Mrs. Ingram told me it was okay for me to read instead. Because . . ."

Frank swallowed hard. A dense lump of guilt slid down his throat and *plopped* into his roiling gut. He'd forgotten Mother's Day was on Sunday. "Go on," he said, his tone softer than before.

"And I was fine with reading, I really was. Until Ricky started running his mouth, calling me that stupid name. And then the others started laughing, too. So, I had no choice."

Frank sighed, taking a long moment to collect his thoughts. This was not the first time Danny had been in trouble at school, but usually, it was his mouth writing the checks, not his fists. Though he seemed to be justified in *this* instance, it was just another episode in what Mrs. Ingram had called "a worrisome pattern" at their last parent-teacher conference.

"It doesn't even make sense," Frank said finally. "Ricky's joke. You're not an orphan, Danny. And you're smart enough to understand the difference."

"But—"

"But nothing. You're also smart enough to understand that we don't hit anyone, regardless of the garbage that comes out of their mouth." He thought of the tiny Tolliver boy, who had a smart mouth of his own and had been on Danny's Little League team the previous year. "Especially when you're twice his size."

Danny opened his mouth, presumably to argue his point, then thought better of it for once, and snapped it shut. He sniffed loudly, wiping at the corners of his eyes.

"Into your room," Frank said, pointing down the hallway toward their bedrooms. "Until the end of the school day. At least."

Danny huffed and puffed, tears finally streaming down his face as he scooted along the wall, walking the long way around the table and out of the dining room.

Frank's heart ached as he watched him go. The boy was his world, the part he could be proud of anyway. And he was so tired of the *bad cop* shit, of always playing the villain, that he was ready to turn in his proverbial gun and badge.

And didn't he deserve a share of the blame? Had he remembered it was Mother's Day to begin with, and taken the time to talk to Danny beforehand, maybe this wouldn't have happened in the first place.

"Hey, pal," Frank called impulsively, freezing the boy at the door. His mind reached back to Dr. Moreland's office and the shrink's final piece of advice: *Create a world you can inhabit together.*

An image of Pop—a black-and-white police academy portrait that had lived in a small frame on the edge of their mantel when he was a boy—flashed unbidden into Frank's mind. Unsettled by the emergence of the long-forgotten photo, Frank tossed it quickly aside, discarding it into the trash heap of time.

Danny lingered in the doorway, waiting, a flicker of impatience flashing over his tear-streaked face.

"That thing still work?" Frank asked. He stared deliberately at

Danny's left hand, then held up his own and pointed to it with his right.

"Does the Pope shit in the woods?" Danny asked, his sadness already forgotten, replaced with his usual cockiness. He raised his left hand with dramatic flair, flexing his fingers for effect.

Frank sighed, deliberated, and let it slide. He had no one to blame but himself. What can you expect when you raise your kid in a fire station, never seeing the inside of a church?

"Then go grab your mitt," Frank said. He reached for Danny's milkshake and took a long pull from the straw. "I'll meet you in the backyard."

PART TWO
DANNY

CHAPTER 12

AGE 12

JANUARY 6, 1993

"So, that's your brilliant advice?" Danny slid his Pepsi and Twix bar across the convenience store's counter, then gave Rory Pryor an exaggerated eye roll. *"Just be honest."*

Danny shook his head in mock disappointment. Coming from the guy who always prided himself on being the smartest kid in the room, Danny expected something better. Something more useful than the kind of crap you'd hear from an *ABC Afterschool Special*.

"Well . . . they say it's the best policy," Rory added lamely, shrugging his narrow shoulders, and offering his usual tight-lipped smile. "Hey, can you cover mine, too?" Rory's sharp blue eyes darted between the Snickers bar in his hand and the disinterested clerk behind the store counter. "I'm a little short on cash today."

In truth, Rory was almost always short on cash. Like the uneven rows of teeth hidden behind his closed-mouth smile, or the fact that he slept on a second-hand couch in the one-bedroom apartment he shared with his mother, it was a point he took great pains to hide. But on those rare occasions when money did come his way, usually limited to Christmas and his birthday, Rory Pryor was generous to a fault.

"Will that be all?" the clerk asked, one pudgy hand rising slowly toward his mouth as he made a lazy attempt to stifle a yawn.

Danny nodded to the clerk, who had already shifted his attention back to the small wall-mounted TV and whatever fake courtroom show he'd been watching when they came in. He rummaged through the jumbled mess of pencils, erasers, and assorted trash in the small front pocket of his JanSport, handed over exact change, then grabbed their items off the counter without waiting for a receipt.

"This is going on your tab, you know," Danny warned, addressing Rory in a deep baritone, his best imitation of his father. He handed Rory his candy bar, rearranging his features into a judgmental frown as they walked from the store. "There's no such thing as a free lunch, kid."

They both laughed at the impersonation, which Danny had been perfecting for months and even Rory agreed was spot-on. Besides his Arnold Schwarzenegger imitation—which he often performed in class, to the amusement of his friends and annoyance of his teachers—it was definitely his favorite. That said, he'd yet to audition this new parody for his father, and he wasn't planning to anytime soon.

"You don't think he'll believe you?" Rory asked, returning to the topic of Danny's latest detention slip, which had been awarded by Mr. Feasel when he booted Danny from English class earlier that day. "I mean, you really didn't do anything . . . right?"

"Right," Danny confirmed, doubling down on the half-truth he'd told Rory inside the store. He squinted as they stepped into the watered-down sunlight of the brisk winter afternoon, considered telling Rory the rest of the story, then decided to save his breath, knowing that Rory's advice would remain unchanged. "But good luck explaining that to my dad."

Danny stopped for a beat to pull the hood of his sweatshirt

over his head. Despite it being only a quarter to five, the sun was sinking fast, and the temperature was dropping accordingly. His black hair—cut in the shape of a bowl, with the sides and back shaved down to the skin—offered little protection against the stiff breeze that made the hairs on his neck stand on end.

"I hate this time of year," Danny complained. He was already dreading the conversation with his father. And seeing no way to avoid an ass-chewing, he was eager to change the subject. "We spend all day in school, then go straight to practice, then it's already dark by the time we get home. It's bullshit." He kicked a bottle cap on the sidewalk and watched with satisfaction as it caromed off the side of a trash can and disappeared underneath a parked car.

"At least we get out early on Wednesdays," Rory countered, his voice upbeat but his words muffled by a dense mouthful of chocolate, peanuts, and nougat. "It gives us a couple more hours of daylight, right?"

Danny and Rory walked in silence through the crowded parking lot, then cut across the grass next to Jack in the Box, circumventing the foul reek of the restaurant's dumpsters before joining the sidewalk just shy of the busy intersection of Marlow and Piner.

Rory stopped at the curb, just short of the crosswalk, dumped his backpack on the ground, and kneeled to tie his size-13 Kmart sneaker. While some kids made fun of his bargain-brand shoes, Danny never did. Rory was more than a pair of shoes. And regardless of what he wore on his feet, the kid could flat-out hoop.

"Oh, shit." Danny gasped as a shot of adrenaline surged through his system, freezing him on the sidewalk. "I totally forgot . . . and now he's *definitely* gonna kill me."

"Forgot what?" Rory asked, his blonde eyebrows arched. He rose to his full height and looked sharply behind them, as if expecting to find a knife-wielding psycho on their tail.

Danny opened his mouth to answer, but his thoughts and words were swallowed by the incessant blaring of a car horn, its persistent drone coming from somewhere in the line of cars behind him.

He spun to face the idling traffic and saw his father's ancient black Chevy, four cars back, waiting for the light to turn green. His dad leaned across the cab and cranked down the window, then shouted for him to meet him on the other side of the intersection.

He nodded emphatically to his father, begging him with his eyes to stop yelling and roll up the window. "He was supposed to pick me up from basketball practice today," Danny explained. He stepped in front of Rory, turning to hide the blush that crept up his neck and across his face. "I totally forgot."

"Ooooh," Rory said, wincing as he looked back over his shoulder at the truck and its ticked-off driver. Rory, like most of Danny's friends, had always been a little bit scared by his father. "He looks pissed, dude. I'm guessing today's not the day to ask for a ride."

"Definitely not," Danny said grimly, again adopting his father's deep voice and judgmental scowl. "There's no such thing as a free ride, either."

This time neither of them laughed.

◇

DANNY BROKE into a jog as soon as the walk sign flashed. He mumbled goodbye to Rory, who loped slowly behind him in the crosswalk, seemingly happy to create some space between himself and the truck.

His father's Chevy rumbled past, its flashers blinking, and came to a stop at the curb on the far side of the intersection. Danny climbed into the cab, dropped his backpack on the spotless mat in front of the seat, and braced himself for the *disappointed dad routine*. Though his father almost never yelled, sometimes Danny wished he would. A little shouting would be a welcome change from his standard response, which sat somewhere between disapproval and embarrassment.

"Well?" his father asked. The word settled like a dense fog in the space between them. He stared at Danny from underneath thick raised brows, one hand gripping the steering wheel while the fingers of the other drummed slowly on his thigh.

"I'm sorry?" Danny tried. He shrugged, adjusted the backpack at his feet, and stared at the neat grooves in the freshly-vacuumed floormat.

"We talked about this when I dropped you off this morning," his father said, the words accompanied by a disappointed shake of his head. "I told you I was picking you up after practice . . . it was written on the calendar on the fridge, for Christ's sake."

"Yeah, I know," Danny shot back, his frustration rising. He stared out the passenger window and rolled his eyes at the mention of the all-important calendar, the tyrannical third member of their disgustingly organized little family. If that calendar were to disappear from the fridge, would his father even remember to put on pants in the morning? "I forgot, *okay*? And I already said I'm sorry."

Danny looked to the middle of the bench seat, where his dusty cleats and mitt were visible in the unzipped gym bag, accompanied by his father's catcher's mask and well-worn mitt. They had planned to go to the high school baseball field today after school. Even during the baseball offseason, Danny threw bullpen sessions with his father twice a week. Though he played other sports throughout the year, there was really no start or end to the baseball season. Not if he wanted to be the best.

"It's not too late . . ." Danny offered doubtfully, looking out the window of the truck to the grassy field on the right. In the center of the field stood a rickety gray barn; the late-afternoon sun hovered just above its sagging roof.

"Nope. Not today." His father shifted the truck into drive, then pulled away from the curb. "It'll be dark soon. And besides . . . you and I have some other things to talk about." He turned toward Danny and shot him a *gotcha* glance. "Like the call I received from Mr. Feasel today after school. Let's start with that."

Danny stiffened as a surge of anger coursed through him. He wasn't surprised Mr. Feasel had gone the extra mile to stick it to him by calling his dad after school. The guy was a first-class dick. And there was no way it was just a coincidence—the fact that his name rhymed with *weasel*.

Stoked by the flames of injustice, Danny powered through the basics of the story. The school was hosting a career day in the auditorium the following week, and his class was instructed to write an essay beforehand, describing their dream job, why they wanted to work in that field, and how and why they thought they could succeed.

"So, today we were just presenting our idea to the class," Danny said, before pausing to catch his breath. "Then the essay is due next Tuesday. But when I presented *my idea* to be a pitcher for the Giants, Mr. Feasel went nutso."

"*Nutso*, huh? Now, why would he do that?" his father asked, his tone mockingly innocent. "It was your choice, right?"

Danny's insides burned. Why did he have to walk his father through the details of a story he clearly already knew? Just like Danny knew that Mr. Feasel didn't like him, that he'd *never* liked him, and that he'd been out to get him for most of the year.

"I guess," Danny said, sensing the trap but seeing no way around it, "he told us ahead of time that our decision had to be *practical*—no actors, athletes, or rock stars. So, when he told me no and embarrassed me in front of the whole class, I had to pick something new. On the spot. So, I told him I wanted to be a teacher."

Danny's eyes cut across the cab to his father, who nodded slowly, his attention fixed to the road as he turned the truck onto their street.

"And that's it?" His father stared across the cab of the truck, his eyes probing, searching Danny's face for confirmation. "You didn't add anything else at the end? Maybe the words 'like you,

Mr. Feasel,' accompanied by what your teacher described as a *smug little smirk?*"

Danny bit down on his upper lip, trying to suppress a smile as he remembered the chorus of laughter the remark had drawn from the class, and how red The Weasel's face had been as he scribbled out the detention slip and booted Danny from class.

They sat in silence, watching the garage door rumble upward, then his father sighed purposefully as he pulled into the darkened garage. That was his dad in a nutshell—the man even sighed with purpose.

"Hold on a second," his father said, freezing Danny with one foot in the truck and the other hovering above the concrete floor of the garage. He paused for a beat, waiting for the noisy garage door to close, then gestured to the gym bag resting on the seat between them, its features barely visible in the dim light of the garage. "Why do you think we do this, Danny? All the practice, I mean."

Danny swung his leg back into the truck but left the door open. "So that I can get better?" He shrugged his shoulders, fighting the urge to add the word *duh* to the end of his response.

"Yeah, that's part of it," his father acknowledged, his voice sounding tired and thin in the near darkness. He reached for the bag, zipped it up, and pulled it into his lap. "But it's more than that, Danny. Some of the most important lessons I ever learned were taught to me on a baseball diamond. It's where I learned about respect—how to earn it and how to show it. And how to act like a man . . . both on *and off* the field."

Danny avoided his father's eyes. His shoulders sagged as the wind drained from his sails. It wasn't the first time he'd heard some version of this speech, and it always had a way of taking him down a notch, reminding him of what his dad and Uncle Hal always preached: *Character counts.*

"You're so smart, Danny, and you have so much potential. Not just as a baseball player, but as a man. As a leader." He reached across the seat, patted Danny's knee, then reached for his door. "And if you do end up playing pro ball someday," he continued, opening the door to swing one thick thigh out of the cab, "you know damn well I'll always be your number one fan. But if that's *not* in the cards for you, and you have to find another use for all your talents . . . you could do a helluva lot worse than being a teacher."

⬦

DANNY JUMPED IN HIS SEAT, accidentally knocking his pencil case to the floor, startled by the sound of his father's knuckles rapping loudly against the solid frame of his closed bedroom door.

"Hold on," he called, huffing and puffing as he picked up the collection of spilled pencils, still upset about being banished to his room like a child after their discussion in the truck. He bookmarked his page and tossed the thick US history book onto the cluttered surface of his small writing desk.

Despite his theatrics, Danny was actually happy to be interrupted, having read and reread the same paragraph at least five times, his mind constantly straying from the words on the page and revisiting those of his father in the truck. *You could do a helluva lot worse than being a teacher.*

He understood his dad's roundabout point. Teachers, even the shitty ones like Mr. Feasel, deserve to be shown respect. But that wasn't why he couldn't concentrate. Though he hadn't given it any thought before he shot off his mouth in class—he'd never really considered *any* future that didn't include hurling fastballs for the San Francisco Giants—he could see the appeal of teaching. It was almost like being a coach, right? But if he did become a teacher someday, maybe after his hall-of-fame baseball career was over, he would definitely teach history, his favorite subject, and not English. And he would never stray to the dark side of The Force, and never, *ever*, let himself become anything like The Weasel.

"Yeah?" Danny listened from behind his closed door, then he

opened it a sliver and stared sullenly at his father through the narrow breach.

"Dinner is ready," his dad announced. He extended a bear-size paw through the slender gap. "Clean slate?"

Danny stared at the hand like it was coated in dog crap, then reluctantly pulled the door wide and gave it a lackluster shake. "Yeah, clean slate."

He trailed his father down the hallway, annoyed at how quickly his dad could turn the page and move on after an argument. It always took Danny longer to wipe the slate and set his anger aside. Grandma Ruth said he was a lot like his mom in that way. And in a lot of other ways, too, but he'd have to take her word for it.

Danny grabbed two TV trays off the wooden stand in the dining room. Though they owned a fancy dining room table, that table—and the entire dining room, for that matter—was mostly for show. Almost all of their meals, on the nights they were at home and not at the fire station, were eaten in the family room, sitting on the couch in front of the TV.

"How much do you want?" his father yelled from the kitchen. "Big helping or huge?"

Danny seated the sliding mechanism of the second TV tray and turned toward the kitchen. Though the air was thick with garlic, basil, and tomatoes, he didn't need to smell the sauce on the stove to know what was for dinner. It was Wednesday, which meant spaghetti. Always. Anyone who consulted the calendar on the fridge knew that.

"Big, I guess," Danny answered. He closed both eyes and stood with his hands on his hips, waiting for his father's predictable response.

"Huge it is. You don't want to be a little guy forever, right?"

It was a running joke between them. Danny was by no means a *little guy*, at least not compared to kids his own age, but he still had a long way to go if he wanted to catch his dad. Which, of course, he did.

"Don't worry about the settings," his father said, walking into the room with a heaping plate of spaghetti in each hand, the napkins and utensils clutched below each plate. "Go grab a couple of Cokes from the fridge, though."

Danny stared at the calendar on the front of the refrigerator, resisted the urge to rip it in half and throw it in the trash, and snagged two cans from the six-pack on the bottom shelf. From the family room, he heard the first notes of the theme song from *Home Improvement*. His father issued a series of grunts from down the hall, a tribute to the show's main character, Tim "The Tool Man" Taylor. *Home Improvement*, like his dad's spaghetti, was a Wednesday night tradition.

"More power," his dad said solemnly as Danny joined him in the family room. He grabbed the Coke from Danny's hand and grunted again in the direction of the screen, where Tim was talking to his wife, Jill, promising to remodel and upgrade her cluttered closet.

That was Tim's catchphrase, *more power*, and it was usually a good sign that things were about to take a turn for the worse. Though Danny appreciated the show's wacky humor, what he liked most about *Home Improvement* was that the Taylors were a family. An actual family. The "normal" kind, with a mom, a dad, and a bunch of kids.

Watching Tim and Jill together, the way they laughed and joked and bickered without ever really getting mad, it was hard not to wonder what his own parents would be like. What they *had* been like. He remembered almost nothing about his mom, or his parents together, and his father sure as hell didn't provide many clues. He was ten years old before Gram finally told him the whole truth about his mom's accident, about the baby and all. Not many people had known she was pregnant at the time, and no one, including his dad, had mentioned it to him since.

"You want some more?" his father asked, mumbling cartoonishly through a knot of spaghetti noodles, nodding in the direction of Danny's already empty plate.

Danny shook his head and settled back into the sofa, arms folded across his chest, watching the predictable comedic drama unfold. This week, Tim was butting heads with Brad, his eldest boy, who had gotten into a fight on the playground after some jerk teased him for hugging his dad in front of the school.

Danny planted an elbow on the arm of the couch and supported his head with his hand, hiding the deep flush that spread across his cheeks as Tim and Brad shamelessly poured out their emotions on the screen. He cringed every time they used the word "love." It was not a word Danny was accustomed to—*love*—certainly not one he and his father ever used. Even when signing birthday cards—or Father's Day cards, if he remembered to make one—Danny always got hung up at the end, usually going with something stuffier, like *sincerely* or *truly*, down at the bottom.

Danny stole a glance at his father, watching him as he watched the show. If he was as uncomfortable as Danny, as bothered by the gross outpouring of emotions, his blank expression offered no hints. Danny squirmed deeper into the cushions of the couch, wishing now that he'd just stayed in his room.

By the end of the episode, which couldn't come soon enough for Danny, Tim and Brad had made up, and a compromise had been struck: no hugging in front of Brad's friends, and the pair would use "How 'bout those Lions?" as a football-based code, a secret way for them to say "I love you" without embarrassing Brad in front of the other kids.

Danny didn't even wait for the closing credits to roll. He jumped from the couch, snatched his empty plate, and made a beeline for the door. Tonight's show had been more serious than usual, more *emotional*, and it had gotten under Danny's skin in a way he didn't fully understand. Or like. Or want to discuss with his dad.

"Whoa, you okay?" his dad asked as Danny booked it for the kitchen.

"Yeah, I'm fine." Danny hesitated at the doorway, then bolted down the hallway, mumbling a lame excuse about "homework" as he marched toward the kitchen.

"Hey, come back for a second," his father called, his voice carrying that firm edge that Danny knew better than to ignore.

Emitting a long sigh that sounded petulant even to his own ears, Danny returned to the edge of the family room. He straddled the doorway, one hand on his hip, staring impatiently down at his father. In the dim light of the living room, his dad's face looked different somehow. Older, maybe. And sadder, too.

"I know today was tough, Danny. And I just wanted to tell you . . ."

His father shifted awkwardly on the couch, his face looking strained like he needed to poop, then began again. "I just wanted to say . . . *how 'bout those Giants?*"

Despite his mood, Danny smiled, somehow pleased by his father's quick adoption of Tim and Brad's code. He eyed his dad, who moved his TV tray aside and stared up expectantly from the couch.

"Yeah, Dad," Danny answered. Unable to meet his father's gaze, he admired his sauce-smeared plate instead. "How 'bout those Giants."

CHAPTER 13

AGE 16

MAY 24, 1996

Danny couldn't help but stare. The entire group—eleven of them in all, crammed like man-sized sardines into the front row of the bleachers behind home plate—stood out like a sore thumb. Dressed in their pressed khaki pants and colorful golf shirts, watching the game intently from underneath caps or visors, it was obvious to everyone who they were. Even without their clipboards and radar guns, Danny would have pegged them from a mile away. Major League scouts.

"What the hell did I tell you?" Dell Greene chastised, startling Danny and ripping him back into the present.

The grouchy coach, his attitude more bark than bite, lowered his considerable bulk onto the bench, occupying a sizeable chunk of the wide swath of pine that separated Danny from the rest of the team. Coach Greene was old school. He knew the protocol—never mess with a pitcher while he's throwing a no-hitter—and up until now, he'd ensured the rules were enforced.

"I wasn't looking," Danny lied, crossing one ankle over the other, playing it cool. His eyes cut quickly to his coach, then back to the action on the field, where Rory Pryor, their last chance at notching an insurance run, was digging into the batter's box.

In truth, Danny had been staring for the whole damn game, and now, after six innings of dominant no-hit ball, he knew that at least some of the scouts were finally staring back. He understood they weren't there for him, but he knew that didn't matter. Their presence alone represented an *opportunity*. It was a chance for him to make a statement, a loud one at that, and to officially put himself on their radar.

"Well, I sure hope not," Coach Greene answered, the faintest hint of a smile lifting the corners of his goatee-encircled mouth. "Me either." He spit a stream of brown tobacco sludge into an empty Gatorade bottle, hoisted himself off the bench, and looked Danny square in the eyes. "Now that we have that straight, how 'bout you pull your head out of your ass and go finish this thing?"

Danny chuckled wryly. He watched Coach Greene lumber back to the front of the dugout, then turned to peer through the diamond-shaped openings in the chain-link fence. His dad sat behind the first base dugout at the far edge of a lively crowd of parents in the first row of bleachers. His focus was trained squarely on the field, his maroon Piner Prospectors cap pulled low to block the bright afternoon sun.

Like Coach Greene, Dad was an old-school gamer, and he knew baseball's superstitions and unwritten rules better than anyone. He'd steered clear of the dugout fence since the middle of the fourth inning, when Danny had recorded his tenth strikeout of the game and retired the side for the fourth time without surrendering a hit. His father's message was clear—even with the scouts in the stands, Danny was on his own.

The sharp *ping* of a metal bat striking the baseball pulled Danny's focus back to the diamond. His eyes quickly scanned the field, where Montgomery High's first baseman, the undeniably intimidating Chris Meadows, was waving his muscular arms back and forth, positioning himself underneath a harmless fly ball that Rory had launched high into the cobalt sky above.

Everybody knew Meadows was a big deal. He was one of the nation's top prospects, and this was the final game of his headline-grabbing high school career. With the Major League draft only three weeks away, he was the reason the swarm of professional scouts had descended on today's game, clipboards in hand, eager to get one last glimpse of Mr. Big Shot before draft day.

Danny tried not to envy the prick as he drifted gracefully into foul territory, then made the catch only feet from the Piner dugout, marking the third out of the bottom of the sixth inning.

Nervous energy flooded Danny's body as he rose from the bench and slid his damp right hand into his glove, preparing to retake the field for the seventh and final inning. He sucked in a deep breath and held it for a count of five, trying to slow the jackhammering of his heart inside his chest.

He snuck one last look at the row of scouts, scrutinizing each of their faces, then cleaned the slate, banishing them from his mind. This was his moment, and no one, not even *Chris-fucking-Meadows,* was going to stand in his way.

⋄

"THIS ASSHOLE . . ." Danny muttered, not caring if the kid heard him or not. He toed the rubber, watching through narrowed lids as Montgomery's second baseman and number-two hitter stepped into the batter's box, then stalled by calling for time.

Danny stepped off the mound, the words *three more outs* playing on repeat in his mind as he stared at the lit scoreboard above the center field fence, slowly flexing and unflexing the fingers of his left hand. Clinging to a 1-0 lead, with only these three outs standing between him and a no-hitter, the drama of the moment was not lost on him. This was more than just an *opportunity*; it was the stage he'd been waiting for his entire life. His chance to be great.

The second baseman, known to Danny only by the number

12 on the back of his jersey, was the singular reason Danny was pitching for a no-hitter right now and not a perfect game. The kid had taken a 3-2 fastball back in the fourth inning and been rewarded by the umpire with a questionable base on balls.

Danny's blood boiled as the little shit finished digging in and the umpire signaled for the game to resume. He remembered that pitch, which had surely clipped the outside corner for a strike, and he already regretted the missed opportunity, knowing damn well what could have been.

He pushed those thoughts aside, peered behind the plate, and waited for "Tank" Sizemore to flash the sign. Tank, a two-time state champion wrestler, with the compact physique and mangled ears to prove it, quickly flashed his index finger, angled toward first base, to signal a fastball on the outside part of the plate.

Danny wound up, reached back, and fired a fastball that sailed high and outside for a ball. Tank rose from his crouch, signaled for a timeout, and walked toward the mound.

"All good," Danny yelled to his catcher, his glove outstretched, waiting for the ball to be returned. Though Tank was a senior and two years older than Danny, the two had grown close over the past two seasons. And with closeness came trust. Tank nodded, fired the ball back, and returned to his post behind the plate.

Despite falling behind in the count 0-1, Danny collected himself, brought the count to 1-2 on successive foul balls, then retired the hitter when he swung over the top of a vicious curveball that started at the letters but dropped precipitously—below the batter's knees—by the time it crossed the plate.

Danny pumped his fist energetically and let his eyes rove over the crowd, basking for a moment in the glow of their uproarious applause. He located his dad, who had abandoned his seat and was pacing back and forth in the gravel next to the bleachers, chewing on a fingernail and sweating like a whore in church.

Danny waited as the next batter, Montgomery's rangy center fielder, stepped to the plate and took his sweet time digging into the batter's box, doing his best to disrupt his rhythm. Danny ignored his antics, delivered the pitch, and jammed him on a nasty slider that cut sharply in on his hands.

The ball dribbled weakly toward the mound. Danny charged, fielded the ball cleanly, then fired it to Rory Pryor at first base for the second out of the inning.

Danny pumped his fist again, received the return throw from Rory, and gave his friend a confident nod as he drifted slowly back to the mound, reveling in the noise of the crowd, which had swelled to a crescendo. He looked to the on-deck circle, where Chris Meadows took two more unhurried practice swings, then sauntered toward the plate, staring at Danny with *you banged my sister* intensity the entire way.

"Time!" called Coach Greene, yelling into a cupped hand from his perch at the mouth of the dugout.

"Ah, c'mon," Danny complained. He kicked at the dirt and stared in disbelief, outraged that the coach was breaking his rhythm in order to visit the mound. Greene, joined by Tank Sizemore and all of the infielders, converged on Danny, who made no attempt to mask his irritation as he waited for the entourage to arrive.

"You want to take over?" Danny challenged, spitting in the dirt before offering the baseball to Coach Greene as he arrived at the mound.

"Cut the shit," Greene said gruffly, ignoring Danny's jab. Dell Greene wasn't in the habit of taking flak from any of his players, but he'd become accustomed to Danny's competitive streak. He knew his fiery outbursts came from a good place, and he extended him more leeway than most. "I know you're raring to finish this thing off—hell, I am, too—but don't forget, this kid has much more on the line today than you do."

Danny looked at Tank, who stared back and nodded slowly, as if to emphasize the coach's point.

"You and Tank have done a great job keeping him off balance so far," the coach continued, "but it only takes *one* mistake to tie the game. And after you embarrassed him with that strikeout earlier, I guarantee he's walking up there this time trying to square one up and hit it into next week." Greene paused, his hooded eyes darting between Danny and Tank, allowing time for his previous statement to sink in. "Just be smart and pitch your game, Danny. And try to keep the ball in the park, huh?"

Danny rolled his eyes at the coach's last remark and watched him amble back to the dugout. He returned his attention to the plate, where Chris Meadows, an ominous scowl etched into his dark features, called for time, then stepped deliberately into the batter's box. The massive lefty methodically adjusted each of his batting gloves, the muscles in his forearms pulled taut like steel cables, while he continued to stare menacingly toward the mound.

Danny returned Meadows's stare, refusing to be intimidated. He held it for a moment, then shifted his focus to Tank, who flashed the sign from behind the plate.

Danny wound up, released the pitch, and snapped a perfect curveball that fooled Meadows badly, causing him to dive back from the plate as the ball clipped the inside corner for a called strike.

The crowd hooted and hollered, but Danny did his best to block out the noise, channeling his focus and worrying only about the next pitch. He wiped his damp left hand on the leg of his pants and looked to Tank for the next sign.

He wound up and delivered again, this time a four-seam fastball, thigh-high and over the center of the plate.

As soon as it left his hand, Danny recognized it for what it was. *A fucking mistake.*

Meadows' eyes lit up as he lifted his front leg and tracked the ball from Danny's hand to the plate. He swung hard, his long metal bat whipping through the strike zone with brutal efficiency, then connecting with such force that the sound of the bat meeting the ball made Danny wince.

Danny jerked his head toward right field.

He watched helplessly as the ball sailed on a high arc toward the creek beyond the right field fence, then curved at the last moment, hooking only inches to the right of the yellow foul pole.

The mammoth shot drew low whistles from the Montgomery contingent, who knew Meadows had narrowly missed a home run that would have broken up the no-hitter, tied the game, and taken a royal shit all over Danny's afternoon.

Danny stalked toward third base. He tried to regain his composure, replaying the previous pitch in his mind as the umpire procured a new ball from the bag attached to his hip and dropped it into Tank's waiting hand. Danny caught Tank's throw, walked back to the mound, and wiped the sweat from his brow while Meadows settled back into the batter's box.

Tank flashed the sign, calling for a changeup, and Danny fervently shook him off. He wasn't in the habit of second-guessing his catcher—he rarely needed to—but they had struck out Meadows on the same pitch sequence in the second inning, and Danny's gut told him the hulking slugger would be sitting on the changeup again.

Tank hesitated, a look of exasperation visible through the bars of his mask, then flashed a new sign. Calling for a curveball this time, he raised his glove, ready to receive the pitch.

Danny nodded and came set. He subtly adjusted his grip on the ball inside his glove, being careful not to tip his pitch, then again delivered a perfect curveball, freezing Meadows in place as the ball *whooshed* past his body and over the inside corner of the plate.

The next moment stretched into an agonizing eternity.

The trio at the plate—Meadows, Tank, and the home plate umpire—remained frozen in time. The crowd, on the edge of their seats since the beginning of the inning, waited breathlessly.

Then, in a sudden flash of movement, the umpire raised his right fist, struck a fast blow in the air at his side, and bellowed the word "Out!" in a throaty roar that was quickly drowned out by the cheers of the Prospector fans and the shouts of Danny's teammates, who rushed to greet him at the mound.

Danny was stunned. Overcome by a surge of emotions—equal parts elation, pride, and relief—he stood motionless on the mound, his hands hanging limply at his sides. He turned to look for his father, eager to share the moment, but lost sight of the crowd as he was dragged to the earth and trapped under a jubilant mass of writhing torsos and limbs.

As the on-field celebration waned, and the crowd began to slowly disperse, Danny walked toward the dugout, where his father waited, speaking to Coach Greene in hushed tones as his teammates filed noisily past.

"Helluva game," Coach Greene remarked, producing the game ball from the pocket of his maroon windbreaker and handing it to Danny.

Danny examined the dirt-stained ball, which Coach Greene had already marked with a black Sharpie, recording the date, the opponent, and the score of the game. He had underlined the words "First No-Hitter," as if certain there were many more to follow.

"Thanks, Coach," Danny said, accepting the ball from Coach Greene with a smile. He started to apologize for his heated remarks on the mound, but the coach waved him off and nudged him toward his father.

"Come here, kid." His dad's voice was strained by emotion as he pulled Danny into a bear hug. "I knew you could do it," he whispered into Danny's ear, squeezing him tight. "I'm proud of you, son. So goddamn proud."

A warm glow spread over Danny's now-exhausted body. He'd barely slept the night before, knowing that he'd be pitching in front of big-league scouts, and running through all the possible scenarios in his mind. He thought he'd prepared himself for every outcome, but the joyous reality of this moment was beyond anything his imagination could conjure.

"You mind holding this while I grab my stuff?" Danny asked.

He handed the game ball to his dad, who grasped the ball like it was made of glass, then turned it in his hand to read the inscription.

"Sure thing, bud. But you can leave your stuff for now." His father's face broke into a sly smile as he scanned the remnants of the crowd, then pointed to a cluster of scouts who were waiting in the gravel next to the bleachers. "There are a few gentlemen over here who'd like to congratulate you before we go."

◊

"YOU OKAY, DUDE?" Rory asked, bringing the car to a halt as the light turned red at the deserted intersection of Guerneville and Fulton. He craned his long neck to get a better view of Danny, who was slumped between Tank Sizemore and the linebacker-sized Luke Dalton in the tiny back seat of Mrs. Pryor's white Corolla.

Every group of friends has that one parental figure, the lone voice of reason who errs on the side of caution and makes sure everyone gets home safely at the end of the night. For Danny's group, it was Rory Pryor. And tonight, Rory had spent most of his evening—and all of his patience—trying to keep Danny out of trouble.

"I think you better pull over," Steve Janecke cautioned. The center fielder peered out from below the brim of his Yankees hat, his almond-shaped eyes darting between Danny and Rory. He leaned forward in the passenger seat, reached toward the dash, and silenced Tupac mid-verse. "I'm serious, bro, he looks pretty rough."

"I'm good," Danny slurred. He raised his eyes to the front seat, where two versions of Rory stared back from behind the wheel, both of them looking like they'd had enough of Danny's shit.

As rough as Danny might have looked, he surely felt even worse. Riding high on the wave of excitement that followed his no-hitter and the subsequent conversation with the big-league scouts, Danny had hit the town ready to let loose.

Everywhere they went, people were pumped to hear of the afternoon's drama; Danny, reveling in the spotlight, had told the story of the final at-bat at least ten times, his dramatic fervor escalating with each retelling. But now, after a series of house parties, three shots of Jägermeister, and one keg stand too many, his head was swimming, and he was fighting the urge to expel the contents of his stomach into his Giants hat, which Tank had snatched from his head and placed on his lap.

Willing his eyes to focus, Danny looked up at Rory, who was still eyeing him from the driver's seat. "I'm telling you," Danny began, the garbled words tumbling haphazardly from his lips, "I'm golden, man. Just get me home. I'm already an hour late . . . and my dad is gonna lose his shit." Danny belched loudly, then abruptly clenched his jaws, feeling his insides roil as the Taco Bell quesadilla in his stomach petitioned for an encore.

"Jesus," Rory sighed. He shook his head in disappointment, doing his best Frank Romano impersonation, and pressed lightly on the accelerator, easing the car forward as the light turned green. "Hopefully your dad is sound asleep, man. If he does see you tonight, looking and smelling like this, I think you're screwed."

Though Danny made it home without vomiting into his own lap, the world spun wildly, and he was shaky on his feet as he exited the car and lumbered up the driveway toward the house. He turned to wave to the Corolla, which was still idling in the driveway, then tripped over his own feet, nearly pitching headfirst into the row of shrubs that lined the walkway leading to the front door.

After rummaging through the front pockets of his jeans—which were stuffed with beer bottle caps, loose sticks of Fruit Stripe, and an assortment of trash—Danny located his house key and lurched toward the front door. Though the stoop was well-lit, the entire door seemed to be swaying from side to side, and it took him three attempts to seat the key in the lock and disengage the bolt.

Danny pushed through the door, into the darkened entry hall, and listened nervously for sounds of his father. He peered past the kitchen and down the tiled hallway to the family room, where the light from the television cast shifting shadows against the wall. With any luck, his dad had fallen asleep watching *SportsCenter*, as he often did, and didn't hear him come in.

"Screw you, too," Danny whispered, cursing the double knots in his laces as he struggled to remove his Nikes. He braced his body against the wall for support, then tossed the sneakers haphazardly atop the neat row of boots, cleats, and athletic shoes that lined the wall next to the door. Listening again, and satisfied that he'd entered unheard, he crept ninja-style down the hall toward his bedroom.

"You're late."

Danny froze at the sound of his father's voice, projected down the hallway from the family room.

"I paged you. Twice. Not sure why I pay for the service on that thing if you can't find the time to call me back."

"Sorry," Danny croaked. He winced at the quality of his voice, which sounded even shittier than he felt. "I just lost track of time."

Eager to get the hell out of Dodge, Danny staggered down the hallway and ducked into the safety of his darkened bedroom. He flopped noisily onto the bed, pulled the paperback copy of *The Killer Angels* out from underneath him, then stared up at the ceiling, listening for sounds of movement from elsewhere in the house.

Seconds passed in silence. Then he heard heavy footfalls approaching from down the hall. The hallway light turned on, shooting a sliver of yellow light under his door and onto the gray carpet below.

"We're not done here," his father said, his words sounding clear and crisp, even through the closed door. He barged inside and flipped the wall switch, flooding the room with harsh artificial light.

Danny shielded his eyes, then swung his legs over the side of the bed, rising unsteadily into a seated position. Awkward seconds crawled by as his father stared from above, examining him like a piece of roadkill hopelessly enmeshed with the grill of his truck. Danny tried to match his gaze, then wilted under its heat and let his eyes slip to the floor.

"You're drunk," his father said. It wasn't a question, but a statement of fact. He closed his eyes and shook his head from side to side, the standard preamble to the *disappointed dad routine*. "Unbelievable, Danny. Absolutely unbelievable."

His father never drank, and he had an almost irrational loathing for alcohol. While Danny understood that his dad carried baggage from his youth—*emotional scars* that Gram alluded to from time to time, but only when his father wasn't around—he couldn't comprehend why *he* was expected to share in that burden.

His father's words, steeped in his typical notes of disapproval, elicited a feeling of shame, which manifested in a heat that began at the base of Danny's neck and spread quickly upward to engulf his entire face. Then, in an instant, the feeling of shame was quelled, replaced with a flash of defiant anger.

"And?" Danny challenged, his voice booming in the small confines of the bedroom. He lifted his eyes to meet his father's gaze. "So, what if I am, Dad? Maybe, that's okay sometimes. Maybe, every once in a while, it's okay to have fun—to do something spontaneous that isn't listed on a schedule or a stupid calendar."

Danny chuckled joylessly and rose clumsily to his feet. He swayed at the side of the bed, eye to eye with his father. "Maybe," he continued, his words fueled by alcohol and contempt, "it's okay for me to have a fucking life."

"A life?" his father asked incredulously, throwing his hands up in the air. He took a step forward, closing the distance between them. "And this is how you want to live it, Danny? Getting drunk? Partying? Risking everything you've worked for?" His voice grew louder and more intense with each question. "Some life, kid." He paused, his hands planted on his hips, letting his words sink in.

"Well, Dad," Danny whispered. "At least *I* have a life. That's more than I can say for you."

His father's eyes widened. He stepped backward, shocked disbelief electrifying his features.

Danny hesitated, considered folding, then doubled down instead, driving the knife home. "She's dead, you know. She's dead, and she's gone, and she's never coming back!" He ignored the hot tears streaming down his cheeks. "And at some point, I'm going to be gone, too. And you'll still be here, by yourself, alone and miserable. And maybe then you can start living your own life instead of trying to control mine."

Danny drew in a jagged breath. He wiped his nose with the back of his hand and searched his father's face for a reaction. The look of shock was gone, replaced with something different, some alien emotion that was impossible for Danny to read. Seconds ticked by in silence.

"Okay, son," his father said, his voice oddly flat but infused with a note of finality. "Now we're done." He turned to leave, then paused, reached into the front pocket of his hooded sweatshirt, and produced the ball Danny had left in his care after the game.

"It'll run out someday," his father said, staring hard at the ball as if counting every red stitch. "Your luck, I mean. It won't last."

He rotated the ball in his hand, read Coach Greene's inscription one more time, then set it on Danny's desk with a dull *thud*.

"I don't care how good you are, kid; not every mistake turns into a foul ball." He shook his head again, stepped into the hallway, and didn't look back as he closed the door behind him.

CHAPTER 14

AGE 18

JUNE 2, 1998

"You think she'll take my last name?" Rory blurted, drawing a handful of judgmental stares from across the darkened classroom. He mouthed a half-hearted apology to *Little Ms. Prim*, Cindy Heffernan, who looked perpetually constipated and accelerated from zero to deeply offended in less than a second, then continued in a whisper. "You know, when we get married, move into a big-ass mansion, and have lots of babies."

Though he was speaking to Danny, who sat beside him in the back row of the second-year Spanish class, Rory's lustful eyes remained glued to the portable TV at the front of the room, which showed the love of his life singing for an adoring crowd and strutting her stuff across the stage.

It was the end of the school year, and the class had little else to do, so Mr. Arriola threw in the towel and showed the first half of *Selena*. A self-certified movie buff, whose credentials were bolstered by holding an after-school job at Bradley Video, Rory had seen the movie when it was first released on VHS and fallen hopelessly in love with its star, Jennifer Lopez.

"Yeah, man, you're definitely her type," Danny replied, all

sarcasm. His eyes darted anxiously back to the classroom door, which had been calling his name since the minute he sat down. "In fact, I'm sure she's out on the prowl right now, all dolled up, scouring the streets of Hollywood in search of a skinny computer nerd with acne and braces."

The words came out harsher than he'd intended, drawing a sidelong glance from Rory, who was never afraid to let Danny know when he was acting like an asshole. Danny knew Rory was painfully self-conscious about his acne. And even more so about his smile. It was the reason he'd quit playing sports and taken the after-school job in the first place—to pay for the braces his mother could never afford.

"Oh, I get it," Rory said, trying to sound nonchalant, but clearly hurt by Danny's remark. He folded his long arms across his chest and glared at Danny from across the aisle. "You're still pissed off at your dad for making you come to school on *the big day*, but he's not here to be your punching bag, so you're going to take it out on your best friend instead."

Danny averted his eyes, examining the faux-wood surface of his desktop and the cartoonish cock and balls that were drawn across it in Sharpie.

Though Rory wasn't wrong, Danny was in no mood to concede the point. He *was* pissed off about going to school, on this of all days, but there'd been no way around it. He had his history final later that afternoon, a requirement for graduation, and both his father and his teacher had stubbornly refused to budge. So, he'd grudgingly dragged his ass to school in the morning, only to grow more and more annoyed with each passing hour.

Still angry with his father and reliving their lengthy discussion from the night before, Danny reached into his backpack. He withdrew the single sheet of yellow legal paper from his binder and set it on the desk in front of him. The note, written in pencil and littered with childish erase marks where his father had corrected his spelling, had been placed on the kitchen counter this morning when Dad left for the gym. It was short, to the point, and absolutely dripping with his dad's parental sensibility:

> Danny,
>
> No matter how today goes, don't feel pressured to make the call right away. I'm not trying to decide for you. I just want you to take your time, think it through, and make the RIGHT choice.
>
> Stay focused at school and keep your eye on the ball. You'll know as soon as I do.
>
> —Dad

Danny held the letter in both hands. He read his father's irritating message one more time, resisted the urge to crumple it into a tight little ball and whiz it into the trash can in the corner, and slid it back into his binder instead.

While he knew Dad was trying to be helpful, he was still annoyed. His father had made no secret of his preferences regarding Danny's future or what he considered to be the *right choice*. And as well-intentioned as the letter was, it was just another distraction, another angry siren blaring inside his brain, making it that much harder for Danny to focus while his life and his entire future were hanging precariously in the balance.

Danny drummed his fingers on the desk, then made up his mind. He stepped into the aisle—planning to grab the laminated bathroom pass and kill time pacing around the campus—then froze when the classroom phone jangled angrily from behind the teacher's battered metal desk.

Danny watched as Mr. Arriola, a barrel-chested man with a black pencil mustache and an infectious laugh, jumped from his seat and snatched the vintage 1970s receiver off its wall-mounted hook. He turned his back to the class and spoke in a hushed whisper to the person on the other end of the line.

After an exchange that dragged on for a lifetime, he seated the receiver in its cradle, then turned to face the class. He locked eyes with Danny, flashed an electric smile, and motioned eagerly for him to join him at the front of the classroom.

Danny's heart thundered. He looked to Rory, who sat up in his seat, his annoyance with Danny seemingly now forgotten.

"Ooooohhh, shit!" Rory cried, interrupting the movie again, and again drawing a pretentious sneer from Cindy Heffernan.

Rory knew the score. Like many of Danny's classmates and teachers, he was well aware of the significance of the day, and he was nearly as eager as Danny to hear the news. To know once and for all whether Danny had been selected in the draft.

"Just promise me," Rory began gravely, grabbing Danny by the forearm and staring up from his desk with serious blue eyes, "that when you're rich and famous, you won't forget about me." He released Danny's arm and broke into a wide grin, the genuine article that showed all his teeth. "And that you'll set me up with Jennifer Lopez."

◆

DANNY STRODE across the open-air campus—which was empty, save for the lone campus security guard who patrolled up one corridor and down the next—crossed the tree-lined quad, and booked it to the school's front office.

He paused outside the glossy maroon door, next to the glass-enclosed bulletin board, and struggled to catch his wind. A cold trickle of sweat slid down the back of his neck and beneath the collar of his T-shirt, making him shiver as it disappeared into the space between his shoulder blades.

The light in the office was unexpectedly dim. Danny stepped into the small reception area and waited for his eyes to adjust from the brilliant morning sunshine to the low lighting of the windowless space. There was his father, standing at the counter, still dressed in his gym clothes and propped up nonchalantly by an elbow. He faced away from the door, carrying on an animated conversation with Mr. Jackson, the school's intolerable jackass of a principal.

"Ah, there he is," Mr. Jackson called, subtly adjusting the cuffs of his plum-colored suit. "If it isn't the man of the hour." Jackson flashed a toothy grin, which almost seemed genuine at first, then lingered on his face long enough to sour into something else.

Danny hesitated in the doorway, then pulled the door shut behind him. He and the principal were not on good terms. Jackson had never been a fan of Danny's in-class antics to begin with, and this was the first time he'd spoken to the man since *the incident* a week prior.

Danny, along with a handful of his friends, had been implicated in the execution of an elaborate senior prank. The details of the scheme, which had spread across the school like wildfire, involved the kidnapping and transportation of two wild geese, the force-feeding of prescription-strength laxatives, and the explosive sullying of the teacher's breakroom.

Danny had been summoned to Jackson's office in the aftermath and grilled for more than an hour, treated like the prime suspect in one of Rory's shitty detective movies. Though Danny had convincingly argued his innocence and walked away unscathed, he knew Mr. Jackson was not as stupid as he looked. And that the prank would not soon be forgotten, much less forgiven.

"Your father was just filling me in on the news," Jackson said, the phony smile still plastered across his shiny face. He pulled an olive-green handkerchief from the pocket of his ridiculous suit, mopped beads of sweat from his forehead, and motioned for Danny to join them at the counter.

Danny returned the smile robotically, then shot a *what-the-hell* glance at his father. Couldn't Dad have waited, instead of jumping the gun and spilling the beans to Mr. Jackson first?

His dad, perhaps sensing the temperature of his mood, offered an apologetic shrug, then gestured for Danny to take the lead as they followed Mr. Jackson out of the reception area and into the narrow hallway beyond.

Danny trailed Mr. Jackson down the corridor, his eyes roving from side to side as he admired the series of framed photographs that were hung at regular intervals along the off-white walls.

There was a picture of Danny on the righthand side, standing atop the mound. His face was locked in a grimace as he stretched toward home plate, milliseconds away from releasing the ball that was frozen forever on his fingertips. The picture was taken in the final inning of his no-hitter more than two years earlier and appeared on the front page of the *Press Democrat*'s sports section the following morning.

"This is our conference room," Mr. Jackson bragged, waving them into the forgettable space like it was the oval-fucking-office. "You guys can make yourselves at home and take as long as you need."

Jackson shook both their hands—first his father's, then Danny's with much less enthusiasm—and retreated from the room, pulling the door closed as he went.

Danny rolled a chair back from the large rectangular conference table. He settled himself in its cushy upholstery and waited impatiently for his father to do the same.

"Well?" Danny asked, unable to contain himself as his father meandered granny-style across the room.

"Well . . ." Dad took a seat toward the far end of the table, opposite Danny. He clasped his hands on the surface of the table, then stared out from beneath thick furrowed brows, which suddenly looked grayer than Danny remembered.

"There's good news and . . . some not-so-good news, son. Pick your poison."

Danny's pulse quickened, and a knot of anxiety churned in the depths of his stomach. He wished for the thousandth time that he'd blown off the history exam and stayed home from school, where his father had been glued to the computer, constantly refreshing the dial-up internet connection so he could monitor the progress of the Major League Baseball draft, pick by pick and round by round.

"Let's start with the good news," Danny croaked. He licked his lips, swallowed the golf-ball-sized lump in his throat, and prepared himself for the imminent kick in the balls.

"The good news," his father began, the corners of his mouth betraying a smile that quickly spread across his entire face, "is that you were drafted. Fifth round, 158th overall." He paused, still smiling, waiting as Danny processed the monumental news.

Danny breathed an audible sigh of relief, and the tension drained from his neck and shoulders. While he knew going into the day that he wasn't going to be picked in the first round—unlike the Sabathia kid from Vallejo, who already sported big-league stuff and basically walked on water—he hoped to be selected within the first five rounds. His fear, which thankfully hadn't been realized, was to be overlooked entirely on the first day of the two-day draft, sliding later and later into the subsequent rounds.

"And the bad news?" Danny asked, the black cloud of dread settling in the air above him.

The smile faded from his dad's mouth and eyes, and he sat ramrod straight in his chair. He cleared his throat, looking even more uncomfortable than he had at Cousin Sheila's wedding reception when a woman had foolishly dared to ask him to dance.

"Unfortunately, the 158th pick, the one you were drafted with . . ." His father paused, the corner of his mouth twitching. He stared down at his hands, before finally looking up to meet Danny's eyes. "The pick belonged to the Dodgers."

The words landed like a sucker punch to Danny's gut. He leaned back in his seat, stared up at the water-stained ceiling tiles, and let out a long groan. Of course, he knew this was a possibility—being selected by the one team in baseball that he, and every other Giants fan, truly hated—but with thirty teams between the two leagues, the possibility had seemed remote.

Danny released his white-knuckle grip from the arms of the chair and frantically searched for a silver lining. He opened his mouth to speak, to ask if there might have been a mistake, then swallowed the question whole. His father was watching him from across the table, biting his lower lip, and his face had darkened to an absurdly crimson hue.

"Wait," Danny said suspiciously, his mind reeling. "Are you screwing with me?!" He leaned forward in his chair, searching his dad's oddly contorted features for answers. "You've had *eighteen years* to be funny, and this is the day you miraculously grow a sense of humor?"

His father broke into an uncontrollable fit of laughter. He launched his chair back from the table, bent forward at the waist, and slapped his knees. Irked by the prank but giddy with relief, Danny joined in the laughter.

Eventually bringing himself under control, his dad wheeled his chair back to the table and placed his palms down on its surface. He looked Danny in the eye and spoke softly. "It was the Giants, kid. Round five, pick number 158, it belonged to the Giants."

Danny sat motionless, frozen inside a cube of stunned disbelief. He searched his mind and heart for the right words—the ones to express the joy, gratitude, and excitement that bubbled inside him—but he came up empty-handed and fought back tears instead.

"But just because it's the Giants," his dad cautioned, all business now, "doesn't mean that you treat this decision any differently. Got it?"

Danny nodded, barely listening, still soaking up the moment. *It belonged to the Giants.*

"You weigh the pros and cons," his father droned on, "then do what's right." He waved both hands in the air in front of him, ensuring he had Danny's full attention. "As exciting as this is, it may turn out that college is still the best option."

Danny let out an exaggerated sigh, his shoulders sagging as the wind drained from his sails. He closed his eyes, turning these last words over in his mind, trying to see them from his father's perspective. For months now, including the night before, his dad had been hammering away, pressuring him to put pro baseball on the back burner and accept one of the many scholarships he'd been offered.

In a few years, he'd argued, Danny would be more experienced, more *mature*, and better prepared to compete at the highest levels. Danny's participation in Operation GOOSE JUICE, though hilarious and never proven by Mr. Jackson, had done nothing to alleviate Dad's concerns about his lack of maturity.

"Yeah, Dad," Danny replied, wishing he could recapture the excitement he'd felt before his dad had predictably pissed on his parade. "I get it." He stood and reached for his backpack, adding sarcastically, "I need to get back to class. Don't forget, I have a history final today."

"Okay," his father said, staring patiently from across the table. "But one more thing: We're going to have a house full of people tonight. And all of them are going to want to know what comes next. When they ask you—and believe me, they will—just tell them you're thinking it over, okay?" He waited for Danny's grudging nod, then moved around the table and pulled him into a hug.

Danny returned his father's hug, then quickly pulled away and moved to the door. "And thank you," Danny said, his hand on the handle, his gratitude almost an afterthought. "For coming here, I mean. And for everything else, too. For helping me *get here*. To this point." He jiggled the door handle as a shy blush crept over his cheeks, wishing he had the words to express how he really felt. "How 'bout those Giants, huh?"

Dad stared back at him, confusion etched into his sun-bronzed face. Sentimentality was not their strong suit, and it had been years since either of them had used their *secret code*. Then, as if a lightbulb went on, recognition flashed across his features, and his eyes shone with pride.

He met Danny at the door and hugged him again. "Yeah, son," he whispered, squeezing Danny tight, "How 'bout those Giants."

◇

"You know, kiddo, I remember you being much better at this whole *hide-and-seek* thing when you were little."

Hal Baker smiled from the entrance to the family room, where Danny had retreated under the guise of checking in on the College World Series. The window shades were drawn to block the late afternoon sun, with the only light coming from a shaded floor lamp standing in the far corner of the room, to the right of the TV.

"And I remember you guys letting me stay hidden for an hour at a time," Danny fired back from the couch, returning Baker's smile. "Probably so you could watch the game in peace."

Baker laughed and joined Danny on the gray upholstered sofa, the two of them separated by the pair of elderly Siamese cats who were curled up beside each other, fast asleep with their furry bodies intertwined.

"Your dad asked me to come and grab you," Baker said in his gravelly voice, shifting his Budweiser to his left hand so he could pet Basil with his right. "I think he's going to make a toast."

"Oooh, that'll be epic," Danny said, coating his response in his thickest layer of teenage sarcasm. His father was good at a lot of things. Public speaking wasn't one of them, but, apparently, predicting the future was.

Danny hadn't been away from the backyard barbeque for long, but his absence had provided a welcome break from the unending barrage of inquiries from family members and friends. His father had been right, of course: With the draft now behind him, everyone was pushing and prodding, eager to hear *the plan*, and to know what he would do next.

"Is this the championship game?" Baker asked, gesturing to the boxy wide-screen TV as he nimbly shifted the topic of conversation.

On the screen, the Mississippi State pitcher wore a pissed-off expression that Danny understood better than most. He handed the ball to his manager, who had evidently seen enough. The skipper grabbed the ball, waved to the bullpen, and gave the kid a cursory slap on the ass as he stalked toward the dugout.

"Nah, not yet. But getting close," Danny said. "It's an elimination game for both teams, but it looks like USC is going to close it out."

Danny looked over to Uncle Hal, whose eyes remained trained on the television. It was hard to believe the dude had just turned sixty. Wearing cargo shorts and a Gold's Gym T-shirt that barely managed to restrain his biceps, he was still an impressive specimen. And he was still the last guy Danny would want to square up with in an arm-wrestling competition.

"So that's the other option?" Baker asked. Right on cue, as if reading Danny's mind, he raised a well-muscled arm and pointed toward the television with the neck of his beer. "If not the Giants, then college at USC?"

Danny only nodded in response. The recruiting process had been running balls to the wall since the beginning of his junior year. Most of the big baseball programs had come knocking at their door, but the recruiting pitch from Coach Gillespie, the head coach for the University of Southern California, had stood out from the rest. And with this year's squad in contention to win the College World Series, accepting the offer would mean joining a strong team that was already poised for success.

"Everything's still on the table," Danny answered cautiously. Even with Uncle Hal, he was trying to heed his father's advice. To toe the party line. "We're not looking to rush into anything without weighing our options, you know?"

Baker smiled knowingly. He took a long pull from his beer, still watching the action on the screen, then turned his broad torso to face Danny at the other end of the couch. "So, you'd probably want to take the college route, right, kiddo? Get some more experience under your belt, so you'll be better prepared to take the next step. Is that what your dad says?"

Danny nodded again, slower this time, as he read between the lines and started to understand the purpose of this chat. Though

Uncle Hal's tone was light, his expression was serious, and Danny could tell from the firm set of his square jaw—and the words he used, almost identical to those of his father—that he and his dad were of the same mind. He wouldn't be surprised, in fact, if Dad had orchestrated this little talk. There was no one on Earth Danny trusted or respected more than Uncle Hal.

"Well, Danny," Baker continued, groaning as he hoisted himself off the couch, "your dad has a pretty good head on his shoulders, you know? And if that's his take, I think you'd be wise to listen."

"Sure," Danny answered, his tone noncommittal. He had plenty of points of his own, a whole list of convincing arguments to counter those of his father, but now that he understood that the deck was stacked, he saw no need to show his cards.

Baker walked to the door, turned, then continued in a more somber tone. "That was a dream of his, you know, to play college ball. And if things had gone differently, with your grandparents and all, then I'm sure he would have. Would have been damn good, too." Baker scratched at the gray stubble on his cheek and stared at the collection of trophies lining the top shelf of the bookcase on the opposite wall, a faraway look in his eyes.

"Yeah, I know," Danny said, tossing the words into the still air just to dispel the somber mood that had settled in the room.

Though his father had never spoken to him about that night, the night his grandparents died, Danny had thought about it a lot. He'd known from an early age that those hours had changed his dad and reshaped his life in ways that Danny would never fully understand. He also knew, without ever having to be told, that more than just his grandparents had perished in those flames. Those were feelings to which Danny could relate.

"That's life, though, right?" Danny asked, the words sticking in his throat, then emerging from his mouth, sounding thin and strained. He reached impulsively for the remote, then stared at its neat rows of buttons as he tapped it on his thigh. "Shit happens every day, right? Big shit, little shit. And sometimes it's impossible in the moment to tell the big things from the small things, the important from the unimportant. Or to know what's coming around the next bend, and how our lives will be changed." He paused to catch his breath and looked to Uncle Hal for a response.

Baker sighed long and hard, then ran a hand up and over the gray ridge of his flattop. He shifted his weight awkwardly, seemingly frozen by the changeup Danny had floated across the outside corner of the plate.

"It's okay," Danny said. He jumped from the couch, switched off the television, and joined Baker in the doorway. "C'mon," he said, gesturing toward the hallway. "Let's go see about that toast."

Danny followed Uncle Hal through the house in silence. The pair exited through the sliding glass door and emerged into the crowded backyard, where no fewer than thirty friends, teammates, coaches, and family members had assembled to celebrate Danny's selection in the draft.

Many people—including Danny's grandparents, who had pressed for this celebratory barbecue, even over his father's objections—were seated at rectangular folding tables, which had been set up at regular intervals across the freshly mown lawn. Others stood in tight circles across the pebbled concrete patio, carrying on loud conversations and eating hot dogs and hamburgers off of paper plates.

"Danny!" his father called. Wearing a grease-stained apron and drinking a Diet Coke, he waved from behind the smoking Weber grill, then beckoned for Danny to join him and Uncle Sammy on the far side of the patio.

"Danimal!" Uncle Sammy yelled. It was his nickname for Danny since before he was old enough to walk. Sammy carefully shed the toddler that was draped from his back like a cape, then leaned in for a hug and offered his congratulations.

Sammy's youngest son, child number five and boy number two, scurried out from under foot and trotted in the direction of his mother, who was seated at a table on the grass with the rest of their noisy clan.

"I was just telling Uncle Sammy," his father began, his eyes glued to the grill as he expertly flipped a row of hamburgers, "about your newfound interest in geese. And laxatives."

Danny stifled a laugh and fist bumped Uncle Sammy, a gesture his father ignored, then waited as his dad removed his apron and passed off the spatula. He threw a heavy arm over Danny's shoulder and guided him to the edge of the patio, where the concrete yielded to the emerald grass.

"Excuse me," his father shouted, his voice cutting through the din, bringing the competing conversations to a sudden close. "The man of the hour has returned, so I'd like to take this opportunity to say a few words." He waited while guests filtered off the patio, skirting around them to join those who were seated at the tables on the lawn. "First off—"

"Thank you for coming," Danny interrupted, surprised by the sound of his own voice. He shot a quick glance at his father, who was just as surprised by the interruption as Danny. He hadn't realized he was going to speak until the words spontaneously rocketed from his lips. Now, with the words out there and all eyes trained on him, he found himself enjoying the moment, savoring the spotlight.

"There's something that I'd like to say," Danny continued, his voice gaining strength. He could feel the heat of his father's glare, so he stepped forward, continuing to gaze into the sea of faces assembled in front of him. "When my dad broke the news today at my school, we agreed that there was no rush to reach a decision. We agreed that I have plenty of time to *weigh my options* before I choose the next step."

"And you do, son," his father said from behind. "You have all the time in the world." He spoke quietly, his voice a cautionary growl.

"But the truth is . . ." Danny continued. He felt his father's hand on his shoulder and took another step forward, shrugging off the hand but refusing to look back. "The truth is," he repeated, locking eyes with Grandma Ruth, whose lips were pressed together, her round cheeks raised slightly, betraying the faintest hint of a knowing smile, "that we never know how much time we have. For anything."

Danny peered back at his father, noted his uncomfortable smile, and felt the tug of indecision. He looked back to Gram, who swept a silver wave of hair back from her lined forehead and offered a subtle nod.

Danny returned her nod, then took the plunge. "And that's why I'm glad you're all here," he continued, the butterflies in his stomach now put to rest. "So that I can share my decision with all of you tonight."

Chapter 15

Age 21

August 24, 2001

Fuck around, get fucked around. It was one of Coach Greene's favorite sayings, a profanity-laced adaptation of the old "mess with the bull" expression, and now it was blaring in the forefront of Danny's mind, a warning sign he'd be foolish to ignore.

He was no stranger to locker room pranks, having *fucked around* with more than his fair share of teammates over the years, but Danny was more accustomed to staring down the sights and squeezing the trigger than being the poor asshole caught in someone else's crosshairs.

Resigned to his fate, Danny crossed the threshold of the Fresno Grizzlies locker room and pretended not to notice when a host of conversations, many of them loud and boisterous only seconds before, came to an abrupt halt. Though there were still hours before game time, the locker room was already crowded with teammates, most of them rambling through their pregame routines, milling about in various states of dress.

"Fellas," Danny called. He nodded to the masses, addressing the greeting to no one in particular.

Painfully conscious of both the stifling heat and the sudden change in atmosphere, he crossed the space quickly, the only lingering noise the rhythmic sound of a ping-pong ball being batted back and forth at the table that dominated the center of the room.

Danny arrived at his locker, one in a series of identical open compartments lining the concrete walls of the spacious locker room the Grizzlies shared with the Fresno State Bulldogs. He dropped his gym bag to the floor and peered inside, discovering the source of his teammates' anticipation.

Taped to the back wall, just below the placard bearing his name and jersey number, was a laminated poster with the words "Butterflies of North America" printed across the top in large black script. Below the lettering, centered within green boxes set against an off-white background, were illustrations of twenty-four of the continent's most common butterfly species. He didn't recognize most of the winged insects, but that wasn't the point. Their message was clear: His time was running out.

"Pretty damn funny," Danny shouted. He ripped the poster from the wall, then let it drop to the bottom of his locker. He scrutinized the faces of his teammates, one after the next, before fixing his stare on Rex Fader, the self-proclaimed chairman of the Romano tattoo committee.

"Don't look at me," the red-haired second baseman said innocently. He paused from his ping-pong game, glanced around the room, and placed his worn paddle onto the scarred surface of the green table.

Fader, who was three years older than Danny and in his second year with the San Francisco Giants' Triple-A affiliate, had initially been a royal pain in Danny's ass. But after nearly a year together in Fresno, he had evolved into Danny's partner in crime, their friendship based largely on a shared fondness for Taco Bell, Steel Reserve, and postgame jackassery.

"First off," Fader said, playing to the audience, "you know I don't mess with starting pitchers on game day. And second, you know damn well I settled on the monarch weeks ago."

Fader looked slyly around the room, the party end of his fiery red mullet pouring out the back of his backward-facing cap. He let the tension build as teammates snickered, then picked up his paddle and joined Danny next to the locker.

"The only question now," Fader continued, as he drew back his paddle, "is where we're gonna put it!" He punctuated his words with a sharp smack to Danny's ass, then erupted in a fit of laughter, which was joined by the rest of the team. They were all in on the joke, eager to turn the tables and have a rare laugh at Danny's expense.

Danny joined in the laughter. In fairness, he knew he deserved all the shit his teammates could dish out. The butterfly joke, now months in the making, had stemmed from a wild night of drinking early in the season. The team had been celebrating two milestones—Danny's twenty-first birthday and his first complete-game shutout—when he foolishly let his mouth write a check his ass had yet to cash. Stoked by his performance on the mound and multiple tequila shots, he'd held court at the team's favorite bar, The Crowe's Nest, and compared himself to a majestic butterfly, newly emerged from the cocoon and ready to spread its wings and launch into flight.

As if the shitty butterfly comparison weren't bad enough, he'd followed the ridiculous metaphor with an even more cringe-worthy pledge: If he wasn't called up to the big leagues by the end of the year, he would get a butterfly tattoo (species and location to be determined by the team) to commemorate his epic failure. Now, with most of the season in the rearview mirror and only a month of games still to play, it seemed more and more likely that Danny would end the year in Triple-A and be paying the piper come October.

The chorus of laughter was cut short by a sharp call originating from the doorway of the tunnel that led from the locker room to the team's offices and the playing field beyond. The voice, scratchy with age and recognized by all, belonged to Chip Nugent, the team's septuagenarian pitching coach.

Nugent, who had long ago parlayed a short and unmemorable major league pitching stint into a long and distinguished coaching career, often joked that he had forgotten more about baseball than Danny would ever know. And though Danny wasn't willing to concede that particular point, he was quick to admit that Nugent was one hell of a mentor and more responsible than anyone for Danny's season-long string of successes. And for helping him discover the maturity and consistency—both on *and off* the field—that had held him back in the past.

"Let's go, Romano!" Nugent called again from the doorway of the tunnel, his Alabama twang cutting through the stillness of the sweltering room. "Skipper wants to see you A-S-A-F-P. Don't worry about changing over, son, just *giddy up*."

Dressed in his gray Nautica T-shirt that had been certified as "lucky" and was now worn every day he pitched, Danny trailed Nugent nervously up the concrete tunnel, past the empty training room and a series of small offices that lined both sides of the narrow passage.

"Any idea what he wants?" Danny asked, probing for insights into the manager's agenda. It wasn't unusual for Chuck Greenlaw to summon the starting pitcher on game day, but those conversations were strategy-based and always included Marty Hillman, the team's starting catcher. Based on the confused look on Hillman's ruddy face when Danny passed him on the way out of the locker room, this conversation was a departure from the norm.

"Oh, I reckon I have a notion," Nugent replied. He came to a stop outside the manager's office, then paused for a beat with his hand clutching the doorknob. "But an old-timer like me knows well enough not to steal the skipper's thunder." He winked, a kindly gesture that always reminded Danny of his grandfather, then opened the door and motioned for Danny to head inside.

"Hey, Skip." Danny cringed, embarrassed by the nervous tremble in his voice. He lingered in the doorway, waiting for the manager to invite him in. "I heard you were looking for me."

A serious man with a serious mustache, Greenlaw waved to

the nearest of the two chairs parked in front of the desk, then waited for Danny to sit.

In his playing days, the manager had been an all-star third baseman for the St. Louis Cardinals before a series of back injuries derailed his promising career. While some guys on the team thought the skipper's blunt disposition could be attributed to residual back pain, Danny had formed his own medical opinion, and he was convinced that the manager's surliness was the result of an undiagnosed stick up his ass.

"As I'm sure you're aware," Greenlaw began, leaning back importantly in his chair and fixing Danny with hard eyes, "you're no longer starting today."

Danny looked to Nugent, who met his gaze and offered a single nod as confirmation. He leaned forward in his seat, his breath coming in short gasps as his hopes rose and his chest constricted in nervous anticipation.

"It turns out," Greenlaw continued brusquely, "that the issue with Estes's ankle is worse than they thought. He hit the disabled list this morning, leaving a hole in the Giants' rotation for the next couple of weeks."

Danny's stomach roiled as he digested the meaning of the coach's words. Shawn Estes, a long-time staple of the Giants' five-man starting rotation, had been battling an ankle injury for the past few months. That said, he and the team had seemed confident that he could pitch through it, and Estes had yet to miss his turn in the rotation.

"What the Skipper is saying," Nugent offered, taking a step forward and annunciating each word with unusual precision, "is that you need to pack your bags." A slight smile formed at the wrinkled corners of his mouth as he leaned forward and placed a liver-spotted hand on Danny's shoulder. "You're headed to the show, kid."

Though Danny had waited for this moment his entire life—had spent countless sleepless nights envisioning every possible scenario, then used his waking hours trying to transform those fantasies into reality—now that the call had finally come, he found himself speechless, overwhelmed by the enormity of the moment.

"I'll walk him through the travel arrangements," Nugent promised Greenlaw, tugging gently on Danny's arm and coaxing him from his seat. "Maybe help him find his tongue, too."

Still suspended in a state of disbelief, Danny rose to his feet. He accidentally kicked the leg of the chair, apologized to Greenlaw, then shuffled toward the door.

"You know, it's a shame," Greenlaw called, freezing Danny at the threshold. He waited for Danny to turn, then continued, his wry smile partially hidden underneath the wire brush of a mustache. "You've earned your shot, kid. No doubt about that. But I was sure as hell looking forward to seeing that tattoo."

◆

"CAN I CLOSE OUT, MABEL?" Danny shouted, struggling to be heard over the ancient jukebox that blared from its position at the far end of the bar, next to the door that remained open to trap the slightest hint of a breeze. Nearing midnight, it was still at least ninety degrees outside, and even hotter within the sticky confines of the crowded pub.

The Crowe's Nest—with its sagging roof, wobbly tables, and lone neon sign that simply read "BAR"—had been the preferred hangout of the Fresno Grizzlies baseball team for longer than anyone could remember. The place was something of a paradox: Decorated in a weird maritime motif, its walls covered by cheap oil paintings of Colonial-era ships, the bar's décor tacitly ignored the realities of geography. Fresno, located smack dab in the heart of the San Joaquin Valley, was far removed from the sea, the nearest coastal town almost a three-hour drive to the west. Despite the bar's location, only a mile from Pete Beiden Field and the Fresno State campus, the university crowd largely shunned the tavern, and it would likely have shut its doors years before had it not been for the baseball team and its players' appreciation for cheap beer and greasy food.

"Sure, love, just give me a second," Mabel replied, her meaty hands encircling empty mugs and plucking them from the surface of the bar. The woman, like the bar, was a paradox in her own right. Kind and thoughtful one minute, ready to pounce from behind the bar and break up a fight the next, Mabel had also been a favorite of the team since time out of mind.

"Leaving already, sport?"

Chip Nugent stood behind him at the bar, leaning in close to be heard over the voice of Alan Jackson, who was extolling the virtues of the Chattahoochee River from the jukebox in the corner. He'd traded his baseball uniform for starched jeans and a colorful windbreaker, seemingly unfazed by the night's heat.

Danny looked to his half-empty beer—only his second of the night, which he'd been nursing for the better part of an hour as he'd waited for his father to *finally* return his call—and then to the crowd of teammates, some gathered around the pool table, others scattered at round wooden tables across the room. He nodded in the affirmative. He'd been reluctant to join the party in the first place, but his flight to San Francisco didn't leave until late the following afternoon, and Fader and the boys would not be denied. First-time promotions to *the show* were always an event to be celebrated.

"Let me get that," Nugent offered, nodding to Danny's mug, then pulling a crisp bill from his ancient leather wallet. "I'd like to bend your ear for a minute before you take off for the night." He slid the bill across the slick surface of the bar, then flashed Mabel, who was at least a decade his junior, one of his patented winks.

Though it was hard to be sure in the low light of the bar, Danny thought he saw a slight blush creep up her fleshy neck. He averted his eyes and pretended not to notice. Now *that* was some shit he'd never seen Gramps do.

Danny followed Nugent out of the bar, into the hot night, and around the edge of the building to the small parking lot that sat adjacent to the 7-Eleven. The pair paused next to the wall of the bar, standing in the weak halo of yellow light that was projected from a rusty fixture attached to the wall.

"You know, it dawned on me today, kid," Nugent began, his drawl thicker than maple syrup, which generally meant that some precious nugget of wisdom was about to be unearthed, "that you've probably thought all this time that I was preparing you to reach the majors." He dug in the pocket of his windbreaker, pulled out a pack of Marlboros and a Bic lighter, and lit the tip of the cigarette.

Danny examined the words in his mind's eye, assessing them from every possible angle. *Stump the chump* was one of Nugent's favorite games; it was also one that Danny hated to lose.

"That's part of the job description, right?" Danny asked, buying time as he reflected on the countless hours Nugent had spent simplifying his delivery, refining his mechanics, and teaching him how to pitch and not just *throw*. "But I reckon that's too easy," Danny said, slipping into his near-perfect imitation of Nugent's southern drawl. "So, I bet you have something else up that sleeve, huh, old-timer?"

Most players would never dream of speaking to Chip Nugent that way, but their bond gave Danny a certain latitude he wasn't afraid to exercise.

"Yep, I figured as much," Nugent answered, rolling his eyes at Danny's impersonation. He took a long pull on the Marlboro and blew a cloud of smoke upward, scattering the handful of moths that fluttered around the light. "I never needed to prepare you to *reach* the majors. By the time you worked your way up to Triple-A and got to me, you were already well on your way. No, son, what I was preparing you for was to *stay in the majors* once you got there. And that, my friend, is about more than that golden left arm of yours." Nugent raised his hand, the cherry of his cigarette coming within a millimeter of his temple. "It's about what's up here, too."

Danny smiled. Though he'd never thought about it from

that perspective, having always been focused on just getting his foot in the door, the idea resonated in his heart. And this was a lesson that Nugent, whose time in the big leagues was little more than a flash in the pan, would understand better than most.

"Things are going to be different up there, sport. I guarantee it. Some days you'll be the hammer, other days the nail. But if you keep that temper in check and worry about the things you *can* control rather than those you *can't*, you're going to be around that league for a long time."

Danny cleared his throat, which was achingly tight.

"Thanks, Coach," he managed, his voice infused with the gratitude he lacked the words to express. "And for everything else, too. I mean that."

"I know you do, kid." Nugent looked Danny up and down, shook his hand, and flashed a knowing smile. "All right, kid. Those were my final two cents for you. Best spend 'em wisely." He tossed his cigarette butt to the ground, flattened it with his heel, then walked back toward the bar.

Danny watched the old man shamble off, saddened by the realization that this was really *goodbye*, and not just *see ya later*. He hoped that someday, when all was said and done, and his playing days were behind him, he could be half the teacher, coach, and mentor Chip Nugent had been to him.

"I'm gonna go check on Mabel," Nugent called back over his shoulder, already rounding the corner of the rundown building. "We'll see if she's finally going to accept that marriage proposal of mine. And I'll let the boys know you said *adios*."

⟡

"Holy shit," Danny complained, small beads of sweat breaking out across his brow as he slid behind the wheel. The inside of the car—a sleek BMW coupe that had cost Danny a large chunk of his signing bonus when he'd ignored his father's "sound advice" and purchased it brand new off the lot—was stiflingly hot, almost unbearable.

Danny cranked the A/C, cracked the windows to let out the hot air, and lowered the volume on the stereo, which was blasting Jay-Z's "Hard Knock Life" with enough bass to rattle his teeth. The seat below him was still warm to the touch, making him wonder for the millionth time why he'd settled on the black leather interior, which absorbed the heat of the California sun, trapping its energy and turning the car into a perpetual oven.

Easing the car out of the parking lot and onto First Street, Danny shifted his weight in the plush seat and drew his Nokia phone from his pocket. He consulted the phone's illuminated display. Still no missed calls. Despite leaving multiple messages on the home machine and annoying the shit out of the guys at the station, he'd yet to hear back from his dad. For a man with virtually no social life, who stubbornly refused to even dip a toe in the dating pool, the guy was proving annoyingly hard to reach.

Frustrated with his father, and still dying to share what was undoubtedly the biggest news of his life, Danny tossed the phone onto the passenger seat, then watched with irritation as it bounced off the tight leather and tumbled to the floor below.

"Well, screw you, too," he said curtly. He leaned over to snatch it off the floor, then sat upright, deciding it was not worth risking an injury to his back on the precipice of his major league debut.

Current paternal annoyance aside, Danny's relationship with his father was better now than it had ever been. Living on his own for nearly three years—almost a year in San Jose, then a season in Shreveport with the Double-A club before the promotion to Fresno—had provided him the opportunity to forge a new life, no longer constrained by the watchful eye and strict rules of his father. While that time and distance had allowed for growth, it had also provided him with greater perspective and a newfound respect for the man who had raised him almost single-handedly. The two had patched things up fairly quickly after his rash draft-night announcement, and things had only improved in the years since. And now, with any luck, his father would be able to fly to New York on Monday, when Danny was scheduled to make his first start, playing at Shea Stadium against the Mets.

The engine hummed as Danny navigated the turn onto Gettysburg, shifted gears, and accelerated down the deserted lane. Between the roar of the engine, the rush of the wind coming in from the windows, and the music still playing in the background, he almost missed the sound of the phone, its mechanical ringtone chiming from the floorboard below.

He reached to the dashboard to silence the stereo, scanned the open road in front of him, then leaned his body across the center console, flailing with his right arm for the phone, which was sitting next to the passenger door, its screen glowing green in the darkness.

Dragging the phone closer with his fingertips, he managed to lunge forward and grab it in his hand. Afraid the caller—hopefully his father—would hang up, he located the silver button, pressed with his thumb to connect the call, and shouted "Hold on," to his dad, or whomever it was on the other end of the line.

Danny groaned as he righted his body in the seat. His eyes flashed back to the road, his mind processing the incessant blaring of the horn in the same millisecond that his eyes locked on the set of brilliant headlights, two glowing discs bearing down with a terrifying intensity that shocked his body into action.

Phone still in hand, he jerked the wheel, forcing the BMW back into its lane and narrowly averting a collision with the oncoming car, a featureless white blur hidden behind blinding headlights.

Danny fought the car as it lost traction and entered a slide.

He gripped the shuddering wheel and struggled to bring the BMW under control. His mind registered the sound of skidding tires followed by sensations of tumbling and weightlessness, then an impact so loud and vicious—so jarring—that it hit him like a shockwave, penetrating deep into the marrow of his bones.

Danny struggled to open his eyes. He didn't realize he'd shut them in the first place, and he had no idea how long they'd been closed. His mind was foggy, his vision blurred. In his mouth, the metallic taste of blood. In his ears, a ringing so deafening that it made the world around him spin. The air inside the car was heavy with the acrid smells of burnt rubber and gasoline.

Danny moaned in frustration and pain. He tried to move, but his legs were trapped beneath the crumpled dash, and the airbag pinned his body against the seat.

From his left arm, which was crushed between his body and the battered car door, came an excruciating pain, more devastating than anything he'd ever imagined. The sleeve of his shirt, which was ripped near the elbow and covered in shards of broken glass, concealed the form of the mangled and blood-soaked limb.

The pain was unbearable. Danny moaned again, a pitiful sound, then strained to listen. From somewhere far away, he heard a familiar voice calling his name, speaking to him from what sounded like another dimension.

He ignored the pain in his neck, slowly turned toward the voice, and saw his phone, its screen still lit, resting on the back seat amid shards of glass. He tried to draw air into his lungs and respond to his father's desperate cries, but the pain was too much, and he let his chin drop to his chest, exhausted by the effort.

Danny let his eyes close again, purposefully this time, and just for a minute.

He listened again for his father's voice but heard only his own ragged breaths. He waited like that for an eternity, silent and alone.

And as the sirens closed in and the world went black, Danny dared to hope.

Chapter 16

Age 23

September 2, 2003

It was the scream that woke him.

His own scream, like always, though Danny wasn't sure now whether it had actually erupted from his lips or only echoed within the confines of his mind. Regardless, he was thankful it had come, thankful it had wrested him from the grips of the nightmare and brought him back to the present. To safety. To the here and now and out of that *fucking car*.

Danny untangled his long legs from the sweat-soaked sheet and flung it to the foot of the bed. He grounded his feet on the wooden floor and sat with his head cradled in his hands, trying to put some distance between himself and the nightmare, between his waking body and the cruel memories that haunted his nights.

The floorboards groaned as Danny stood, but Jason was oblivious, snoring lightly in his bed on the opposite side of their cheaply furnished room. Jason had stumbled home sometime in the early hours of the morning, muttering incoherently in his thick Australian accent, stinking of spilled beer and menthol cigarettes.

He crossed the small room in two strides, shook his comatose friend by the shoulder, and waited until Jason's eyes opened.

Barely visible between two puffy slits, they struggled to bring Danny's face into focus in the darkness of the room.

"Hey, dickhead," Danny whispered, their standard greeting. "Sleep in this morning." He picked up the digital alarm clock from their lone nightstand and held it in front of Jason's face. It was 5:26, four minutes before Jason's alarm was scheduled to sound. "I'll set up for breakfast and get the laundry started. Just make sure you're downstairs by eight o'clock; that's when I need to be out the door."

"Thanks, mate," Jason muttered, pulling the sheet up to his scruffy chin, and falling instantly back to sleep. Jason rarely gave two shits about anything; it was a quality Danny envied. If he was curious why Danny was covering his morning duties on his only day off, he certainly didn't show it.

Danny reset the alarm to seven thirty, then dressed quickly in his standard work attire—striped board shorts, weathered flip-flops, and a faded T-shirt—before running a brush over his teeth and slipping noiselessly from their room and into the long hallway that lay beyond.

Danny had been working at Paradise Hostel, one of the many small outfits that catered to the host of backpackers transiting through Hanoi's Old Quarter, for the better part of two months, long enough to realize that the name of the joint, allegedly a tribute to Jack Kerouac's character, Sal Paradise, in *On the Road*, was complete bullshit. He'd taken the job for practical reasons, namely that he needed money to survive but had almost none of it left; but now, he was beginning to question how much longer he could endure the mind-numbing monotony of his day-to-day duties.

Though Danny usually coveted his mornings off, when he didn't have to rise before the sun to begin the day's tasks, he knew it would be impossible to get back to sleep in the suffocating stillness of the humid room. The recurring nightmare, a jarring and unwelcome visitor from a past he'd worked tirelessly to forget, had certainly seen to that.

Danny descended the narrow staircase and strode through the cramped lobby and into the large dining area that lay beyond. There was no night clerk in Paradise, so the morning desk clerk, usually Danny, was responsible for setting the tables and preparing the dining room for breakfast, which began promptly at six o'clock.

"Mornin', Anh," Danny called from the swinging doors to the kitchen, as much to announce his presence as to greet the hostel's cook. A small and efficient Vietnamese woman with zero tolerance for laziness, Anh spoke little English and wasted none of it on pleasantries.

Bent and gray, with a sheen of sweat already covering her creased forehead, Anh held a large metal mixing bowl, furiously whipping eggs. She nodded her head in Danny's general direction, like she always did, but didn't look up from her task to acknowledge his presence.

Guests would soon be filtering down from the dorms. He left Anh to her labors and worked quickly through his tasks, eager to finish setting the tables for breakfast and assume his post at the front desk. Tour guides would be arriving at the hostel soon, and it was Danny's responsibility to ensure the right guests were paired with the right guides. It was a tiresome chore, complicated by innumerable language barriers, and it often left Danny questioning the series of life decisions that had landed him in Paradise in the first place.

"Gooooood morning, Vietnam!"

The jarring voice clobbered the serenity of the morning, scaring Danny shitless and causing him to drop a coffee mug, one of many he'd balanced delicately on a circular serving tray in his right hand. The mug fell to the tiled floor below, landing with a sharp *crack* and shattering upon impact.

"Damnit!" Danny spun toward the doorway as fast as he could without dropping the entire tray's worth of mugs and stared accusingly at the owner of the voice. "You know you're an asshole, right?"

Rory Pryor, looking like a fish out of water in his khaki pants and white-and-red-checkered shirt, stepped further into the room, a sheepish expression hanging from his freshly shaved face. "Sorry, man. Couldn't help myself. Great movie, though, right?"

So much had changed in the two years since they'd last met. It was more than just the obvious—Rory's more muscular physique and his billboard-quality smile. He also seemed older now. More confident and self-assured. And his blonde hair—once shaggy and parted in the middle—was now cut short on the sides and swept up in the front, making him look like the missing cast member from *Friends*.

"Breakfast isn't ready yet," Danny said, hearing his own voice and knowing he sounded like a jerk. He dug deep, trying to unearth a more hospitable tone. "But help yourself to some coffee." He gestured to the serving tables in the front of the room, where the industrial-size coffee maker gurgled and spurted next to the last in a series of empty serving vats.

"I thought this was your day off." Rory walked to the front of the room, watching with a curious expression as Danny kneeled next to the table to pick up the scattered pieces of the broken mug, then poured a cup of coffee.

"You're up early this morning," Danny countered, discarding Rory's observation in favor of his own. "I didn't expect you down here for another couple of hours."

Their brief reunion the night before had been unexpectedly tense. They'd exchanged awkward pleasantries in the lobby when Rory arrived just after midnight, then agreed to meet in the dining room at seven thirty to have breakfast before their planned day of sightseeing.

Still kneeling, Danny searched the floor, collecting ceramic shards with his right hand, then placing them delicately in the palm of his left. The dexterity in his damaged left hand had improved greatly in recent months, but he still favored his right for tasks of this nature, those which required fine motor skills and precision.

"I'm excited to see the city," Rory offered, shifting gears and breaking the uncomfortable silence. He took a seat at the table closest to the serving line and blew on his coffee.

"Yeah, same here," Danny replied, trying to match his friend's enthusiasm but falling noticeably short.

Though he'd been excited when Rory reached out by email and proposed the visit, his initial enthusiasm had been eroded by creeping doubts in the weeks leading up to the trip. As his new life collided with his old, it wasn't shocking that the nightmares had returned.

Danny rose from the floor, satisfied that he'd recovered all the broken pieces of the mug. He deposited the shards into the trash before continuing to set the last table in the row of five. He looked up periodically from his work, eyeing his friend from across the room, still amazed to see Rory Pryor, his best friend from another life, here at Paradise Hostel in Vietnam. He'd traveled the globe for more than a year, doing his best to make a fresh start, to leave that old existence behind. Inviting a piece of that world to Hanoi, or anywhere else for that matter, had never been part of the plan.

"All right," Danny said, consulting his cheap plastic watch and surveying the room one last time. "I need to go man the front desk." He nodded in the direction of the lobby. "But Jason should be down in a bit to relieve me. You should probably finish your coffee, eat some breakfast, and sharpen your prison shank in the meantime."

Danny registered the confusion in Rory's eyes but chose to ignore it, considering it payback for the broken mug. He laughed under his breath and ducked under the low frame of the door, making a quick exit before Rory even had time to ask.

◇

"You know," Danny began, staring at the wood-framed behemoth and speaking in a low tone, "this thing was *way* ahead of its time."

At least fifteen feet tall—its rusty blade suspended between parallel beams that nearly scraped the top of the vaulted ceiling—the guillotine was a relic from the colonial period. It was also a shocking reminder of the French occupation and the cruel practices that had marked their rule.

"Oh, yeah?" Rory asked doubtfully, smelling the horseshit and trying not to step in it. His eyes darted between Danny and the guillotine, waiting for the other shoe to drop.

Danny stifled a laugh, then delivered the corny punchline. "Yeah, it had... *cutting-edge* technology."

"Jesus Christ. You really can't help yourself, can you?" Rory nudged him with his shoulder. "But it's definitely not what I was expecting," he added, also in a whisper. Though the room was deserted—surprising, even for a Tuesday morning—the gruesome subject matter seemed to call for reverent tones.

"That was my first impression, too." Thoughtful now, Danny clasped his hands behind his back as he stared upward at the antiquated tool of justice—or vengeance, depending on where your allegiance rested.

He'd first visited the museum two months earlier, soon after he arrived in Hanoi. Like Rory, he'd been surprised to find that most of the exhibits in Hỏa Lò—known to most Americans as the "Hanoi Hilton"—were dedicated to its history as a French prison, when it was used to confine Vietnamese political dissidents, not American prisoners of war.

Though most of the old prison was demolished back in the '90s, the original guardhouse was preserved and later converted into a museum. Because of its central location, within walking distance from Paradise Hostel and the Old Quarter, the notorious former prison was a popular destination for the city's tourists.

"Honestly, I think most Americans feel that way," Danny said, continuing his thought as he moved slowly toward the door.

He was enjoying Rory's company now and relishing the opportunity to play tour guide. Despite their rocky start, the initial awkwardness had evaporated as the morning wore on, and the pair had fallen back into the easy rhythm of their old friendship.

Danny matched Rory's long strides as they departed the guillotine room and entered a long and narrow hallway. "We—Americans, I mean—come here with a limited understanding of this country's history," Danny explained. "One that focuses mostly on the war our two countries fought. Then, assuming we actually take the time to crack a book or two, we're blown away when we find that there's a much longer, more complex story to be told." This kind of revelation was nothing new to Danny; he'd found this to be the case in every country he'd visited throughout his year of travels.

The pair walked in silence, traversing the length of the hallway, stopping occasionally to look at the framed pictures mounted on the finished concrete walls. Below each picture was a bronze plaque with engraved text in both Vietnamese and English that described the people and events portrayed in the photos. Taken in its entirety, the hallway told the story of decades of oppression and misery, a legacy the Vietnamese would not soon forget.

"But if your primary interest is in the Vietnam War," Danny said, pausing at the end of the hallway while Rory finished reading, "then these last few exhibits should make it worth your trip. I'll warn you ahead of time, though, the propaganda is so thick, you could cut it with a knife." He arched one eyebrow, then flashed a wry smile. "Or a guillotine, if you'd prefer."

Amused by his own dark humor, Danny cackled like a cartoon villain, continued into the next room, and stopped in front of a massive display case. Metal framed, with glass on all four sides, it stood on a wooden platform, its back flush to the gray concrete wall.

"Holy, shit . . ." Rory stepped closer to the display case to better inspect its contents. "Is this what I think it is?"

On the left side of the exhibit, hanging vertically from a steel hook that was affixed to the top of the case, was a white parachute, its surface crusted in reddish-brown dirt. To the right of the parachute, placed over a metal frame that bore the rough shape of a man, were a pair of black combat boots, a tattered olive-green flight suit, and a beaten aviator's helmet, the white paint chipped away from much of its scarred surface.

"Sure is." Danny stepped back so as not to obscure Rory's view. "It didn't take long for the NVA to figure out who John McCain was, the family pedigree and such, so it's not surprising that they preserved these items." Danny turned slowly in a circle, taking in the rest of the small Vietnam War exhibit. "And the rest of the room," he continued sarcastically, gesturing to the photos lining the walls, "is all Christmas parties and volleyball games, and any other staged photos they could dig up to paint a rosy picture of the life of an American POW."

Rory nodded thoughtfully and stepped to his right, his focus shifting from the contents of the display case to a black-and-white photo fastened to the wall next to it.

Danny moved to his friend's side, studying Rory as he studied the picture. In the photo, which also looked like it had been staged for propaganda purposes, McCain was undergoing a perfunctory medical examination, presumably only hours after the Vietnamese retrieved his broken body from Trúc Bạch Lake, where he'd nearly drowned after parachuting from his damaged plane during a bombing run over Hanoi. Lying flat on his back, his arm in a sling, McCain wore a pained expression. It wasn't difficult to envision the suffering he had endured, both in those early moments of captivity and during the grueling five-and-a-half years that followed.

"I can only imagine," Rory began, staring at the image of McCain's broken body, his tone empathetic, "how hard that must have been for him. How alone he must have felt." He looked up from the photo and over to Danny. His eyes settled on the raised purple scars—some of them from surgeries, others more jagged, inflicted by twisted metal and shards of broken glass—that ran down the entirety of Danny's left arm, extending to his wrist and hand.

Danny searched Rory's kind eyes, realizing his friend was no longer talking about John McCain. Suddenly self-conscious, he stuffed his hand reflexively into the pocket of his shorts, then stepped toward the wall, leaning forward to examine the photo more closely.

"Yeah, it was hard," Danny acknowledged, his voice even, his tone flat. He was speaking to Rory but staring deeply into McCain's desperate eyes. "I was hospitalized for nearly a month, you know. There in Fresno."

His mind wandered back to the small recovery room, where he awoke after the accident and his first round of surgeries. It was only the beginning of his agony.

Of being immobilized in a bed.

Of being helpless.

"More injuries than I can remember," Danny recounted. "And so many goddamn surgeries." He paused, picturing the textured ceiling of that damn hospital room, remembering the soul-crushing pain that kept him up each night, the pain that no amount of drugs could ever dull. "Wondering if I'd ever play again."

Though everyone—his father, the doctors, even the team— had been honest with him about the extent of his injuries from the very start, Danny had been stubborn, harboring secret hopes of returning to the mound for far longer than he would ever admit.

Rory closed the distance between them and placed a hand on Danny's shoulder. "I remember," he said softly, carefully, though they were the only two people in the room.

Though he was already going to college in San Diego by then, Rory had been the only one of Danny's childhood friends who had visited him in the hospital in Fresno in the days following the accident. He was the only one who had taken the time. The only one who made the effort.

Danny cleared his throat, breaking the silence, then shrugged off Rory's hand. "Water under the bridge, right." It was a statement, not a question.

Danny bolted for the opposite side of the room, trying to escape the gravitational pull of his past. He gathered himself and closed that door in his mind, the one he so rarely dared to open, then turned to flash a smile that misfortune had taught him to summon at will.

"The next stop on our tour isn't far," Danny said, playing the role of energetic tour guide once more. "And I should have asked this before, but . . . you're good with corpses, right?"

◇

DANNY RETURNED FROM THE BATHROOM, joined Rory at their wobbly table next to the open window, and reached for the bottle of Tiger Beer that had been delivered in his absence. During his time in Singapore, he'd converted to the bargain brand more as matter of economics than preference and remained a loyal customer ever since.

The restaurant was nothing spectacular. Tucked away on the third floor of a sagging four-story building a few blocks from Paradise Hostel, it was indistinguishable from a hundred others in the Old Quarter, but it was one Danny had discovered on his own and visited often in the weeks since. What it lacked in elegance it made up for with cheap food, cold beer, and fast service. And the window tables, which were almost always available, provided a great perch for watching the endless stream of people crawling like ants up and down the narrow lane below.

"You can get that in English," Danny advised. He sipped ice-cold beer, watching with amusement as Rory squinted at a laminated menu that was written exclusively in Vietnamese.

He raised his own menu in his hand, caught the waiter's eye, and mouthed the word "English." The waiter, an older man whose eyes were magnified by impossibly thick Coke-bottle lenses, nodded his head and marched purposefully toward the back of the restaurant, presumably to grab the new menus.

"I've gotta say," Rory began, before pausing to take a sip from his beer, "that experience is now carved into my all-time Mount Rushmore of weird. If I live to be 142 years old, that will still go down as one of the creepiest things I've ever seen."

He was referring to their afternoon visit to Ba Đình Square and the mausoleum of the country's former President, Ho Chi Minh. The mausoleum, an enormous multi-tiered temple, its façade constructed entirely of gray granite, was inspired by Lenin's mausoleum in Moscow but with distinctly Vietnamese flair. Inside the central vault, in a climate-controlled chamber made of polished gray, black, and red stone, lies the man himself. Embalmed and encased in glass under the watchful eyes of a military honor guard, he rests in perpetuity, on display for every Tom, Dick, and Rory to see.

"It's just a different culture," Danny countered, setting down his beer and reaching up to retrieve the menus from their waiter's outstretched hand. "Not better, not worse, and not *weird*. Just different."

After so much time abroad, jumping from country to country and continent to continent, these were the types of cultural differences he'd come to appreciate. This exposure had given him a different perspective on life and a new appreciation for the diverse world around him.

"So how many countries *have* you visited?" Rory asked, seeming to read Danny's mind.

This was Rory's first trip abroad. And though he was only spending a few days in Vietnam, he planned to visit Tokyo and Hong Kong as well, both of which were on the long list of places to which Danny had traveled.

"I'm not sure," Danny said, gears whirring as his brain tried to calculate a precise number. "I was constantly on the move at first. When everything was fresh and exciting. But you can't keep that shit up forever, man. It gets tiring. And expensive."

When Danny left Santa Rosa, following ten grueling months of rehab and a stern ultimatum from his father—enroll in school, find a job, or move out—he hopped a plane from San Francisco to London on little more than a whim. He didn't know a soul in England, and he didn't have much of a plan, but Danny knew he needed to get away, to try to put his circumstances behind him.

After seven surgeries to restore functionality to his arm and legs, and months spent recuperating in his childhood bed with only a stack of books to keep him company, he'd been desperate to break free and escape his trophy-lined prison. And aching to finally explore the wide world he'd spent countless hours reading about in books.

At the time, with most of his signing bonus still sitting in the bank, his options had seemed limitless. Now, with only two-thousand dollars left in his checking account and few opportunities for work other than shitty jobs at even shittier hostels, his carefully constructed illusion of freedom was collapsing on top of him.

"So, tell me about this new job," Danny said, eager to angle the conversation toward his friend and away from his own dwindling prospects.

"Man, where to start?" Rory raised his empty beer, drawing the waiter's attention and signaling for another round.

Over the next hour, Rory filled Danny in on all the milestones of his life in San Diego. After five years of rundown apartments, baloney sandwiches, and working part-time jobs to make ends meet, he'd finally completed his computer science degree in May and then was rewarded for his efforts with a prestigious internship. Rory being Rory, he later parlayed that internship into a cushy job, designing software and pulling down big bucks at an up-and-coming tech firm.

Though Danny wasn't fluent enough in *nerd* to understand all the technical details of Rory's job—and spent much of the meal nodding his head, slurping from his steaming bowl of *phở bò*, and knocking back subsequent bottles of Tiger that were delivered at regular intervals by their waiter—it was clear that Rory had hit his stride. He'd even entered escrow on a beachside condo, an enviable detail that made him seem even more mature and accomplished than his Ross Geller haircut and pressed khaki pants.

"So, what do you think?" Rory asked finally. He leaned back in his chair, his features excited and expectant.

Danny was caught flat-footed. Now four beers deep—and way more interested in the tattooed brunette at the next table than in Rory's plans to renovate his guest bathroom—he realized that he'd lost the thread of the conversation, somehow missed a crucial detail.

"About what?" Danny asked, a hot blush engulfing his cheeks. He registered the flash of annoyance on Rory's face. "I'm sorry, bud," he said, offering an apologetic shrug. "I was trying to get the waiter's attention, so he could bring us the check."

"About *the room*," Rory answered firmly. "The second bedroom in the house." He leaned forward and clasped his large hands together, then placed them squarely on the cheap plastic table. "Listen, Danny, I know how hard the past couple of years have been. The accident, the recovery . . . the shit with your dad. I get it, man. And I understand why you left."

The shit with your dad.

Danny leaned back from the table and fought the urge to laugh. He weighed Rory's words in his mind and found them utterly wanting. The accident, the one stupid mistake that kept him from reaching the heights he and his father had always imagined, had opened a chasm between them that seemed impossible to bridge.

His father had never said it outright—that he blamed Danny for what happened—but he never had to either. The long uncomfortable silences and *disappointed-dad* stares said it all. By reaching across the car for that phone, by causing the wreck, and by failing to become the one thing he'd always been destined to be, Danny had let them both down.

His father had known it all along: *Not all mistakes end up foul balls.*

"But I'm your friend," Rory continued, delivering his words with conviction as he stared Danny in the eye, "and friends are the people who are willing to speak hard truths. And the truth for you, Danny, is that it's time to move on. It's time to rub some dirt on it, come home, and put your life back together. So, if you're ready to do that, if you're ready to start the next chapter, then the room is yours."

Danny took a long pull from his beer, the icy gulps numbing the back of his throat, wondering how many times Rory had rehearsed this little speech. Shocked by his friend's offer—but more so by the forcefulness with which it was delivered—he sat in stunned silence, contemplating Rory's words and the implications behind them.

While Danny viewed his time abroad as a period of personal growth—an opportunity to see the world, expand his horizons, and move on from his devastating mistake—it was clear that Rory did not. Still the smartest kid in the room, and still dispensing advice straight out of an *ABC Afterschool Special*, Rory obviously had a different perspective.

Before Danny could respond, their waiter appeared silently at his elbow. Perhaps sensing the tension between them, he shuffled quickly by, pausing only to slide the check to the center of the flimsy table before continuing on his path back to the kitchen.

"Nah, I've got this," Rory said. He snatched the check from the table, a sweaty wad of bills already in hand, and flashed his perfect smile, genuine but sad. "It's the least I can do."

Chapter 17

Age 26

July 22, 2006

Danny stood bathrobe-clad in his messy room, ear pressed to the door, listening to the low voices emanating from down the hall.

"Dad" and "Mom" had been at it again. They'd been arguing when he awoke half an hour before, bickering back and forth in angry whispers that he wasn't supposed to hear, but the storm seemed to have passed now, rendering the kitchen safe for entry.

"Howdy," Danny called as he moseyed through the doorway of the condo's first-floor kitchen, his voice dripping with false cheer.

He'd overheard much of their fight, enough to know he was the well-chewed bone of their contention. Now he was just hoping to power through a bowl of Frosted Flakes without drawing Heather's wrath. While he thought her position was bullshit—kicking him to the curb to make way for a hypothetical love child they'd yet to conceive—he understood his new place on the totem pole, and he wasn't itching to kickstart World War III over Saturday breakfast.

In the kitchen, they both sat at the bright yellow IKEA table, Rory staring despondently at a plate of bacon and eggs, Heather hunched over her bulging three-ring binder, the contents of which had come to dominate household conversations for much of the last year. With the wedding only six weeks away, the planning—and near-constant friction—seemed to have reached its apex.

"Hey, bud," Rory said, tension underpinning his greeting. He looked up sharply from his plate, cocked his head in Heather's direction, and gave it a quick shake before reaching for the mug in front of him. "There's coffee in the pot and some eggs left in the skillet. I finished the bacon, but there's more in the fridge."

Danny mouthed the word "thanks," both for the eggs and the unnecessary warning, and busied himself making breakfast. He considered taking his food up to the second-floor balcony, which overlooked Ocean Beach and its concrete fishing pier, then changed his mind, refusing to banish himself from civilization, and joined them at the table instead.

"Your dad called. Again." Heather looked up from the binder, acknowledging Danny's presence for the first time. Her job as a realtor required her to show houses on the weekends, so she was already fully dressed, her black pantsuit accentuating both her athletic frame and the curtness of her mood.

Staring at her across the table, it was hard to imagine they'd ever been friends in the first place. She'd found him amusing at the beginning, he thought, and been at least slightly entertained by his snarky one-liners and elaborate pranks. But the gloves had come off immediately following the engagement, as soon as she'd moved into the condo, and he knew damn well she'd been plotting his eviction ever since.

"I saved the message on the machine for you," Heather continued, her voice irritatingly prim. "Maybe you can let him know that you have a cellphone, so he can call you on that instead."

"Thanks for the suggestion," Danny answered politely, after considering and quickly dismissing a few *maybe-you-can* suggestions of his own. "I'll give it a listen before I leave for work."

Despite his promise to Heather, Danny had no intention of listening to the message. Nor did he need to. He knew why his father was calling: to follow up on an invitation to his aunt and uncle's house for Thanksgiving, which was still four months away. In the nearly three years since he'd moved to San Diego and started college, he'd seen his father only twice, both times in San Diego. And he'd yet to visit his extended family in Santa Rosa.

His long absence, and the unspoken reasons behind it, had become a point of friction between them. Every square foot of that house reeked of Danny's failure and his father's judgment. Although he knew he'd have to return home eventually, he wanted to do it on his own terms. When he was ready. Preferably after he'd made something of himself, and he had more to show for his efforts than an incomplete degree and a shitty gig as a bartender.

"We're going out to O'Malley's tonight," Rory offered, seemingly desperate to talk about anything besides the wedding. "They started doing live music again on Saturdays. Should be a good time, if you want to join us."

"Sorry, no can do." Danny looked squarely at Rory while ignoring Heather's pinched expression.

O'Malley's had been Rory's and Danny's favorite bar long before Heather weaseled her way into the picture, but she clearly wasn't interested in watching the pair suck down pints of Guinness while trading obscure movie quotes and reliving their glory days.

"I'm working until nine o'clock; then I need to come home and study," Danny continued, speaking through a mouthful of eggs just to annoy Heather. "I have two tests on Monday that I need to study for."

Seeing Rory's success had made Danny anxious to make up for lost time. He'd been taking classes at SDSU year-round, including summers, trying to graduate in under three years. Assuming all went to plan, which seemed likely, his last semester would begin in late August, and he'd be holding his diploma by the end of December.

Hoping to avoid any conversation about color schemes and centerpieces, Danny rushed through the rest of his breakfast in silence. He washed his dishes and was halfway out the door to the kitchen when he heard Heather clear her throat loudly from the table behind him.

"Um, can you hold up a minute?" Rory asked, using the slightly deeper version of his voice that he usually reserved for meetings, work-related phone calls, and long-winded explanations about shit like *how the internet works*. "We need to talk to you before you leave for work."

His back turned to the kitchen, Danny rolled his eyes, yearning for the days *"we"* referred to him and Rory, not Rory and his sneering bride-to-be. He flexed the fingers of both hands, slowly exhaling as he recalled the details of Rory and Heather's hushed argument earlier that morning. He needed to start getting ready for work, and he knew that a prolonged back-and-forth conversation wasn't going to change the outcome anyway.

"No need," Danny said. He wheeled back toward the kitchen, his tone intentionally light. "I totally get it, guys. And it's not a problem. I'll start looking for a place next week and be out before the wedding."

He nodded diplomatically to Rory, who looked like he'd just been spared from the firing squad, ignored Heather's self-satisfied smirk, and made his way down the hallway and back to his room. Proud of himself for his maturity, he was even careful not to slam the door when he closed it behind him.

"Here you go, ladies." Danny flashed his most engaging smile as he slid a third round of margaritas across the cool surface of the marble bar.

The women—both middle-aged, both platinum blonde, and both obnoxiously flirtatious—were his final customers of the day. Behind them, across the broad terrace and down the long granite staircase that led to the marina, the last rays of the San Diego sun were skipping over the rippled surface of Mission Bay, casting the harbor and its fleet of anchored boats in rich hues of purple, orange, and pink.

"And whenever you're ready," Danny added. He slid their bill across the bar, smiling again as the prettier of the two, the one with the perilously low-cut top and no wedding ring, reached for the check, her hungry eyes assessing Danny over the top of expensive sunglasses that she'd slid to the tip of her nose.

Danny ignored the heat of her stare as he walked to the other side of the enclosed rectangular bar, then continued initialing blocks in his closing checklist. He'd already let the servers go for the night. And with less than twenty minutes until closing time, he was nearly two-thirds of the way down the lengthy sheet, well-poised to be out the door when the clock struck 9 p.m.

"They look like good tippers."

Danny smiled as he peered down into the icebox, which was badly in need of defrosting. From the thick Castilian accent, he knew without looking up that the voice belonged to Luis Gomez, a fellow bartender at The Harborside Hotel. Luis had started working at the hotel the year prior, at roughly the same time as Danny, and the two had formed a casual friendship in the months since. Though Danny had never considered Luis to be *roommate material*, his impending homelessness had him carefully examining all options.

"We'll see," Danny said. He raised a doubtful eyebrow and fought the urge to peer back over his shoulder at the women. He leaned over the bar and continued in a near-whisper. "If I don't show up for work tomorrow, the one in the sunglasses should be the prime suspect. I think she's planning to club me over the head and drag me back to her room."

Both men laughed. It was a fine line they walked—between engaging in friendly banter with customers and writing checks they weren't willing to see cashed—and both of them had become well-practiced in the art of letting women, and occasionally men, down easy at closing time.

"I'm glad I caught you," Luis said. He was speaking to Danny but smiling seductively at the women across the bar, winking as he combed his fingers back through his shoulder-length black hair. "We're running out of small bills upstairs, and I need to make an exchange before you go." He held up a fistful of folded cash, then laid the bills neatly on the bar for Danny's inspection.

Danny counted the money twice, tallied five-hundred dollars both times, then opened his register and began making hundred-dollar stacks in smaller denominations.

"This is the best I can do." Danny placed the collection of twenty and fifty-dollar bills into his register as Luis counted, and recounted, the neatly aligned stacks on the bar.

"How are things going up there?" Danny asked, trying to mask the tinge of envy in his voice.

He'd been toiling at the main bar since noon, roughly the same time that the crowd of musicians—discernible by their colorful personas and the instruments they carted through the doors—had begun streaming into the lobby of the hotel. From his post behind the bar, situated in an annex to the main building that connected the lobby of the fifteen-story hotel to the terrace that lay beyond, Danny had watched the eclectic procession with more than a touch of curiosity.

"Not bad," Luis answered, shoulders shrugged. "A bit of a mixed crowd. No shortage of eye candy, but the starving artists outnumber the bigwigs twenty to one, so the tips have been shit."

The Southern California Singers and Songwriters Expo, from what Danny could tell, was something of a big deal. The annual event, which was hosted by The Harborside every year, drew not only aspiring musicians and songwriters but also representatives from major record labels. During the day, the hotel's various conference rooms were used for an assortment of seminars, workshops, and networking events. Then, in the evening, a stage was erected in the hotel's elegant third-floor ballroom, and the space was transformed into a performance venue, allowing the aspiring artists to showcase their talents and mingle with executives and talent evaluators from the record labels.

Luis collated the assorted stacks of bills into one, thanked Danny in Spanish, then turned on his heels and strutted toward the lobby.

"Oh, I almost forgot," he said, strolling back toward the bar. "They have attendants at the door checking credentials—yellow for staff, blue for performers and songwriters, and green for the record labels—but I managed to get my hands on one of these." He reached into the back pocket of his too-tight slacks and produced a green credential attached to a black lanyard. "The easily charmed young lady at the registration table said it belongs to a no-show. Not sure what your plans are for tonight, but I can think of worse ways to spend an evening."

Danny's eyes darted back and forth between Luis's expectant face and the laminated credential in his well-tanned hands.

He knew the right answer. It was *no*.

He opened his mouth to decline, to do the responsible thing so he could return home early to study for his exams; then the irresistible hand of curiosity reached down his throat and tugged the words "fuck it" up and out of his mouth before he could stop himself.

Luis flashed a knowing smile, winked as if the outcome were never in doubt, and placed the credential into Danny's hand with a flourish. "If you are going to use it," Luis called, glancing back over his shoulder as he crossed the lobby and approached the elevators, "you better ditch that hotel polo shirt first!"

"I'll take a Stella," Danny said, trying to sound confident and nonchalant, like an up-and-coming music executive would, even as a cocktail of guilt and nervous excitement churned in his stomach.

Standing at the bar in the rear of the spacious hall, his back to the stage, he placed one foot atop the brass footrest, quickly scanned the faces to his left and right, and wondered again whether he looked as conspicuous as he felt. He'd never crashed an event in his life, certainly not one being hosted by his employer, and he knew that his time would be better spent at home, hitting the books and Googling phrases like "affordable rooms in San Diego for broke-ass bartenders."

He'd taken Luis's advice—changed out of his teal Harborside polo shirt and into the striped button-down he'd worn to work—yet he was hesitant to complete his disguise by draping the lanyard around his neck. Instead, he'd left the credential in the back pocket of his jeans and been pleasantly surprised when he stepped off the elevators into the mirrored vestibule and found the doors to the ballroom wide open, left unattended by expo staff.

"Here you are, sir," Luis said, projecting his voice to ensure he was heard by the other patrons at the bar. He offered a slight bow of his head as he placed the bottle on the bar. "Compliments of the house, Mr. Romano."

Embarrassed by Luis's antics, Danny accepted the beer amidst curious stares from the people on his flanks. He extended his most discreet *"thanks, asshole"* nod in return, then walked toward the elevated stage, where hundreds of folding chairs had been set up in neat rows, a generous center aisle dividing the left side of the audience from the right.

His paranoia was intense. Afraid he'd be tackled by event security at any moment, Danny wandered to the right, remaining on the outskirts of the crowd. He settled himself in the too-small chair at the far end of the empty back row, then watched as a distinguished-looking man in a black suit, presumably the emcee, introduced the next performer.

"Have you seen him before?"

Startled by the voice at his side, then terrified when he realized the question was directed at him, Danny looked up to see a petite brunette in her mid-twenties, a glass of red wine in one hand and a small clutch in the other. Dressed elegantly in a form-fitting black dress, with a blue credential nestled in her cleavage, she stared down expectantly.

"Mind if I join you?"

Without waiting for a reply, she stepped in front of Danny, slid her lithe body into the seat next to him, then directed her attention back to the stage. Standing in its center was an undeniably handsome man in a black Stetson hat, an acoustic guitar hanging from his broad chest by a leather strap. Dressed in head-to-toe denim, the sea of blue was broken only by a silver belt buckle, its dimensions equal to that of a small serving platter.

"This is my third year coming to this thing," the woman said, still staring at the figure on the stage, who was tuning his guitar and warming up the audience with a colorful story about a three-legged dog named Hank. "Mac has been coming for even longer than that."

She looked over at Danny, her eyes resting briefly on his uncredentialed chest, then gulped her wine and began tapping her toe atop the plush carpet.

"Oh, yeah?" Danny sat up straighter in his seat, fascinated by his bold new acquaintance. He wasn't sure where this conversation was heading, but he was happy to be along for the ride. "And is *Mac* any good?" He was immediately aware of the unwarranted jealousy in his voice and simultaneously hoping she wasn't.

"Good?" she asked, surprise written across her refined features. She turned in her seat, then looked him up and down again. "Of course, he's good. Everybody here is *good*. But good doesn't pay the bills. And it sure as hell doesn't get you a recording deal."

Danny blinked hard and slowly sipped his beer. Unsure how

to respond, or even if he should, he offered his hand instead. "I'm Danny. Danny Rom—"

"Romano. Yeah, I heard *Rico Suave* at the bar earlier. You must be a pretty big deal to drink for free around here." She switched the wine glass from her right hand to her left, then shook Danny's hand. "I'm Natalie. Natalie Cohen."

On stage, Mac had finished warming up the crowd and launched into a sad country ballad, seemingly about his furry pal, Hank. While Danny didn't know much about music—and he knew even less about country music—Mac sounded pretty damn good to his ears.

"Can I tell you a secret?" Natalie asked. She drained the rest of the wine and placed the empty glass on the floor next to her chair. "You know . . . since we're properly acquainted now."

"Absolutely," he replied, leaning subtly in her direction, catching the faintest hint of her vanilla-scented perfume. This woman could recite her entire grocery list and Danny would be riveted, clinging to the edge of his seat.

"After Mac," Natalie said, gesturing toward the stage, "comes Sheila, my former bandmate and the expo's resident Fiona Apple wannabe. Then I'm next. And honestly, Danny . . . I'm terrified." She turned in her seat and fixed him with a pointed stare.

Danny stared back, momentarily lost in her brown eyes, the irises so dark they were almost black. In the dim light of the ballroom, her eyes shone with a certain primal energy, a brand of nervous anticipation Danny intuitively recognized from his years on the mound.

"But you've performed before, right? You said you've been coming here for three years. And that you were in a band, too. So, why is this different?"

"It's *different*," she said, her voice catching in her throat, "because every other time felt like it could be the beginning of something new. Something wonderful." She glanced toward the stage, where Mac seemed to be hitting his stride, then back at Danny. "But I've been chasing this dream for a long time now, you know? Too long. And I promised myself—and promised my father—that if it didn't happen this year, I'd give it up for good and go to law school. So, if it doesn't happen for me tonight, which is seeming less and less likely, then I guess it never will. So, yes, Mr. Danny-drinks-for-free, this is terrifying."

She breathed deeply to catch her wind, her rising chest grabbing Danny's eye, then exhaled slowly through pursed lips.

"Wow. That's a lot." Danny nodded in sympathy, then offered his most reassuring smile. He fought the urge to reach out, to comfort this woman, this beautiful stranger he hardly knew. "Believe it or not, though, I happen to have a little experience in this area."

"Which one?" she asked wryly. "The part about the death of a dream, or the part about living up to the expectations of a demanding father?"

Danny chuckled uncomfortably and weighed his response. These weren't things he talked about—his father's disappointment and the irreversible error he'd made to earn it. And certainly not with a woman he'd just met. "Would you believe me if I said both?"

They laughed in unison—he a little too loudly, she with an endearing snort. The commotion drew judgmental stares from a young couple seated in front of them.

"But that, Natalie Cohen, is a story for another night."

"Thank you," she said. "I needed to laugh." She reached over, rested her hand lightly on top of his thigh, then looked back toward the stage. "It looks like he's wrapping up. I need to get back there."

She reached into her clutch, dug around for a moment, then produced a white business card.

"You should call me," she said seriously, handing him the card. She paused for a beat, a teasing smile playing around the corners of her wide mouth. "Maybe, I don't know, the next time you plan to crash an expo?"

He watched dumbly as she rose from her chair. He racked his

brain for a clever reply—some classy George Clooney line, like you'd see in *Ocean's Eleven*—but his bottomless barrel of one-liners had sprung a leak.

"Don't worry," she said, drawing him in with her eyes. She leaned over, her whisper a warm caress to his ear. "I'll keep your secret if you keep mine."

Chapter 18

Age 26

November 23, 2006

"Is this *really* necessary?" she asked again, making no attempt to hide her exasperation. Natalie's eyes lingered on the ring, its small diamond reflecting bright rays of midday sun that cascaded through the car's window. She rotated it back and forth around her slender finger but made no move to take it off.

The fuse had been lit at the airport in San Diego, when Danny first suggested she remove the engagement ring before meeting his father. He'd thought the matter was settled, but the argument continued in fits and starts during their short flight to San Francisco, while standing in the line at the rental counter, and throughout the hour-long drive from San Bruno to Santa Rosa.

"You want to make a good impression, right?" Danny struggled to mask his own impatience, which simmered just below the surface. He pulled the rental car, a red Honda Accord, parallel to the curb and brought it to a jerking halt just before the driveway to his father's house.

Danny understood her frustrations. She had communicated them well and often, using the same sturdy logic she undoubtedly applied to her legal studies, but his position remained unchanged.

It was no picnic coming back to this house, plunging himself into the thorny thicket of the life he'd left behind; if he was going to lob a grenade in the process, and potentially blow the hinges off Thanksgiving, the pin wouldn't be pulled until he was good and ready.

"Well?" Danny asked, shifting the transmission into park. He turned to face her in the passenger seat, admiring her delicate features as he reached across the divide to sweep a stray lock of hair away from her face, then tuck it neatly behind her ear. Despite the pout, it was a beautiful face.

"You know I do," she said finally, a hint of resignation seeping into her voice. She grudgingly slid the ring from her finger and placed it in a zippered compartment inside her purse. "I just wish you would have told him ahead of time, you know? So we wouldn't have to hide anything."

"I understand," Danny said. "Seriously, I do. But you have to understand my dad. He still sees me as a little kid, you know? And questions every decision I make. He'll lose his shit just knowing we're living together. Engaged after only four months? His head might *literally* explode."

Danny reached over the center console and gave her hand a quick squeeze, then planted a soft kiss on her neck, just below the ear. "But once he gets to know you, once he understands *us*, he'll be fine."

"Okaaaay," she relented, though clearly not convinced.

"You're going to be fine. Trust me." He straightened in his seat, then drew and held her gaze. "Better than fine. *Amazing*."

Danny smiled encouragingly, then popped the trunk release and walked to the back of the car. Though the skies were clear, it must have rained the night before: The driveway was damp, as was the front lawn, which was freshly mown in preparation for their arrival.

Danny raised his hand to knock on the front door, its surface painted a dark shade of green to match the house's trim, then let it drop as the door flew open. His father, his face thinner and more deeply lined than he remembered, peered eagerly out from inside.

"Right on time," his dad remarked, after lifting the sleeve of his burnt orange sweater to consult the watch stretched around his thick wrist. "Come in, come in," he added hurriedly, ushering them off the doorstep and into the house.

He wrapped Danny in a tight hug made awkward by the two small suitcases hanging at Danny's sides, then stepped back and looked appraisingly at Natalie. "And you must be the lawyer, Natalie." He thrust his hand forward, then withdrew it clumsily as she stepped in for a hug.

"Future lawyer," she answered warmly, no trace of their previous disagreement discernible in her voice. "I just started law school a few months ago, so there's a long way to go before I earn that title. And it's a pleasure to meet you, Mr. Romano."

"Please, call me Frank. Mr. Rom—"

"Mr. Romano was my father," Danny finished, slipping seamlessly into the well-trod impression of his father that he'd perfected in his youth. "You need some new material, Dad. That joke's got more miles on it than your sweater."

They all stopped to inspect the sweater. His father owned only three of them, the other two yellow and red, and he'd worn them dependably to commemorate the last two decades of major holidays. While yellow was reserved for Easter, and red for Christmas, the burnt orange was always saved, without fail, for Thanksgiving.

"True enough," he admitted, staring pointedly back at Danny, his sun-bronzed cheeks rising to form the same uncomfortable smile he reserved for large social gatherings and women who showed any hint of interest. "Why don't you two get settled in the guest room? My famous green bean casserole is finishing up in the oven; then, we need to be out the door in fifteen minutes to get out to the farm by two o'clock."

Still holding a suitcase in each hand, Danny waited until his father departed for the kitchen, then rolled his eyes for Natalie's benefit. He'd warned her ahead of time about his father's compulsive punctuality, promising to show her the obsessively maintained calendar that undoubtedly still hung from the front of the refrigerator. Danny slipped off his Vans without untying the laces and walked down the tiled hallway toward the back of the house, Natalie following closely in trace.

"You didn't tell me," Natalie began, a touch of surprise in her voice, "how much you look like him." She stopped at the mouth of the hallway to examine the framed photo from his parents' wedding. His father in a brown suit and grotesque, striped tie, his mother in a flowing white gown, both of them so young and attractive, smiling unabashedly for the camera. It was one of only a handful of pictures mounted on the otherwise barren walls.

"Same height and build," she continued, cataloging his and his father's shared traits. "And same olive skin and black hair." She looked up from the photo, cocking her head to the side as she scrutinized Danny's features. "Except for the nose and the eyes," she added quietly. "Those hazel eyes are all her."

Danny stiffened at the mention of *her*. He lowered the bucket, searching for an appropriate response, but discovered the well was dry. He motioned for her to join him down the hall instead, then gave her arm a light squeeze as she passed.

"This one here?" Natalie asked, leaning her head through the first open door on the right. "Oops, I'm guessing not. Unless your father's guest list consists exclusively of sports-obsessed twelve-year-old boys." She broke into a mock frown and snorted at her own joke. "Which would be kinda weird, right?"

Danny lingered in the hallway, his breath catching painfully in his chest, before joining her at the threshold. The room was depressingly unchanged, untouched in the years he'd been gone.

He peered through the doorway, watching Natalie wander deeper into the bedroom, then stop to admire the Will Clark poster and collection of Barry Bonds memorabilia that covered much of the far wall. Trophy-lined shelves still decorated the near wall, celebrating the triumphs of Danny's youth like a maddening shrine to his once-unlimited potential.

That word—*potential*—was one he'd love to see stripped from the dictionary. To most people, the word was infused with a naïve sense of hope, the promise of good things to come. To Danny, the word symbolized a vacuum, the bleak void left behind when that promise is obliterated in a single moment, never to be realized.

Danny's eyes lingered, his mind registering each trophy and award, the certificates and pennants, and the game ball from the no-hitter he'd thrown at the end of his sophomore year. As much as the room was a shrine to past glories, it was also an acute reminder of *the mistake*. Of everything he'd lost and all the shit that followed.

The pain and despair.

The isolation.

His father's silent judgment.

"Definitely the wrong room," Danny confirmed, tearing his eyes away from the shelves, refusing to succumb to the gravitational pull of his past.

Their eyes locked. Natalie looked down at his feet, which hadn't broken the threshold of the room, then closed the distance between them. He reached for her hand—thankful that she could read him so well, that she could sense his mood and knew better than to push—and gently led her back into the hallway. He pulled the door closed behind him, then grasped the knob a second longer, just to ensure it was tightly shut.

◇

"This place is incredible," Danny observed, speaking to Uncle Carl. "And somehow different than I remember it." He held Natalie's hand as they walked three abreast, flanked by parallel rows of olive trees that stretched as far as the eye could see.

Tucked into the rolling hills of Petaluma, their grassy slopes dotted here and there by tight clusters of coast live oaks, the olive farm had been run by his mother's family for three generations. Though Danny had spent a considerable amount of time here as a boy—staying with his grandparents in the old house, watching black-and-white movies on their ancient TV, and playing tag in the grove with his cousins on hot summer days—it had been a long time since his last visit. Too long. And a part of him had dreaded this return to the farm, wary of their scrutiny, of exposing himself to the prying eyes of countless relatives who would be eager to see just who and *what* he'd become. How the other pieces fit once baseball was removed from the center of the puzzle.

"It reminds me so much of Tuscany," Natalie remarked.

She squeezed Danny's hand and looked beyond the olive grove to the grass-covered slopes, their rolling curves turned a lush green by the autumn rains. She had studied abroad in Italy for a year during college, visiting many of the same places Danny had toured during his months in Europe.

"We hear that a lot," Carl interjected, speaking over his shoulder as he stepped off the fertile soil onto the paved path and began climbing the steep grade that led back to the villa.

The oldest of Danny's mother's siblings, now in his mid-sixties, Carl was also the one who most resembled Danny's grandfather. Tall and rangy, with the same square jaw and straight nose, his resemblance to Gramps was uncanny.

"We definitely had Tuscany in mind when we built the new house," Carl explained, his voice filled with pride but wavering slightly as he trudged toward the crest of the hill. "As I'm sure you could tell on your way in."

The new house was constructed on a hilltop overlooking the olive grove, within a stone's throw of the smaller, porch-lined house where Danny's grandparents had raised their four children and where his Gram still lived. The sprawling new two-story home, with its stone façade and slanted roofs, had been modeled after a traditional Tuscan villa. Carl and Sue built it the year after Danny was drafted, when Gramps passed away and they took the reins of the family business, expanding the operation to include daily tours and a boutique gift shop.

"Looks like they started without us," Carl said, pointing a long arm across the well-manicured lawn, then pausing to catch his breath at the top of the hill.

Beyond the immaculate lawn, the house's expansive patio—its surface shaded from the fall sun by a wooden portico—had been set up for the day's festivities. Two long walnut tables, their benches already filled with at least thirty boisterous members of the extended Snyder clan, were positioned in the middle of the terrace, and a third table was set up buffet-style to hold the assortment of platters, bowls, and crockpots required for the traditional Thanksgiving spread.

"Over there," Danny said. He guided Natalie by the elbow to the nearest table, where his father, hunkered over a plate piled high with thick slices of turkey and all the fixings, had reserved two seats on the lacquered bench.

Danny's heart nearly burst when he saw Gram, who had been napping when they'd first arrived. She was seated across from his father, near the head of the table, commiserating with his obnoxiously loud Aunt Sue. Wearing a hand-knitted shawl around her shoulders to ward off the chill, Gram was carrying on as Danny and Natalie approached, her hazel eyes growing wide with excitement as she recollected some story from her distant past.

Gram had always been an amazing storyteller. Her bedtime stories had been the event Danny looked forward to most when he was little and stayed the night at their house while his father worked. And most of what Danny knew about his mother—the important things anyway, the fine details and little quirks that make a person who she is—he had learned from Gram.

Danny walked to the far side of the table, pecked Gram lightly on her paper-thin cheek, then tried to hide his blush when she announced to the entire table that Natalie was "quite a catch."

Gram wasn't wrong, Danny noted, admiring Natalie's profile as he sat next to her at the table after they'd helped themselves to heaping plates at the buffet. Though Danny had been apprehensive about the visit, about seeing his family again after so long away, not to mention breaking the news of the engagement to his father, he found himself at ease, enjoying their company more than he'd anticipated. And while he'd expected a laundry list of questions about his new life, his *life after baseball*, he was pleasantly surprised to find that those concerns were unwarranted. If anything, he was an afterthought, with most of their curiosity, Gram's in particular, focused on Natalie.

"And where in San Diego do you live, dear?" Gram asked Natalie. Though her tone was light, her eyes were sharp.

His grandmother's questions had been incessant, so much so that Natalie had hardly touched her food, which was now sitting cold on the plate in front of her.

Danny looked up from his own plate, over to Natalie, and placed his hand lightly on her thigh beneath the table. Natalie might be fooled by Gram's demeanor, what his dad and Uncle Hal referred to as her *bumbling inspector routine*, but Danny had seen this act before and knew better than to let his guard down around Mrs. Columbo.

"Uh, I live in Pacific Beach," Natalie answered carefully. "I have a condo there, not far from the water." She took a quick sip of her diet soda, then shot Danny an uncomfortable glance.

Danny was happy to note the use of *I* and not *we*. He discreetly nodded his approval, then gave her leg a reassuring squeeze.

He hadn't decided exactly when he would have *the conversation* with his father, but it wouldn't be now, in front of Gram's inquisitive eyes, during Thanksgiving dinner.

"And is that far from where you live?" Gram asked, pinning Danny between two plastic slides and positioning him beneath her microscope. She subtly shifted her frame on the wooden bench, her eyes narrowing ever so slightly as they darted back and forth between him and Natalie.

Caught flatfooted, Danny scrambled to buy time. "Yeah,

pretty close, Gram." He looked to Natalie for confirmation, then nodded at her as she nodded back at him. "Not far at all."

Danny shot a worried glance to his left, where his father was stuffing his face with pumpkin pie and explaining to Uncle Carl and Aunt Sue why the Detroit Lions always play on Thanksgiving. Despite Gram's best efforts, Dad was oblivious to the Spanish Inquisition she was conducting just down the table.

"And speaking of close," Danny said loudly, nudging Natalie gently with his elbow, "I think we might be close to running out of pie over there. Nat, you wanna come with me to grab a slice?"

Danny slid his long legs awkwardly out from beneath the table, stood behind the bench, and helped Natalie to do the same. She smiled tersely, mouthed the words "thank you," and beelined for the dessert end of the buffet table.

Danny watched Natalie's hasty retreat, then sneaked a peek across the table at Gram. She wasn't looking at him but staring off into the distance instead, a paper napkin raised to her mouth to conceal the hint of a wily smile.

⚾

"They're going to be good, those two," his father boomed, announcing his presence before joining Danny at the edge of the pebbled patio, where the pavement gave way to the bluegrass lawn.

The boys were both lean and tan, both markedly tall for their ages. One eleven, the other only eight, they moved with an athletic grace that made it clear to Danny that they would blossom into good baseball players in the years to come.

"They're *already* good," Danny corrected. He pulled his eyes from the wide swath of grass, where Carl's grandsons were playing catch, to glance at his father on his right. It was always shocking to see him standing at eye level; even now, Dad loomed larger in Danny's mind.

"Reminds me of you at that age," his dad said, pointing to

Seth, the older of the boys. "Tall lefty with a strong arm. Not strong like yours, of course, but strong enough."

Danny nodded. He smiled wistfully at his father's attempt at flattery but remained silent. Baseball was no longer a topic he cared to discuss.

"Anyway, Danny," he continued, dutifully inspecting the grass in front of their feet, "your grandmother suggested we have a little *powwow*. She thought you might have something to tell me."

Danny chuckled. You never could sneak anything past that woman. When he was a kid, she was all-seeing and all-knowing; she used to warn him that she had a magical second set of eyes hidden in the back of her head. Twenty years later, he wasn't convinced otherwise.

"I was going to wait until later, Dad. After we got home." Danny glanced at the tables under the portico. Most of the crowd had dispersed since the meal, when Natalie had been whisked away by Aunt Sue, presumably for a tour of the villa.

Danny turned back to the lawn and watched Seth dip his shoulder, drop sidearm, and unleash a ground-seeking missile in his brother's direction. The ball took a high hop, skipped off the top of Jonah's glove, and rolled across the damp grass, coming to a stop at the edge of the patio in front of Danny and his father.

Danny waved his father off. "I've got it."

He leaned to pick up the ball, then grasped it carefully with his left hand, feeling its familiar weight—and a visceral pang of sadness—before tossing it back to Jonah, only twenty feet away. The throw sailed just wide, but the boy speared it without having to adjust his feet.

"I didn't know you could do that," his father said. "Throw a ball, I mean."

A flash of anger ignited behind Danny's eyes, then flamed out just as quickly. "The arm still works, Dad. At least now, anyway." He looked down at his scarred left hand, balled his fist, then slowly flexed his fingers. "It's the hand that's the problem. My nerves. The grip."

Day-to-day functions—like unloading a dishwasher, driving a car, or even writing with a pen—had long ago become routine. Applying a precise amount of pressure to a seam, while trying to control the rotation and break of a projectile traveling in excess of ninety miles per hour, was another story entirely. His father knew this.

"Anyway . . ." his dad said, subtly shifting his weight as well as the uncomfortable trajectory of the conversation. He lapsed into silence, kicked at a clump of dirt on the patio, then pushed forward. "What's this news, huh? She pregnant?"

"Jesus!" Danny spun to his right and met his father's blue eyes with an admonishing stare. "Are you kidding me? No, *Dad*, she's not pregnant."

"Well, that's—"

"But we are engaged," Danny cut in. "And living together. Happily." He clenched his jaw and braced himself for his father's predictable response.

"I see," his father said flatly. "All this after, what, four months?"

Danny let the question hang, suspended in the crisp air between them. It was late afternoon, and the autumn sun was little more than a sliver above the hills to the west. The temperature was dropping rapidly in its wake.

Though he wanted to explain the connection he and Natalie shared, the magnetism that bound them together, and the unmistakable electricity he felt every time she walked into a room, he knew these concepts were beyond his father's reach. According to Uncle Carl, his dad was more alone than ever, busying himself with softball leagues and thousand-piece puzzles, and any other solitary hobby that could effectively fill the yawning void *she* had left.

"And what about a job?" his dad asked. "A real job, I mean. Don't you think that's an important piece to have in place before you get married?"

"I do . . ." Danny acknowledged.

These were all the questions he'd anticipated. If there was anything he understood in this world, it was the inner workings of his father's ever-practical mind. He had dragged Danny over the coals with a similar line of questioning when he chose the minor leagues over USC, then again when he'd canceled his physical therapy appointments, packed his bags, and hopped a plane to London.

"I have a plan, Dad," he continued, annoyed that he even had to explain himself. "After graduation in December, I already have a job lined up. A good job. Natalie's father owns a bunch of appliance stores in Southern California, and he's already offered me a position."

Danny turned and stared.

There was something about Dad's expression, a pained look in the depths of his eyes and a defeated sagging at the corners of his mouth, which seemed foreign. Out of place.

Danny was rattled. He traced the line of his father's sight to the hills beyond—wondering what his father's eyes could see that his couldn't—then the expression disappeared, replaced with the familiar grimace of *disappointed dad*.

"And that's what you want to do with your history degree? *Sell appliances?*" His father waited with his hands on his hips for a response that didn't come, then sighed long and hard. "I just wish you would take some time," he said finally. "You can be . . . impulsive. You dive into things, sometimes headfirst, without even thinking them through. I just don't want to see you make a mistake."

Mistake. The word traveled from his father's lips to Danny's ear on a bolt of lightning that shocked Danny's mind and brought his blood to an instant boil.

Danny's nostrils flared as he contemplated what other mistakes his father might want to discuss. Foregoing college the first time? Maybe his time abroad and the decision to spend his signing bonus on travel instead of socking it away for a rainy day?

Or perhaps the one errant pitch he regretted every day but

could never take back—his impulsive decision to reach across the car to answer the phone instead of just letting it go to voicemail.

Danny was transported through space and time to his childhood bedroom. He watched his dad shake his head, reach into the pocket of his hoodie, and deposit a baseball onto the desk with a disappointed frown. *Not every mistake turns into a foul ball.*

"I'm not looking to fight," Danny said, though every tensed muscle in his body told him otherwise. He pivoted on the grass and squared his shoulders toward his father. Though only a foot separated their bodies, it might as well have been a mile. "And I'm certainly not looking for relationship advice from a man who's been married to a ghost for twenty-two years."

Danny barely registered the look of shock on his father's face before bolting for the house. This was the way it always went with them: No matter how far he traveled, or how much he accomplished, his father had a maddening way of burrowing under his skin, of making him feel like an angry child pouting in the cab of the truck.

Hardly feeling the ground beneath him, Danny's angry strides carried him under the portico and past the few curious faces at the nearly empty tables, transporting him within seconds to the closed French doors of the villa.

He paused, his shaking hand resting on the ornate handle of the door.

Those words—spiteful words that had escaped his lips before they'd even fully formed in his mind—left a foul taste in his mouth. He regretted them already, wished he could take them back.

Danny almost turned around. His heart yearned to rejoin his father, who continued watching the boys from the edge of the grass, but he resisted the urge. Why should he be the one to apologize?

Danny steeled himself instead, then opened the door and disappeared inside.

Chapter 19

Age 29

June 8, 2009

Dean Martin. The old *King of Cool*.

It was a name from the distant past, from movie nights in the rec room of the firehouse, when he'd reclined on the shiny red beanbag chair the guys kept next to the couch just for him. And it was one Danny hadn't heard in at least twenty years.

But as he assessed the extent of the damage—while trying valiantly to ignore the persistent throbbing behind his eyes—a quote he'd heard in the station as a kid kept traipsing through his mind: *"I feel sorry for people who don't drink. When they wake up in the morning, that's as good as they're going to feel all day."* While Danny appreciated Dean's humor, it was a sentiment he didn't share.

"What?!" Danny shouted.

He winced at the shrill sound of his own voice as he struggled to be heard over the portable water pumps that rumbled noisily in the colossal warehouse. Their motors worked furiously to extract the ankle-deep water that had pooled at the back of the building, farthest from its massive bay doors.

"I *said*," Butch Nicholson repeated, also yelling to be heard over the commotion, "it's a bit funny. You know . . . that it was the *dryers*." He laughed sardonically, then halted when he read Danny's expression and realized his joke had missed its mark.

A retired Marine Corps Master Sergeant with Popeye-thick tattooed forearms and a penchant for ironic humor, Nicholson was a subpar comedian but an outstanding inventory manager. When Danny had first taken the reins of the warehouse operation, a critical cog in the well-oiled machine of his father-in-law's appliance store empire, Butch went the extra mile to show Danny the ropes, despite being passed over for a promotion he rightfully deserved.

"Sorry, boss," Butch said, angling his large buzz-cut head toward Danny to be better heard over the steady howl of the pumps. He motioned for Danny to follow him away from the potbellied plumber and his powerful pumps, then down the broad center aisle, which was flanked on either side by towering industrial shelving units that housed countless boxes, pallets, and crates full of valuable inventory.

Sometime during the night, a water pipe burst in the men's bathroom. After flooding the entire restroom, the water leaked under the door, pooled in the far end of the warehouse, and soaked the bottoms of a row of cardboard boxes. Unfortunately for Danny, those boxes—which contained Whirlpool dryers that had been received from the supplier the previous week and would be shipped to retail outlets in the days to come—had been stacked five high. When the boxes on the first level inevitably collapsed, all the others toppled down as well, forming a soggy and costly heap on the floor of the warehouse.

"I know you've got meetings this morning," Nicholson acknowledged. Now that the noise of the pumps had faded to a dull roar, he spoke in a low Midwest grumble, his version of a conversational tone. "I'll take care of the clean-up, then get on the horn with the insurance folks to see what our options are. I'll back-brief you later today, once I have my shit in one sock."

Danny clapped him on the shoulder, grateful as always for the man's brutal efficiency, and walked down the long center aisle of the warehouse, toward the offices at the front of the building.

My shit in one sock, Danny mused, the wet soles of his shoes squeaking on the finished concrete floor beneath his feet. He'd been secretly keeping a list of Nicholson's pet phrases, which he referred to as *Butch-isms*, and sharing them with Natalie, who was equally fascinated by his colorful turns of phrase. He'd have to remember to add this gem later, once his murderers' row of morning meetings was behind him.

Danny passed through the outer offices, comprising one large room broken into cubicles by a maze of sectional dividers, and shut the door to his office behind him. Though he'd been in the job for five months, the smooth white walls of the windowless office remained purposefully bare.

This position was only a stepping stone. No need to get comfortable. If all went according to Abe's plan, which had only been accelerated since Eli, Natalie's only sibling, had shunned the family business in favor of medical school, he'd be managing his own store by the end of the year. At a location closer to home. One that didn't require a soul-crushing hour-long commute each morning and night.

Danny plopped down in his rolling chair, began the ten-minute-long process of booting up his computer, and reached for the phone. He dialed his father-in-law's office number from memory, having no doubt that Abe would already be seated behind his desk in the company's corporate office, his workweek well underway.

"Danny boy!" Abe thundered from the other end of the line. "You getting a late start today?"

Danny rolled his eyes, shook off Abe's not-so-subtle jab, and reached for the bottle of Aleve he kept in the top drawer of his desk. After lowering the volume on his desktop phone to a more tolerable setting, he dry-swallowed two capsules—then a third for good measure—and glanced at the digital clock on his computer screen. It was only 7:04. He gathered himself before responding, trying to match his father-in-law's fervor despite the mounting intensity of his headache and the shitty turn his Monday morning had taken.

"Hey, Abe. I'm calling because I walked into a bit of an issue at the warehouse this morning."

Danny waited for a response, heard none, and pressed onward. He provided a quick summary of the facts, heaped praise on Butch for his timely response, then paused to let the information sink in. Though he could hear Abe's wheels spinning on the other end of the line, his father-in-law only sighed.

"Abe, you there?" Bad news usually provoked an onslaught of follow-up questions and unsolicited advice. Prolonged silence was the last response he'd expected and far more unsettling.

"Yeah, I'm here," Abe replied, breaking his lengthy pause. "I'm not worried about the flooding, Dan, or the dryers, for that matter." He paused again, the silence interrupted only by the sound of coffee being slurped from a mug. "What I'm worried about, Daniel, is my daughter's well-being. She sounded . . . *distressed* when we spoke yesterday."

Danny bit down on the cap of a highlighter, briefly wished it was the barrel of a pistol, and closed his eyes, trying to stitch together an appropriate response. Yes, the last few weeks had been stressful. *For both of them.* It's hard to keep your balance when your world's been turned upside down. And while he shared his father-in-law's concerns, he didn't appreciate his guerilla-style ambush. This was the last conversation he wanted to have in his office early on a Monday morning while nursing a hangover that only appeared to be hitting its stride.

"She *is* a bit stressed," Danny acknowledged, careful to shave the sharp edge off his voice. "As I'm sure you can understand." His gaze dropped to his cluttered desktop, where a yellow post-it note sat next to the keyboard, with 11 a.m., the time of the appointment, scrawled in black Sharpie across its surface. "But she'll adjust, Abe. *We'll adjust.* And once we do, it'll be fine."

Danny pulled the receiver away from his ear and sighed through another agonizingly long pause.

"Ah, I'm sure you're right," Abe finally replied, sounding unconvinced. He slurped his coffee again, then turned the page. "It's kind of ironic, though, right?" he asked, his voice carrying an annoyingly sly tinge.

"What's that?" Danny's soul groaned, and he rubbed at his temple with the hand not holding the receiver, already dreading Abe's predictable punchline.

"A warehouse floods . . . but only the *dryers* get wet. You can't make this stuff up." Abe cackled at his own joke, broke into a prolonged cough, then hung up the phone without bothering to say goodbye.

◇

"YOU THINK THIS THING GETS ESPN?" Danny pointed up from his chair at the black screen of the idle machine. He followed the remark with his cheesiest open-mouth smile, which Natalie met with a sidelong glance before quickly dismissing him with a narrowing of her mascara-rimmed eyes.

The rest of his morning had been an epic grind. But after slogging through his series of mind-numbing meetings and tying up the loose ends of the dryer fiasco, Danny was trying to turn the page. To start fresh. And imbue the day with the degree of positivity it rightfully deserved.

"Oh, is that what we're doing?" Natalie asked. "Being clever?" She spoke in a sarcastic whisper though they were alone in the cramped examination room. "You'll have to warn me next time, so I can be ready to match your wit."

Danny considered another attempt at humor, then read the room and shut his mouth instead. She was sitting on the edge of the exam table, her tiny feet dangling well above the floor. Despite the sarcastic façade, she looked uncharacteristically vulnerable. Small and fragile. And more than a little pissed off.

Abe was right; Natalie had been stressed. Only four weeks removed from law school graduation, she'd been studying night and day for the California Bar Exam, which would be proctored in less than a month. While she'd already accepted a job offer from a well-respected downtown firm, that offer would be off the table if she tanked the exam. This news, though wonderful and exciting, was wholly unexpected. And it had thrown a massive wrench into their plans.

"I'm sorry for being a bitch." She looked up from the checkered linoleum floor and extended a reconciliatory hand down toward Danny. "I'm just super anxious. And I *really* have to pee! They tell you to come in with a full bladder, then they make you sit in the waiting room for, like, forty-five minutes. Talk about cruel and—"

"Knock, knock!"

Danny jumped in his seat and gawked past Natalie's legs at the door on the opposite side of the room. The words, barked by a stout woman with short graying hair and a wrestler's neck, hung in the air as she charged into the room and fiddled with the knobs and dials of a complicated-looking machine.

"I'm Nurse Terri," she announced, pivoting away from the machine to face the table. She aggressively pumped Natalie's hand, then inserted both of hers into a pair of latex gloves. "I already know who you two are—Mom and Dad—so I guess we can get this party started."

Danny watched with admiration as Nurse Terri, a model of efficiency, continued to prepare the ultrasound machine. Much like Butch Nicholson, this woman clearly had her shit in one sock. She glanced up occasionally, fixing them with sharp gray eyes as she provided an overview of the procedure, firing off crisp and clinical definitions of unfamiliar terms like *transducer, gestational sac,* and *transabdominal.*

"You got all that?" Danny asked Natalie, his words swallowed by the sharp crinkle of exam table paper as she leaned back, raised her blouse to bra level, and unzipped the front of her black capris.

"What we're looking for first," Terri said, ignoring Danny's joke, "is the baby's heartbeat." Foregoing the customary warning about the temperature of the gel, she squirted a mound of it onto Natalie's exposed abdomen. "If you *are* seven weeks along, which we'll also confirm today, then that should be no problem to find."

She used the end of the transducer to smear the gel into a thin layer, then began moving the wand slowly from side to side, searching for the tell-tale signs of budding life.

"And what about gender?" Danny asked, peering up at the monitor from his chair on the far side of the exam table. "Will we be able to tell if it's a boy or a girl?"

He stared up at Natalie's profile; her face, what he could see of it, remained impassive. Their difference of opinion had kicked off a lively debate over breakfast the previous morning. While Natalie was eager to learn the gender, if only for "practical" reasons like purchasing baby clothing and accessories, Danny had pitched his tent in the *practical-schmactical* camp. And he was perfectly content to revel in the mystery all the way up until game day.

"Not today, Dad," Nurse Terri said brusquely, her eyes glued to the monitor as the wand snaked slowly across the slick plain of Natalie's toned belly. "Still too early for that."

Terri pursed her thin lips, then halted her search, holding the tip of the wand in place as she scrutinized the grainy image on the screen. "Well, that's interesting..."

"Interesting?" Natalie repeated breathlessly. She propped herself on both elbows, angling for a better view. Her wide eyes darted over to Danny, then back to the image on the screen.

"You see this little shape here?" Terri asked, using the stubby tip of her index finger to trace the outline of an oblong bean on the screen of the monitor. "Well, that's your baby."

She adjusted a knob, raising the volume on the machine, and a rapid *clop-clop-clopping* droned from its speakers. "That's the heartbeat. Don't worry; it's supposed to be fast. But *that's* not the interesting part."

She beckoned to Danny, then waited as he rose from his seat, walked around the end of the exam table, and leaned closer to the monitor.

Danny reached for Natalie's hand, ignoring the sting of French-tipped fingernails digging into his flesh. Though he knew little about this process, about ultrasounds, he'd done enough internet searching over the weekend to understand that they were used as a screening tool—to identify problems early in the pregnancy.

"And this," the nurse continued, turning away from the screen to lock eyes with both of them before again running her finger in an oval-shaped pattern across the screen, "is your *other* baby."

Danny's knees buckled.

His hand, the one *not* being pulverized in Natalie's vise-like grip, shot forward to grab the edge of the exam table, narrowly rescuing him from an embarrassing collapse to the floor.

The nurse's words zoomed around the periphery of his mind like a racecar encircling a closed track. *Your other baby.*

"Congratulations, Mom and Dad." Nurse Terri's colorless cheeks rose to form an abstract painter's representation of a smile, her first since she'd entered the room. "You're having twins."

✧

"I can't help feeling, Daniel, like I was seriously misled." Natalie laughed, then snorted as she rolled onto her back. She looked up at Danny and tapped him lightly on the chest with her index finger. "Big time."

Her head rested on a pillow in his lap, her torso and legs stretched languorously over the cushions of the sofa. She reached for the remote control and lowered the volume on the television as the closing credits of the movie cascaded down its screen.

For the first time in weeks, Danny had made it home from the office relatively early. He'd fumble-fucked his way through the afternoon, wandering in a distracted daze, then eventually thrown in the towel and hopped into the car, hoping to beat the crush of rush hour traffic on I-5. He'd come home early, wanting to talk about the appointment, about the ultrasound and Nurse Terri's *revelation*, but by the time he'd arrived at the condo, all the words had dried up. So, he'd suggested the movie instead.

"I could be mad at you," she continued, still staring up at him, "both for your devious ruse and for dragging me away from my studies. But the truth is, I needed the break."

"My *ruse*?" Danny feigned innocence. "You must be mistaken. It's literally right there in the title of the movie —*Twins*." He leaned over her head, reached for his glass on the coffee table, then sank back into the soft cushions of the couch when he realized it was empty.

In truth, Natalie was an easy mark. She'd never seen the hit '80s comedy before, so it had been easy for him to sell it as a foundational experience for expectant parents of twins. It hadn't taken her long to realize, though, that the hilarious Schwarzenegger-DeVito comedy—about genetically engineered twins who are reunited in adulthood after being separated at birth—was wholly inapplicable to their current situation.

"In all seriousness, though . . ." She sat up, moved to the other end of the couch, and crossed her legs beneath her. "Is there something you want to talk about? You're not that hard to read: You default to Schwarzenegger whenever you have something on your mind. Some people have comfort food; my husband has the Terminator."

"Easy, lady," Danny warned, rising from his spot on the couch and grabbing his empty glass off the table. "That's your governor you're talking about."

He walked toward the kitchen and paused at the sliding glass door that led to their small balcony. The summer sun was just beginning to set over the ocean, sending a kaleidoscope of colors off the rippled surface of the Pacific. And although it was a Monday, the street below was packed with summer tourists and obnoxious college kids, all streaming down the lane toward the various bars and restaurants of Pacific Beach.

"Seriously, Dan. Can you not walk away while I'm talking to you?"

He wheeled to face her, his jaw clenched, brows furrowed. "It's okay, Natalie," he assured her, pumping an imaginary shotgun and slipping easily into his near-perfect Schwarzenegger impersonation. "I'll be back."

Danny strutted into the condo's small kitchen, inordinately pleased by his own pun. He tossed a few ice cubes into the bottom of his glass and doused them with a liberal splash of Jack Daniels before rejoining her on the couch.

He pretended not to see her staring at his glass as he leaned back into the soft leather. Even before she'd learned she was pregnant and had to forego all drinking, his *habits of consumption* had become a sticking point between them.

"They're lucky, you know." His eyes roved over her abdomen, its flat surface betraying no hint of the dynamic duo growing inside it. "You're going to be a terrific mom. The kind they deserve." He took a long sip, felt the sting of the liquor as it slid down his throat, then rested the glass on the meat of his thigh.

The past few weeks had afforded him plenty of time to think. Maybe too much. And while much of that time was spent dwelling on the realities of parenthood—and wondering whether he was truly up to the task—some of that time had been spent thinking about his own parents. The loss of his mother. And the unbridgeable gap between him and his father.

"I bet you miss her," Natalie said, her words couched in compassion. "Your mom, I mean."

"It's complicated," Danny acknowledged, before sipping his drink. He rarely spoke about his mother, and Natalie rarely pried. "It's hard to miss someone you barely remember, you know? She's like a faceless statue that lives in my mind, standing atop this pedestal my dad and grandma have built. Perfection personified."

Danny swirled the glass in his hand, then watched the three

shrinking cubes trace its inner wall as he searched for the right words.

"But sometimes, I think of her more like a void, an empty pit in our lives—his more than mine—that can never be filled. Though, I doubt either characterization is fair."

Natalie sat motionless at the far end of the couch, her legs still folded beneath her. She watched him through patient eyes, waiting.

"But life isn't fair either. *He* knows that. Maybe better than I." Danny regretted his words immediately. He knew Natalie would pick up the thread and where she would take the conversation next.

"Have you called him yet?" she asked predictably. "Told him the news?" She swept a strand of dark hair away from her eyes, tucked it behind her ear, and stared at him expectantly.

"No. No, I haven't."

He had seen his father only once since their Thanksgiving argument at the farm, when Danny had let his anger get the best of him. His father had come to San Diego for their wedding the following spring, but even in the midst of the celebration, the tension had been palpable. They'd spoken only sporadically on the phone since, their conversations becoming short and cursory, marked less by what was *said* than what was left *unsaid*. Like "I'm sorry," which Danny regretted not telling him in the first place. But with so much to apologize for—harsh words, poor decisions, and dreams torn recklessly asunder—it was hard to know where to begin. Or whether his dad even cared. The dude wasn't exactly an open book.

"But I will," Danny said. "Maybe tomorrow." He offered his most reassuring smile though they both knew he'd made this noncommittal proposal before.

He rose from the couch, feeling the heat of her stare as he finished the watered-down whiskey in his glass in one quick gulp.

"I'm going to read for a while before bed." He grabbed the thick hardback biography from the edge of the coffee table. This time it was Churchill. Before Sir Winston, it was Honest Abe. And Gandhi before that. His thirst for history was unquenchable, provided it wasn't his own.

Danny placed his hand gently atop Natalie's stomach. He kissed her lightly on the lips, then smiled as he slipped seamlessly back into his sunglasses and bullet-riddled black leather jacket. "Hasta la vista . . . babies."

Chapter 20

Age 32

October 28, 2012

What do you call an office printer that doesn't print? The answer, as Danny well knew, was *a worthless piece of shit.*

Unfortunately, when you're the boss, there are certain standards to uphold. And kindergarten rules still apply—if you don't have anything nice to say, don't say anything at all.

He'd been pacing between his desk and the printer for the better part of fifteen minutes, wearing out the carpet in the shared office that overlooked the showroom floor. He was trying in vain to print the lengthy transactions report for the weekly sales call the following morning, and he was dangerously close to losing his shit.

Danny planted his hands on his hips, blew out a long stream of air, and stared down through the window of the office. Below the elevated workspace—in the store's massive showroom—the size of the crowd was encouraging, even by Sunday standards.

"Did you try turning it off, waiting for thirty seconds, then turning it back on?"

Danny scrutinized Phil Westerman's doughy face, trying to ascertain whether he was genuinely trying to help or only poking the bear. Judging by the pained look on his assistant manager's face, as if *he* were solely responsible for the printer's considerable shortcomings, Danny gave him the benefit of the doubt and assumed the former.

"If you'd like," Phil said, using the sleeve of his ill-fitting button-up shirt to wipe away the beads of sweat that dotted his forehead, "I could print it out for you later. When the printer is . . . printing."

"Thanks," Danny said curtly. While Westerman toed the line of competency as an assistant manager, his perpetual kindness was his redeeming quality. And his subtle interventions were usually successful in reducing Danny's anger to a low boil. "I might take you up on that."

Danny walked across the brightly-lit office and checked the thermostat, which was set to seventy. During the fall and winter, when they ran the heat in the morning to maintain a comfortable temperature down on the showroom floor, the store's office, which was built in a loft atop the employee breakroom, became a veritable oven. Danny adjusted the setting to sixty-eight degrees, returned to his desk in the back corner of the office, and again consulted the printing queue on his computer screen.

He was about to cancel the print job, a futile act of resistance that he'd undertaken three times already, when his cellphone chimed from beneath a stack of papers on his cluttered desk. It was Natalie, again, texting to remind him about the party later that afternoon. He switched the ringer to silent, placed the phone facedown on the corner of the desk, then turned his attention to the handful of inconsequential emails that remained in his inbox.

These Sunday trips to the office were a rarity when he first took over the company's Miramar store, but they became more common as he'd settled into the position and felt the full weight of his father-in-law's expectations. They were sometimes a necessity, other times an act of avoidance. While some days it was hard to divine his true motivation for holing up in the office on his day off, today it was abundantly clear.

He'd slept like shit. *Again.*

His morning started just after five o'clock when Will crept into their darkened bedroom, TV remote clutched in his pudgy little hand. He woke Danny with a one-word demand, *"Caillou,"* which the boy chanted into Danny's ear with escalating intensity until he finally yielded, carried him football-style down the stairs like a pajama-clad sack of potatoes, and turned on a DVD of the annoying cartoon. After getting Will settled on the couch, Danny tried to get some shut-eye in the recliner, only to hear Matty wailing from the boys' shared bedroom upstairs.

By the time breakfast was done, a messy affair consisting of mostly uneaten pancakes, a spilled bowl of Cheerios, and the incessant use of the word "no," Danny was physically and mentally exhausted and ready for relief. Despite it being Natalie's negotiated day to sleep in, he woke her soon after seven o'clock, floated a vague excuse that landed like a turd in the punchbowl, then made his hasty escape to the office.

"Well, I'll be darned," Phil said, responding to a low hum that originated from the opposite side of the room. He pointed to the printer, a boxy multifunctional contraption that looked far more capable than it was, then broke into his punchable Ned Flanders grin as it rumbled to life and began spitting crisp white sheets into its output tray.

Danny rose from his chair, intending to retrieve the report from the printer, then collapsed back into his seat as the office phone blared from the back corner of the desk. He consulted the caller ID display, then sighed heavily before picking up the receiver.

"Hey, Nat," Danny answered, coating his voice with a layer of cheerfulness he didn't feel. "Hold on just a second." He locked eyes with Phil, jerked his head in the direction of the exit, and waited until Westerman's ample backside disappeared through the door. "What's up?"

"What's up?" she repeated, incredulous. "You would know *what's up* if you read my texts."

In the background, one of the twins, though it was impossible to tell which one, chanted "monster truck" in close proximity to the phone. Danny cringed and turned down the volume setting on the base of the phone. As much as he loved those boys, every day was a fucking marathon. Run at a sprinter's pace. Uphill, barefoot, and over snow.

"You know the party starts in an hour, right?" Though phrased as a question, her sentence had the hard edge of a challenge. It was the same tone that drew objections from opposing counsel for badgering the witness.

Danny's eyes darted to the clock in the lower right corner of his computer display, below the border of his nearly empty digital inbox.

"Yeah, of course." He squeezed his eyes shut, pinched the bridge of his nose, and compiled a mental list of all the shit he would rather do than attend this party. It wasn't a short list. "I'm almost done here. I'll just wrap things up and meet you at the park at one o'clock."

He listened to her soft breathing on the other end of the line followed by muffled footfalls as she moved through the house, away from the intermittent screeching of the boys.

"Dan, I need you to be on time today." Her voice was quiet but firm. "I need you to be on time . . . and I need you to be present."

Danny clenched his jaw and smeared the sheen of sweat that had materialized on his forehead. *Present.* She'd adopted the term from *The 5 Love Languages*—or one of the countless other self-improvement books she'd been carting home from Barnes & Noble in recent months—then started injecting it into their arguments with increasing frequency ever since. As annoying as her habit was, he knew she wasn't wrong.

Danny swallowed a hard lump of pride, opened his mouth to reply, then cursed instead, realizing Natalie was no longer on the line.

⬦

"Would you believe," Danny began, cutting his eyes slyly to the right to take in Natalie's profile across the park bench, "that he's *this close* to finding a cure for cancer?" He held up his hand for her to see, his thumb and index finger separated by less than an inch.

She rolled her eyes and continued staring passively at the playground, where Will and Matty, dressed in khaki shorts and short-sleeve plaid shirts, were trying to help the birthday boy climb atop a rocking seahorse. Little Preston, nine months younger than the twins, was less interested in mounting the purple seahorse than exploring the contents of his left nostril, where his finger had been lodged for the last thirty seconds.

"That's nothing," she said finally, adjusting the bottom hem of her knee-length white skirt and warming to their game despite herself. "Heather told me that he completed work on his prototype time machine. Assuming the Libyans come through with the promised plutonium, he'll be visiting the year 2355 tomorrow... after his toddler yoga session and just before his afternoon nap."

"Good one." Danny chuckled under his breath, awarding extra points for the subtle nod to *Back to the Future*.

In the two years since his birth, Rory and Heather's son had convinced his mother, if no one else, that he was a certifiable genius destined for unparalleled greatness in a broad spectrum of career fields and disciplines. Gossiping about *Baby Einstein's* achievements had become a wellspring of happiness for both of them, making otherwise shitty events like these easier to stomach.

Danny reclined against the warm concrete of the park bench, tilted his face skyward, and closed his eyes. The sun had risen high in the cloudless San Diego sky; though the temperature was only in the upper sixties, it felt much warmer in the direct light of the sun.

"We need to talk about it," she declared, setting down their game in favor of a weightier topic.

Though his eyes remained closed, he could feel her gaze moving over him, searching his countenance for cracks and seams. He opened his lids slowly. Their eyes met for a brief second, then he shifted his focus past the playground to the thin strip of beach and the calm body of water that lay beyond. Across Bonita Bay, on the other side of the Mission Bay Channel, he could see the imposing tower of the Harborside Hotel, the windows of their meeting place reflecting the light of the afternoon sun.

"They're just dreams, Nat." Even to his own ears, the assessment was unconvincing. He slowly flexed and unflexed the fingers of his left hand, watching bone and tendon shift beneath faded purple scars.

Not surprisingly, the nightmares had started again the previous week, the first recurrence in almost eighteen months. He'd woken up violently—his body slick with sweat and his nose filled by the acrid smells of gasoline and burnt rubber—at least twice a night in the days since. And Natalie was no dummy; she understood the timing was not a coincidence.

"They're not *just* dreams," she said, pivoting on the bench to face him, her dark eyes radiating intensity. She leaned closer and placed her bare arm over the back of the bench. "They're—"

Danny saw her staring at a point over his left shoulder and turned to follow her line of sight. It was Heather. Her long legs carried her briskly down the narrow path that separated the playground from the grassy park where the canopies and tables had been set up for the party. Somewhere in her second trimester, she walked with a hand cupped below the tiny bulge in the midsection of her sundress. It was less a protective measure than it was a signal to the world, alerting all of humanity that she was, in fact, pregnant and hadn't just let herself go.

"Hey guuuuys," Heather gushed, the lightness of her tone at odds with her constipated smile and the severe ponytail that stretched the skin of her face into a taut mask. "He's been behaving, I hope." She looked to the playground, where the three boys were now sitting together in the sand, huddled around a red plastic bucket.

Will and Matty—dark-haired, olive-skinned, and identical in all ways except for the color of their shirts—gripped tiny plastic shovels, industriously filling the bucket with scoops of sand. Blond little Preston, who had discarded his shovel on the ground next to his feet, scooped at the dry sand with his hands, dumping most of it on his shorts rather than inside the bucket.

"He's been perfect," Danny said, flashing the plastic smile that he reserved only for Heather. "Downright brilliant," he added, assuming the upper-crust British accent that he'd pilfered from *Downton Abbey*. He winked at Natalie, a gesture she ignored.

Danny excused himself, under the pretext of helping Rory at the grill, and made his way down the cracked asphalt path, amongst the towering queen palms, to the grassy plain where Rory and Heather had set up camp for the party.

Relieved to escape both Heather's presence and Natalie's inquisition, Danny weaved through the throng of people, most of them members of Heather's extended family. He smiled and nodded politely, circumvented a group of older children bandying about a soccer ball, then joined Rory at the large charcoal grill overlooking the bay.

"There he is," Rory called, his wide smile exposing brilliantly white teeth. "The heir apparent."

Danny waved off Rory's elaborate bow and laughed at their inside joke, which had basically written itself. His father-in-law's name, Abe Cohen, was strikingly similar to that of Abe Froman, the fictional "Sausage King of Chicago" in *Ferris Bueller's Day Off*. Now that Danny had been groomed to replace Abe after his retirement, Rory had dubbed him the "heir apparent" to Abe's appliance empire.

"I thought you might need some help over here." Danny surveyed the grill, where neat rows of burgers and hot dogs sizzled over the charcoal-fed flames. Next to the grill stood a black folding card table, its surface covered with plates, buns, and all the fixings for the burgers and dogs.

"Sure, you did." Rory set down the metal tongs and wiped his hands across the black apron that protected his khaki cargo shorts and salmon polo shirt. His eyes roved back toward the playground, where Heather had assumed Danny's seat on the bench next to Natalie.

Though Danny's relationship with Heather had marginally improved in the years since his abrupt eviction, it was clear that theirs would never be more than an uneasy truce. But childhood best friends were hard to come by. And if keeping the good times rolling meant putting up with Rory's untamable shrew, then so be it. Especially when Rory, a model husband and father if ever there was one, seemed to be so unassailably happy living under her man-size thumb.

"Your dad must be stoked," Rory said, shifting the subject away from Danny and his wife. "I'm sure he's got his broom on standby."

Danny stiffened at Rory's mention of his father and the allusion to baseball. He wheeled away from the grill to survey the glittering bay, its surface nearly flat on the windless afternoon. Of course, he was aware—painfully so—that the Giants were up 3-0 over Detroit in the best-of-seven World Series, poised to sweep the Tigers with another win later that evening.

But he hadn't watched a single baseball game since his former team's *last* World Series victory, almost two years before, when his months-long depressive spiral began. And it had been ages since he'd spoken to his father, despite a series of text messages and missed calls that he couldn't bring himself to return in the weeks since the playoffs began.

"I'm sorry," Rory said as if sensing Danny's changed mood and realizing his misstep. He cleared his throat, reached a long muscular arm toward the card table, and grabbed his beer from the edge, draining the last dregs from the bottom. "Can you grab me another?" Rory asked, pointing with the base of the empty bottle toward the cooler at Danny's feet.

Danny bent at the waist, acutely aware of his soft midsection as his gut spilled over the rim of his jeans. His physique, *new* but certainly not *improved*, was just another bullet point on Natalie's long but justified list of gripes and concerns. He surveyed the contents of the cooler, wrapped one hand around a Kona Longboard, and simultaneously grasped a Diet Pepsi with the other.

Danny groaned as he stood and closed the cooler, wondering when the hell he'd gotten so old. And resenting that Rory seemingly hadn't.

"Here you go, bud." Danny handed Rory the beer, then enviously watched him pop the cap with a bottle opener and take a long swig.

The hairs on Danny's forearms stood on end as he registered the magnetic pull of the cooler. He'd promised Natalie he wouldn't drink at the party; it was only 2 p.m., and experience had taught them both that an early start guaranteed a sloppy finish.

He was about to pop the tab on the soda, then reconsidered. He reached again for the cooler and exchanged the can for a cold bottle of Longboard.

"Screw it," Danny said, avoiding Rory's eyes as he reached for the bottle opener. "One beer won't hurt."

◇

DANNY CLOSED his right eye tightly and squinted with his left. Though comparatively bright in the darkness of the night, the screen of his iPhone had become increasingly hard to read, the words blurring as his inebriated eyes battled for dominance and struggled to focus in tandem.

Partially reclined atop a chaise longue on the second-story balcony of the house, he could see the lights of Ocean Beach twinkling between the regular gaps in the slats of the balcony's wooden siding. The view had been a major selling point when they'd purchased the house the year before. From its elevated vantage at the top of the steep hill, they could peer down the entirety of Niagara Avenue to the point nearly a mile away where the massive wood and concrete pier jutted away from the coast and into the waters of the Pacific.

Danny groped for the whisky tumbler that was situated between his thighs and gulped unsteadily. He replaced the glass, spilling some of its contents onto the floral cushion below, then continued to scroll through the recap from the evening's game. If nothing else, he was a glutton for punishment.

The Giants won, of course. A so-called "thrilling" ten-inning victory, capping the team's sweep of the Detroit Tigers and marking the franchise's second championship in the last three years. He wished he could say it was bittersweet, but at the moment, the former sentiment had a stranglehold on the latter. Though he hadn't watched the deciding game *this time*, as he had two years earlier when Brian Wilson closed out the Texas Rangers with a swinging strikeout and the team mobbed him on the mound in Arlington, the outcome was the same. He was hollow inside. Gutted and raw. Acutely aware of his mistake, his loss, and everything that should have been.

"They're bathed and in bed," Natalie said, speaking quietly through the screen of the sliding glass door that connected the balcony to their bedroom.

"Thanks," Danny replied flatly. He rested the phone on his chest and stared out into the darkness. He'd been relieved to be excused from the bedtime routine. It was a taxing chore, a painful nightly ritual that consumed the better part of an hour as well as his small reserve of patience. As guilty as he felt, sometimes he just didn't have it in him.

Natalie lingered at the door, then joined him on the darkened balcony, settling into the chaise longue to his left. The two chairs were separated by a small glass-topped table, its surface bare, save for a half-empty bottle of Glenmorangie that he'd opened only hours before.

"Do you ever wonder," Danny thought aloud, motionless except for his lips, "if this it? If this is all life has to offer?" He craned his head to the side, bleary eyes trying to focus on her worried features.

Natalie bit her lower lip and rubbed the palm of her right hand up and down her jean-clad thigh. "I don't know how to respond to that, Dan." She issued a long sigh, then continued in a more forceful tone. "I do know that I try to be patient with you, for whatever that's worth. That I try to be understanding. I try to have *empathy* even when you disappear into a place where I can't reach you. When you take your entire life for granted. Your job . . . this house. *Me and the boys.*"

He knew she was waiting for a response, but he held his tongue, which felt lazy and bloated in the dryness of his mouth. She was right, of course; these were points he'd conceded before. The last time the Giants won it all, when he'd abandoned hope and sought refuge in the bottom of a bottle. He'd nearly lost his marriage in the process, needing three months and a stint in AA to dig his way out from beneath his avalanche of self-pity and guilt.

She swung her legs over the side of the chair and sat up to face him in the dark. "You act like you're the first person in the history of the world to lose something, Dan. Like you're the first person to watch a dream die." She sniffed loudly and wiped a tear from her cheek. "I lost something, too, you know. And it hurt. Sometimes it *still* hurts. But I keep moving."

Danny stiffened, an electric jolt of anger surging up his spine. He stifled a wry laugh and continued staring forward, down the hill of lights, and toward the blackness of the ocean. "It's apples and oranges, Nat. Your music and my baseball."

He took a swig from his glass and swirled the scotch in his mouth, trying but failing to drown the bitterness of his circumstances with the lemony gold notes of the whisky.

"Singing was your hobby," he continued bitingly, "something you did for fun. An exciting little diversion that you thought, for a minute, could be something more. Baseball . . . baseball was our life."

"*Our* life?" she asked, gently tugging at the thread of his argument.

Danny brushed off her question, ignoring its implications. Ignoring the thought of his father and of what Danny had cost them both.

He knew what Dad wanted—to bask in the team's triumph and pretend nothing had happened—but it was a wish Danny couldn't grant. Most wounds heal with time, others just fester and reek, rotting the flesh until the only remaining option is to remove the afflicted limb. Danny's had proven to be the latter.

He groaned as he clumsily flopped his legs over the side of the chaise. His glass fell to the deck with a dull *thud* as he reached a tenuous sitting position, their faces only a foot apart.

"From the time I was the twins' age," he continued, "to the day I rolled that fucking car, it was always about baseball. It was my life, God damnit! So, if you think, *for even a second*, that those two things are the same, then you're crazy."

He planted a hand on the cushion behind him, steadying himself as he watched her cry silent tears. This time, she made no move to wipe them away.

Natalie stood, her beauty momentarily obscured by a mask of shock and betrayal, and walked around the foot of the chaise, behind him, and back toward the door.

"They're not the same," she said quietly, addressing the back of his head from the doorway. Her tone was resolute. "*Life and baseball*—they're not the same thing, damnit! They're not . . . inextricably bound!"

She slid the screen door open, hesitated, then stepped through its frame.

"You lost one, Dan. Baseball is gone. Forever. And it's not

coming back. At least not the way you want it to. So now you have to decide: Without one, can you still stomach the other?"

The glass door slid shut, then jerked open again a second later. He shifted his body on the chaise and turned to see her svelte outline backlit in the doorway.

"And another thing," she said, pointing to the half-empty bottle of scotch, "you better sober the hell up, Dan. I'm due in court tomorrow morning, so you're taking the boys to daycare."

Natalie closed the door behind her again, this time with a note of finality, not even waiting for his response.

Danny retrieved his tumbler from the deck, poured himself another generous splash, and laughed hollowly into the night. He was no expert in the five love languages, but he'd perused the list and was damn sure of one thing: Their conversation didn't check the box for "quality time."

Chapter 21

Age 34

October 29, 2014

"Fuck off . . ." Danny moaned, his voice muffled by suffocating bedding. He pried open swollen eyes and freed his head from the uncomfortable crevasse between two overstuffed hotel pillows.

The nightstand was a mess, a disturbing metaphor he chose not to dwell upon. He groped blindly atop its unfamiliar surface, scattering the collection of empty minibar bottles that perched perilously on its edge. He finally found his phone, and though he silenced the obnoxious alarm, the pounding in his head continued unabated.

The phone's display, which was offensively bright in the otherwise dark hotel room, read 8 a.m. Just enough time to shower and dress. And to nurse his hangover before meeting Abe in the hotel lobby to begin day two of his father-in-law's grand farewell tour.

The previous day had been a brutal grind. They visited four of the company's Orange County locations—meeting with the store managers, reviewing sales reports and quarterly projections, and effectively installing Danny as the new head of the organization. The Big-Fucking-Cheese.

With four more visits to come, followed by all the San Diego locations on Thursday and Friday, Danny's stomach revolted at the prospect of another day's worth of small talk and schmoozing. But he'd reluctantly come to appreciate the importance of these functions, the necessity of *relationship building*.

Unready to face the day, Danny flopped onto his back in the king-size bed, pulled the starched sheet up to his chest, and unlocked his phone. He cringed at the image that greeted him. The internet browser was still open from the night before, displaying the Major League Baseball page from ESPN's mobile site.

Despite his best efforts, and his slew of well-intentioned promises to Natalie that he would avoid a repeat of his depressive spirals of 2010 and 2012, he had fucked it away again. The torturous pull had been too strong, and he'd allowed his liquor-fueled curiosity to take him down a path he knew was better left unexplored.

Danny closed out the tab and tossed the phone across the bed, unwilling to revisit the story he'd been reading the night before. It was Bumgarner, of course. A nauseating recap of the kid's historic playoff run, detailing how the Giants' southpaw had thrown the team on his back, bringing the squad to within one win of its third World Series victory in the last five years. Though he'd pitched the Giants to victory in game five of the series, a complete game shutout in San Francisco, there was talk of him being available to pitch in game seven, working on only two days' rest. The story would be inspiring, for sure...were it not so soul-crushingly depressing.

He downed a handful of Aleve and shuffled to the spacious bathroom, careful to avoid his reflection as he waited for the shower to warm. The water was scalding. He lingered in the steam, hoping the water would have a regenerative effect, erasing some of the damage from the night before. Almost dressed, and dangerously close to being late, Danny was struggling to knot his tie when his phone rang, its persistent call coming from somewhere within the tangle of sheets.

The number was unrecognized, but the preceding 707 area code threw him for a loop. He still received the occasional phone call from Santa Rosa but rarely first thing in the morning. And never from an unfamiliar source.

"Hello?" His voice was scratchy and strained, sounding just as hungover as he felt.

Baseball hadn't been the only topic on Danny's mind the night before, when he'd returned from dinner and laid waste to the minibar; he'd been thinking of his father as well. Of the years he'd spent pushing the man away and running from his own failure. And of the unspoken wishes that had only become more pressing and urgent as the nightmares returned yet again—that, despite it all, he might somehow find his way back and that all might still be forgiven.

That was the way it went with his father and baseball: Thoughts of one led inevitably to the other, the two being hopelessly intertwined in his mind. Like the red-stitched seams that encircle the ball itself, though seemingly separate at first glance, trace their lines far enough, and the two are always destined to meet. And though he doubted Dad would call from an unrecognized number, especially after almost two years of regrettable silence, he still half-expected to hear his father's familiar timbre on the other end of the line.

"Hey, kiddo."

Though not his father, the gravelly voice was familiar, nonetheless. Older than he remembered, with a certain weariness that made the hairs on Danny's arms stand on end, but familiar all the same. And come on, who else would call a thirty-four-year-old man *kiddo*?

"Hey, Uncle Hal."

Danny swallowed hard, trying to expel the lump of guilt that obstructed his throat. It had been years since he and Uncle Hal had spoken. Since Baker and Aunt Dot had driven down to San Diego for his and Nat's wedding. The years of silence were not by design. There had been no argument between them, no falling out; they had just drifted apart with time.

"What can I do for you?" Danny asked stiffly, trying to regain his composure. He felt like a child again, off balance, unsure of what to say or how to say it. A deep blush engulfed his face, and he rubbed at the back of his neck as he processed the stupidity of his question.

Danny waited for a response but heard only the crackle of static on the other end of the line. The room was suddenly hot. Unbearably hot. He loosened his tie and fumbled with shaky fingers for the top button of his collar, thinking again of his father and bracing himself for the worst.

"Listen, Danny," Baker said finally, his voice trembling. "These calls never get any easier, and God knows I've made my share of them over the years." He paused for a second that stretched into eternity, then coughed away from the phone. "I don't know quite how to say this, kiddo, so here it is."

◇

DANNY SLAMMED ON THE BRAKES, stopping inches shy of the sticker-covered rear bumper of the black hatchback that was tucked into the parking spot, completely hidden from view by the darkness and the large SUV parked next to it.

"God damnit!" he screamed, slapping the dashboard of Abe's Mercedes with window-rattling force. It was yet another close call. Just the latest in a series of near misses that punctuated his chaotic drive from Orange County to Santa Rosa. It was amazing he'd made it in one piece.

Abe had been surprisingly understanding at the hotel. He'd handed over his keys without hesitation, assuring Danny he would make his own way home to San Diego, then ushered him out of the lobby and placed his small rolling suitcase into the trunk before waving goodbye.

Danny threw the Mercedes into reverse. He wanted to scream, but he raced up and down the rows of the crowded hospital parking lot instead, eventually finding a vacant spot marked with a sign designating it as employee parking. Having expended his last fuck somewhere on the long stretch of I-5 that spanned central California, he pulled into the spot, turned off the engine, and shut his eyes.

Most of the drive had been a blur. A fevered nightmare from which he couldn't wake.

Uncle Hal had remained in contact throughout the day as Danny—vacillating between panic and shock—made the long and traffic-riddled drive north from San Clemente, up Interstate-5, through Oakland, then on to Santa Rosa.

Baker was listed as his father's emergency contact, and he was notified soon after his dad was rushed to the hospital. He'd nearly died of the initial heart attack, Baker said, and Danny couldn't scrub the horrific image from his mind. His father clinging to life, facedown in a puddle of coffee, his limbs splayed on the concrete sidewalk next to the fire station off Piner Road.

But as Baker had pointed out, there are few better places to suffer a near-fatal heart attack than in front of a building full of EMTs. The crew at the station provided life-saving aid, used a portable defibrillator to restart his father's heart, then rushed him to the emergency room. He'd regained consciousness only briefly, they said. Just long enough to plead for the presence of his son.

Danny didn't understand all the jargon, but when "less invasive" means of clearing the arteries failed, they'd asked for Danny's consent to perform emergency coronary bypass surgery. In the five hours since, nurses had emerged from the operating room periodically to provide updates, but the scant reports, which Baker relayed by phone, did little to unravel the knot of dread that had taken up residence deep inside Danny's gut.

"Just breathe," Danny said aloud in the darkened car, before continuing to chant the words again and again in his mind. He drew a massive breath, forced it deep into his lungs, and pressed his shoulders back into the soft leather of the driver's seat, willing his heartbeat to slow.

He'd been good at this once—controlling his emotions, summoning the strength he needed to own the moment. To make the right pitch when it mattered most.

Danny took one last deep breath. He unbuckled his seatbelt, then paused with his hand on the door handle, the unanswerable question running through his mind for the millionth time since Uncle Hal's first call: Would he even get the chance to make things right?

◇

DANNY ROUNDED THE CORNER, embarrassingly winded and damp with perspiration after foregoing the crowded elevator and bounding up four flights of stairs.

He paused at the threshold, his heart jackhammering behind his sternum, and scanned the dozen or so forlorn faces that were scattered at irregular intervals throughout the surgical ward's fluorescent-lit waiting room.

Uncle Hal spotted him first. He waved, then beckoned from the far end of the long rectangular room, looking much older than Danny remembered. Though his hair was still cut in his customary flattop, only the gray wall in the front had stood the test of time. Behind it was mostly exposed scalp, uniformly pink and marred by dark clusters of liver spots.

"No change," Baker said quietly, his face looking drawn in the artificial light, his wide forehead etched with deep lines of concern. He pulled Danny into a quick embrace, then held him at arm's length while inspecting the lines of his charcoal suit, his gaze lingering on the striped tie.

Danny had grabbed the suitcoat out of habit as he raced from the car. Now, he felt silly for wearing it, like a child caught playing dress-up.

"No remote either," Baker added flatly, finally losing interest in Danny's tie and nodding toward the television across the room. He gestured to one in a row of identical, blue-upholstered chairs, then walked to the opposite side of the room and lowered the volume on the wall-mounted television, which was tuned to the World Series broadcast from Kansas City.

Danny eyed the television warily, wishing it wasn't playing the game. Wishing it wasn't tormenting him from across the room, pouring salt into the self-inflicted wound he'd opened the night before.

He settled into one of the chairs, then watched Uncle Hal shuffle back over and ease his body into a seat two chairs down. They fell into an awkward silence, Baker watching the muted game, Danny watching a spot on the polished floor in front of him.

"What's that?" Danny asked. He jolted to attention, unsure how much time had passed, embarrassed that he'd become lost in his thoughts. Thoughts of Dad.

"I said you look good," Baker repeated, eyeing Danny from across the arm of his chair, his eyes lingering first on Danny's soft midsection, then again on the red and white stripes of his tie. "The furniture business must be treating you well."

"Appliances," Danny corrected, as if it mattered. He shifted in his seat, still feeling ridiculous in his suit and tie, and now acutely aware of his paunch. "Washers, dryers, refrigerators, et cetera. It's my father-in-law's business," he continued, speaking faster than normal, "but he's about to retire. So . . . I guess I'm the guy."

"The guy, huh?" Baker smiled politely, then shifted his gaze away from Danny, his eyes settling again on the flatscreen TV.

Danny's eyes drifted reluctantly to the screen, where the Giants' center fielder, Gregor Blanco, stood in the batter's box. Blanco's bat waved slowly back and forth as he awaited the delivery from the Royals' pitcher, some dude named Herrera who Danny didn't recognize. According to the graphic in the corner of the screen, San Francisco was clinging to a slim 3-2 lead, with the bases empty and no outs in the top of the fifth.

"It's been a tight seventh game," Baker said, seemingly oblivious to Danny's discomfort. "Both teams scored two in the second; Tim Hudson got the early hook, then we plated another in the fourth."

Danny cringed at Baker's use of *we*. He averted his eyes and searched for a new favorite spot on the floor in front of his feet. Although he sucked in a deep breath, trying to expand his lungs, no amount of air could relieve the tightness that gripped his chest.

"Well, that answers that," Baker said, pointing a thick index finger in the direction of the screen, an unmistakable hint of satisfaction permeating his voice.

Danny forced his eyes back to the television, where the broadcast had cut away from the duel at home plate. The camera panned to Madison Bumgarner. The kid stood alone in the Giants' bullpen, the only pitcher warming up. Stoically tossing warm-up pitches, his much-anticipated entrance into the game now seemed inevitable.

Danny's pulse quickened. He dragged the sleeve of his coat across his face, smearing the beads of perspiration that dotted his forehead.

"Ah, hell," Baker said, responding to a muffled *ding* that emanated from somewhere beneath his chair. He leaned forward in his seat, pulled an antiquated flip phone from his back pocket, then held the phone at arm's length as he struggled to read a message on its tiny display.

"I'm going to have to take off for a bit," Baker announced, glancing first at Danny, then out the darkened windows of the hospital. "Dorothy was here with me for most of the day, then went home for a bit to rest. She's ready to come back now, but it's been years since she's been comfortable driving at night."

Danny only nodded in response. He watched Baker slowly type, erase, then retype a response to his wife.

The realization hit Danny like a freight train as he watched

Baker struggle to find the right words to share with Aunt Dot. Danny bit his lower lip and blinked back tears, recognizing what a selfish prick he'd been. He'd spent all those hours in the car alone, thinking first about his father, and then about himself. Regretting all the things he'd said and done . . . and all the things he hadn't. He didn't once consider what this was like for Uncle Hal, this man who loved his father like a son.

"You going to be okay here?" Baker asked, looking up from the phone and rubbing at the corner of one eye with the calloused heel of his hand.

"Yeah, of course." Danny offered his most reassuring smile though he was positive it wouldn't fool anyone, especially Uncle Hal.

"Okay, kiddo." Baker patted Danny's thigh and groaned as he rose from his seat. "I'll see you soon." He glanced meaningfully at the muted television across the room, then back at Danny. "And I'll drop by the nurses' station on the way out," he added, "let 'em know that you're here in case they need you."

Baker took two hesitant steps toward the door, then stopped dead. He wheeled back around, then stared down at Danny, his features contorted by emotion.

"He always blamed himself, you know," Baker said.

Danny stared up from his seat, confused, searching Baker's face for clues to his meaning.

"For your accident," Baker continued, again wiping at the corner of his eye. "For calling you in the car that night. And for everything that followed. It wasn't his cross to bear—and I told him that—but that's just the way he is, son. The way he's always been."

Danny sat in stunned silence, trying to comprehend the incomprehensible. He made a move to stand, but Baker waved him off.

"Nah, I gotta get going, kiddo. But I've watched this tragedy unfold for long enough, and I just thought you deserved to know."

Danny nodded reflexively, too shocked to speak, then watched as Baker slowly covered the length of the waiting room, eventually disappearing around the corner and down the hall.

Alone with his thoughts, Danny's mind raced back through time. Back to the months following his accident.

To the silent dinners and the long, awkward pauses.

To the tense nights spent watching TV, occupying opposite ends of his childhood couch.

Then back to those first miserable nights in the hospital in Fresno, when his dad loomed at his bedside with crossed arms, staring down through disappointed eyes at his broken son who would never become what he was born to be.

Was it even possible, what Uncle Hal had said? That his father blamed *himself* for the accident, not Danny? An image of his father flashed into his mind. The two of them arguing on the edge of the grass at the farm. He remembered the pained look in his father's eyes, his sagging features, and the inexplicable expression Danny just couldn't fathom.

Could he have been so wrong, *about everything*, for so very long?

The air in the room was impossibly thick, making it hard to breathe. Danny struggled free from his tie, which had tightened like a noose around his neck, and tossed it aside. His eyes gravitated back to the TV on the wall. Bumgarner had indeed entered the game, and he now stood commandingly atop the mound, glaring toward home plate, waiting for Buster Posey to flash the sign.

Feeling trapped like a caged animal, Danny sprung from the chair and lurched across the room. He reached to turn off the TV, then halted, adrenaline coursing through his body, his hand trembling in midair.

He stood frozen in place, then his hand fell limply to his side. He watched as Bumgarner—the number 40 emblazoned across his broad back—delivered the first pitch to home plate, which missed the strike zone for a called ball.

Danny steeled himself. He again raised a shaky hand, his finger hovering over the power button on the side of the television. He wanted to push the damn button, to be done with this shit, but his body just wouldn't comply.

He lowered his hand slightly, his movements compelled by a force outside his control. He *raised the volume* on the television instead, then retraced his steps, slumping back into the soft padding of his seat.

"THROW THE GODDAMN BALL!" Danny shouted.

His fists were clenched at his sides as Juan Perez, the Giants' left fielder, finally secured the twice-fumbled baseball at the foot of the wall in left center field, then planted his feet and hurled it back toward the infield.

By the time the ball reached Brandon Crawford's glove in shallow left field, the blue-and-white blur that was Alex Gordon had come to rest atop third base, having delivered the Royals a two-out, bottom-of-the-ninth-inning miracle. One that brought the potential winning run to the plate in a game that had seemed all but decided only moments before.

"Sorry," Danny said brusquely, tearing his focus away from the television just long enough to issue the half-hearted apology to the redhead seated a few chairs to his left, a small child in her ample lap and a look of scorn written across her foundation-caked face.

Danny retrieved his suit jacket and tie from the floor, where they'd fallen in his excitement, draped them over the back of the chair next to him, and reclaimed his seat in front of the television. His apprehension and angst were forgotten, his dread replaced with nervous anticipation as Madison Bumgarner retired hitter after Royals hitter—fourteen straight before Gregor Blanco's critical error on Gordon's line drive—and the Giants continued clinging to a slim 3-2 lead.

Bumgarner had been incredible. Pitching on only two days' rest, after tossing a complete game shutout in game five, this was how October legends were born. These were the moments, when the chips were down and the game was on the line, which had always ignited Danny's competitive spirit. And now they were the moments he missed the most.

"C'mon," Danny sighed, wiping his sweat-soaked palms against the meat of his thighs. "Just keep making pitches."

That's exactly what Bumgarner had done throughout his four and two-thirds innings of relief. Sixty-two of them thus far, according to Fox's longtime announcer, Joe Buck, following the 117 he'd thrown in game five and the 106 he'd hurled in his victory in game one.

Danny flashed back to the article he'd drunkenly skimmed the night before. One of those 106 pitches from game one had been crushed for a home run by Salvador Perez, the Royals' mammoth catcher, who was now strutting to the plate, representing the potential game-winning run.

Danny's body hummed with nervous energy. He fought the urge to stand as Perez arrived at the plate, settled his massive frame into the batter's box, and waited for the first pitch while the rabid Kansas City crowd went apeshit in the stands.

Bumgarner got ahead in the count quickly, throwing a first-pitch fastball around the letters that Perez swung hard at but missed.

Then Perez calmly worked the count to 2-2, with Bumgarner feeding him a steady diet of the high heat, resulting in another swinging miss, two takes, and a foul ball that Perez missed putting a charge into by the narrowest of margins.

"Jesus Christ," Danny exclaimed, reacting to Joe Buck's announcement that the preceding pitch had been Bumgarner's 290th of the seven-game series.

Danny's own arm ached in sympathy for the kid. Though he still looked undaunted atop the mound, Danny knew that was horseshit. He understood that Bumgarner's calm exterior was only a façade, a mask for both his fatigue and his competitive fire, and the torrent of other powerful emotions raging inside of him.

Danny released his death grip on the wooden arms of the chair, which he'd been unconsciously clutching since the beginning of the at-bat, then stood as Bumgarner looked to Posey for the sign.

Bumgarner nodded to Posey, acknowledging the sign. He wound up, delivered, and challenged Perez yet again, climbing the ladder once more with a fastball high in the strike zone.

Perez was ready for the pitch. He took a mighty cut, connected with the ball, and launched it high into the air, into foul territory, and down the third base line.

Danny held his breath.

He clutched his fists against his chest and gravitated toward the TV as the Giants' third baseman, Pablo Sandoval, drifted farther into foul territory, settled underneath the ball . . . then made the catch.

"Yes!" Danny roared.

He pumped his fist in the air, then brought his hands together in a series of deafening claps that reverberated through the entirety of the waiting room.

"That's what I'm talking about!" He pumped his fist again, ignoring the judgmental stares from redhead *Debbie Downer* and everyone else scattered throughout the room.

Danny laughed aloud, unabashed, as Posey and Bumgarner embraced in front of home plate, then disappeared into the heart of a joyous scrum of bodies that swirled around the infield grass.

He collapsed back into the chair, exhausted, his shirt soaked in acrid sweat, his limbs shaking uncontrollably as he watched the victory celebration unfold.

An inexplicable wave of elation swept over him, lifting Danny high and carrying him back to a place he had all but forgotten.

To the feel of the seams beneath his fingers.

To the sound of the ball *popping* in the webbing of his father's mitt.

To the smell of the freshly cut grass, carried gently on a spring breeze.

It was a simpler place, where the slate was always clean and only the game mattered. It was a place, Danny realized, which he'd dearly missed. It was a place that felt like home.

⬩

ALONE IN THE WHITE-TILED BATHROOM, Danny waited for the water to warm, then bent over the sink to rinse the oily residue of excitement from his face. He forced himself to confront the reflection in the water-spotted mirror: the soft roundness of his features, the still-bloodshot eyes, and the dark circles beneath them that made him look just as old as he felt.

It was an unsettling image, a shocking testament to how far he'd strayed, but also a sobering reminder of where he was and why he was there.

The thrill of victory evaporated by the time he emerged from the bathroom, his momentary joy replaced with a hard pit of worry, lodged in the depths of his gut.

"Excuse me." Danny apologized, sidestepping to avoid the man who strode out of the waiting room.

"Mr. Romano?"

Younger than Danny, with sweat-stained surgical scrubs and a shock of damp dirty-blond hair swept back from his forehead, he nonetheless had an air of confidence and authority.

Danny's heart galloped. He willed his lips to form the word *yes*, found them unable, and nodded instead.

"I'm Dr. Northey." The man wiped his hand on the leg of his scrubs before offering it to Danny. "I've been operating on your father."

Danny nodded again, unwilling to trust his voice, then waited in excruciating anticipation for the young surgeon to continue.

"I'm not going to sugarcoat it," he began, staring up at Danny with piercing blue eyes. "It was touch and go for a while there.

But your father is strong, Mr. Romano, and the procedure was ultimately a success. Your dad's going to be okay."

The world swam before Danny's eyes, and he leaned against the wall for support. He let out a breath he didn't know he was holding, thanked a god he didn't believe in, and stared down at the doctor's strong hands, which were surprisingly large for his stature and at odds with his boyish features.

"Thank you," Danny said simply, his heart flooded with gratitude. He reached again for the doctor's hand, then pumped it until the surgeon finally pulled his away. "Thank you for bringing him back to me."

◇

TOUCH AND GO.

Dr. Northey's words, delivered outside the men's room nearly an hour earlier, echoed in Danny's mind as he trailed the young nurse through the swinging double doors, then followed her through a maze of identical corridors, each new passage indistinguishable from the last.

He'd said more, of course, offering a detailed accounting of the surgery, filled with jargon that was impossible to retain, but those were the words that had lodged in Danny's mind. A maddeningly mundane expression—one he'd probably used so frequently it became routine—to describe that razor-thin edge separating life from death.

"Keep in mind," the nurse said, her black braided ponytail swinging between her shoulder blades as she walked briskly down the hallway, two steps ahead. "He's been through a lot, and he's still going to be really out of it. He needs his rest right now, but he also needs *you*. And to know that you're here for him."

"I understand," Danny said, his confirmation barely a whisper. His father wasn't the only one who was *out of it*. Bone tired and mentally spent, he was still trying to find his emotional footing after the dizzying series of events that had brought him to this place, to this moment in time. He'd struggled to regurgitate the doctor's report for Uncle Hal and Aunt Dorothy when they'd returned to the hospital, providing them with only the most critical information: His dad was out of surgery, and he was going to be okay.

The nurse, who was older than Danny initially thought, with small crow's feet stretching from the corners of her brown wide-set eyes, stopped outside a wood-paneled door.

"I'll be back for you in a few minutes," she said, smiling encouragingly and patting him on the arm. She reached for the stainless-steel handle, then held the door wide, motioning for Danny to enter.

"Thanks," Danny said. He slid past her, then watched as she pushed the door closed behind her, leaving them alone in the stillness of the room.

Standing at the threshold, Danny's eyes drifted slowly across the landscape of the private room. His father, dressed in a mint green hospital gown and flanked on each side by an assortment of machines and displays, was partially reclined in the adjustable bed that ran perpendicular to the wall. Lit from above by a lone fluorescent tube, he appeared to be asleep—his eyes closed, his chest rising and falling softly underneath a thin blue blanket.

Danny positioned himself at the foot of the bed. Looking pale and drawn in the harsh artificial light, his father seemed different now. Older, yes, but more fragile, too. Vulnerable and exposed in a way Danny had never seen or even imagined.

His father's blue eyes fluttered open, then came to rest on Danny, still standing at the foot of his bed.

"You came," he said. He paused, seemingly to gather himself, his mind groping for words that were hidden in the post-anesthesia fog. "I wasn't sure you would."

Danny flinched as a spear of guilt lanced deep into his chest. His mind conjured images of a time when their roles were reversed. When his father stood at the foot of *his* hospital bed, secretly blaming himself for a tragedy that was not of his making.

"Jesus, Dad. Of course, I came."

Danny retrieved a heavy wood-framed chair from the opposite side of the room and positioned it on the right side of the bed.

"Uncle Hal said there would be free donuts," Danny joked, lowering himself into the chair. "But apparently those didn't make it into the ambulance with you."

His father took a moment to process the joke. He laughed lightly, then grimaced in pain and clutched a hand to his chest. "There was coffee, too," he croaked. His mouth turned up slightly at the corners, his best attempt at a smile.

Dad motioned with his free hand, the one not attached to wires and tubes, beckoning for Danny to come closer. "I'm glad you're here." His mind and mouth seemed disconnected as if struggling to work in tandem. "I'm glad . . . we have time."

Danny leaned closer to the bed. He waited for his father to continue and watched as his eyes fluttered again, then closed.

"Time for what, Dad?" he asked, needing so badly to hear the words, whatever they might be. Danny reached for his father's hand, leaning closer still.

"Time . . . for anything," he replied, his eyes still closed, his head sinking farther into the softness of the pillow. "Time for everything."

Danny held the words in his mind's eye, examined them from every angle, then squeezed his father's hand in response. There were still so many things to be said: decades' worth of apologies and regrets, stacked up like railway cars abandoned on a long-deserted track, stretching as far as the eye could see.

But his father was right: There was still time. *Time for everything.*

A faint vibration emanating from the right front pocket of his slacks pulled Danny from his trance. He retrieved the phone, saw the missed call from Uncle Sammy, and tried to make sense of the series of text messages.

The first part was clear: Sammy's flight from Portland had landed in San Francisco, he was on the airport shuttle heading north, and he was eager for an update. The second part, some nonsense about a gift shop and the *biggest fucking bear on the shelf*, was a mystery Danny couldn't unravel.

Danny held his dad's hand a moment longer, watching the blanket rise and fall as his breathing slowed and he drifted off to sleep. He knew he should return Sammy's call, but he didn't want to disturb his father. He rose from the chair, placed his dad's hand gently atop the blanket, then eased open the door.

"Wait..." his father called. His voice was a scratchy whisper.

Danny turned, his foot propping the door ajar, and stared back into the darkened room.

His father struggled to reposition himself in the bed. He raised his head with great effort, angling his gray-stubbled face toward the door, then paused.

"How 'bout those Giants?" Dad asked.

Danny couldn't help but laugh. Though he'd momentarily forgotten about the wild rollercoaster of a game, he wasn't surprised that his father hadn't.

"The game's over," Danny replied. He shrugged his shoulders, unsure where to begin. He scoured his mind and heart for the right words, those sufficient to describe the transformation he'd undergone in the waiting room; then, he realized, in a flash of clarity, what his father had *really* said.

The hidden meaning behind his question. Their long-abandoned *secret code*.

"I know," Danny acknowledged softly, the warmth of a thousand summer afternoons radiating outward from his body.

Danny returned to his father's bedside, let the door whisper shut behind him, and finally unearthed the words that had been there all along. The words he'd never been able to say.

"I love you, too, Dad."

Epilogue

Ages 36 & 63

May 17, 2016

Danny read the last sentence of the essay again, found it to be just as insightful and well-constructed as the first, then reached for his red pen and marked the top of the front page with an oversized A+. Leaning back in his chair, he stared out across the rows and columns of empty desks, marveling again at the boy's abilities. The kid could write.

Courage, grit, and fortitude.

These were the virtues Danny had been preaching to both his baseball players and his sophomore US history students throughout the school year. They were traits Danny understood well. It had taken a metric fuck-ton of courage to march into Abe's office, look his father-in-law in the eye, and break the news that he wouldn't be coming back. Then, it took a year's worth of grit and fortitude to reshape his life, leave his self-loathing and regrets behind, and translate his ill-formed dream of teaching and coaching into a substantive reality.

Danny wasn't naïve. For most of these kids, his impassioned lectures went in one ear and out the other. But in the case of Bryce

Hoffmann, who embodied these qualities both inside and outside the classroom, the message had clearly struck a chord.

His final essay of the year—a thoughtful analysis of FDR's wartime leadership, which posited that the president's ongoing battle with polio actually *enhanced and informed* his ability to lead the nation in the early years of the war—was easily the finest piece of writing Danny had read during his first year as a teacher.

On the baseball field, Hoffmann's talents were less pronounced, and he'd made the JV team this season by the skin of his teeth. But if he worked hard over the summer—and learned to hit and field half as well as he could write—Danny might be able to find a spot for him on the varsity team the following season. Because character counts, and every team needs a Bryce Hoffmann. Even if he's only leading from the bench.

Danny reached across the wood laminate desktop for the next paper in the stack, then jumped in his rolling chair as his iPhone clattered to life, vibrating from its place atop the beaten podium to his left.

He grabbed the phone, read Natalie's reminder, and was about to respond with a text of his own when he changed his mind, deciding to call instead.

"Hey, mama," Danny opened, dusting off the A.C. Slater impersonation that always made Natalie swoon.

"Hey, yourself," she replied seductively. "Wanna change into your wrestling unitard and meet me at The Max for a burger and shake after school?"

Danny glanced at the clock on the classroom wall. No time for *Saved by the Bell* role-play. It was almost 5 p.m.; if he didn't leave soon, they were all going to be late.

"Sorry, babe," Danny said, a cheesy smile plastered across his face, "but I have somewhere else to be this evening. And if I don't get pedaling now, we're going to have two wildly disappointed six-year-olds on our hands."

He said goodbye, neatened the stacks of paper on his desk,

and changed into his biking attire, which he kept in the lower righthand drawer of his crappy standard-issue desk.

Already wearing his backpack and helmet, Danny locked the classroom door behind him and strolled through the heart of the deserted Point Loma High School campus to the nearly-empty bike rack next to the attendance office.

Danny was excited for the evening, eager to get the night underway. This was a rite of passage for the boys—one he'd put off for far too long, waiting in thrilled anticipation for the moment to be *just right*. He was excited for Will and Matty, of course, but also for himself. And even more so for his father.

◇

"CAREFUL," Frank cautioned, placing a protective hand on the small of Carole's back, guiding her off the top of the escalator and into the throng of Padres fans swarming the crowded concourse of Petco Park.

"Thanks, love." An appreciative smile played at the corners of her wide mouth. "I was distracted by those two." She pointed a few yards ahead to Will and Matty, who walked side by side, trailing in Danny and Natalie's wake. "They're just so cute in their little jerseys."

Wearing gray vintage Giants jerseys, the numbers 22 and 9 emblazoned below the players' last names on the back, the twins certainly looked the part of diehard fans despite this being their very first game in a big-league park.

"He still claims it was a happy accident," Frank remarked, rolling his eyes. He reached for Carole's left hand, careful not to squeeze the golden band that still made his heart flutter every time its attached diamond caught his eye.

"*Will and Matty*," Frank explained, seeing the confused expression painted across her beautiful face. "You know, *Clark and Williams*," he added, pointing at the names emblazoned on the boys' backs as they snaked through the crowd.

She raised both eyebrows and shrugged apologetically.

"That's okay," Frank said with a smile, "I'll explain later."

He pulled her gently forward, trying to match Danny's blistering pace as he guided them all through the crowd. Carole wasn't raised with baseball, so she didn't understand the game like Frank did. But that was okay; she understood him—perhaps better than he understood himself—and loved every part of him. And that's what really mattered.

"I'm going to catch up," Frank announced, releasing Carole's hand and hustling off through the crowd. He maneuvered around a large gaggle of parentless teens, split the gap between the boys, and reached for his son's shoulder.

Danny had been sober for more than sixteen months, and the changes were dramatic. Wearing the Madison Bumgarner jersey Frank bought him for Christmas, he looked out of place in the crowd, so fit and trim that he still seemed better suited for the field than the stands.

"You okay?" Danny asked, halting next to a hotdog cart, a worried expression on his sun-bronzed face as he looked his father up and down.

"Of course," Frank said, touched by his son's concern. "But do you mind if I take them from here?" Frank glanced over his shoulder at the boys, then back to Danny, who smiled knowingly and nodded his consent.

"Okay, fellas," Frank said solemnly, grabbing each of the boys by a small hand, the one not buried in a dusty mitt.

He guided them around the curvature of the stadium, closer to their assigned section, then paused and took a knee. "You're flying blind from here out," he warned, searching their inquisitive little faces for signs of understanding.

Butterflies swarmed in Frank's stomach as he watched Will and Matty cover their identical faces with their identical mitts. He guided them carefully forward, past the restrooms, and into the concrete breezeway that connected the concourse with the box seats below.

Frank led the boys away from the congestion. He paused for a moment at the far end of the tunnel, his eyes scanning the seats below before gravitating to the emerald grass, its blades cut in a crisscross pattern, just as they should be.

He closed his eyes and breathed in the rich scents of the ballpark. The sounds and smells of the stadium washed over him, carrying him back in time to another evening at a different ballpark—much colder and windier than this one—when he stood with his own eyes covered, waiting breathlessly as a hand much larger than his own guided him forward.

"All right," Frank said finally, pulled from his trance by the insistent tugging on his arm. "You boys can look now."

He watched through misty eyes as the boys lowered their mitts and slowly panned from side to side, overwhelmed—just as he had been—by the enormity of the moment and the sheer size of the field.

"It's awesome!" Matty exclaimed, his voice cutting through the din and echoing off the concrete walls.

"Amazing!" Will added, never one to be outdone.

"It's more than that," Frank told them, but if the right word existed, he surely didn't know it. He locked eyes with Danny, who had arrived unnoticed at his side.

Frank gestured for Danny to take the lead, made way for Natalie, then watched as his son and grandsons descended the stairs, hand in hand.

He paused to bask in the soft glow of gratitude. A tear slid down his cheek, but he stilled his hand, resisting the urge to wipe it away. Like the thrill of the ring around his finger, it was a sensation he was finally ready to embrace.

"You ready?" Carole asked.

Frank answered with a smile, the special smile that started in his heart, shone through his eyes, and was reserved exclusively for her.

Carole returned his smile, then guided Frank by the hand as

they emerged from the breezeway together—out of the shadows as one, and into the dazzling light.

Acknowledgments

I am a runner. I say that proudly . . . now.

I discovered long-distance running at the age of twenty-nine, and it's a passion that has shaped and enriched my life ever since. All the same, it took no fewer than ten marathons before I was comfortable calling myself a *marathoner*. As much as running had already become a part of my identity, believing I'd earned the title and gained membership to the exclusive club felt like a tremendous stretch. Eventually, I got there.

The same can be said for writing. Though I'm not yet comfortable calling myself an *author*—it's daunting to consider my feeble efforts in the same category as those of the *real* writers I hold in such high regard—I will allow that I've always considered myself to be a decent storyteller. For now, that will have to do.

With all that explained, I must admit that the story of Frank and Danny Romano, though conceived in my mind and heart, never could have been told without the guidance, patience, and friendship of a wonderful tribe of human beings who supported and mentored me along the way.

First, there's Nicole Criona, my fantastic writing coach who saw some glimmer of talent—even as I struggled through my opening chapters—and eventually helped me find my confidence and voice. You believed in this book *long* before I did, and for that I'm grateful.

To Derrick Alvestal, thanks for helping me invent Frank's world as a firefighter. Your experience and anecdotes helped me imagine his life in the firehouse, and I never could have dropped poor Snickers into a pool without you! As with nearly every other facet of this book (everything from pop culture and fashion to game notes and the broadcast dates of television shows), I aimed for uncompromising accuracy. I did my best to paint your profession in an informed and realistic light; apologies if I missed the mark!

Special thanks go out to the team at Acorn Publishing for helping me make this book a reality. Thanks to Holly Kammier and Jessica Therrien for enabling me to understand my own expectations and desires for this book, then showing me the path to achieving my goals. To Jessica Hammett: Thank you for keeping the trains running on schedule and leveraging your project management skills to shuttle this book down the home stretch. And to Kat Ross, my amazingly talented and insightful editor, thank you for exposing the book's flaws, encouraging me to dig deeper, and helping me to shape this final version into a novel I can be proud of.

Many have trotted beside me for portions of this two-year marathon; thanks to Danielle George for joining me for the final leg. Your advice and support have carried me across the finish line. Alas, I don't have a medal to give you, but I hope a copy of the book will suffice!

And finally, thank you to Julie. October of 2014, the month when this story begins, was one of the hardest of my life. We lived it together—the highs and the lows—and shared so much more in the years before and after. When I first said I wanted to write a novel, you never doubted I could. And when I finally decided to try, you supported me every step of the way, even when the whispers of doubt in my mind almost got the best of me. I hope you enjoy this story, even if you didn't always enjoy the process. And please . . . don't let a couple of "Desperado" references come between you and a good time!

About the Author

Patrick Holcomb is a long-retired Little League right fielder whose passion for the game far outdistanced his unremarkable talent. After hanging up his cleats for good, he found his true calling, earned the title *US Marine*, and spent the next twenty years traipsing around the globe alongside some of the brashest and boldest women and men this country has to offer. Running is his passion, and backpacking is his joy. And to this day he still hungrily admires each mountain with the same boyish question tumbling through his mind: *Can I climb that?*

Book Club Questions

If you're using *Where the Seams Meet* for a book club, these questions are recommended to stimulate dialogue and help explore nuances within the text. To avoid spoilers, don't review the questions for each part of the book until you've completed your reading!

Part I—Frank

- The time capsule in the park takes on increasing meaning to Frank as the years pass. What does it come to represent, and how is it important to understanding Frank's character?
- Baseball holds a special place in Frank's life. What does the game represent to Frank as a child, and how does his relationship with baseball change as he enters adulthood and becomes a father?
- How does Frank view his mother? How does his perception of her change as the years pass?
- Frank is haunted by his father's ghost. How do Pop's memory and legacy affect Frank as he begins his new

life in Santa Rosa and faces the challenges of career, marriage, and fatherhood?
- Explain the Opening Day metaphor. What does it represent for Frank, and what changes does Frank undergo on that fateful afternoon in April 1976?
- The final two chapters of Part I foreshadow future conflict between Frank and Danny. What are some examples of this foreshadowing?

Part II—Danny

- Words left unspoken play a powerful role in shaping the dynamic between Frank and Danny. What are some examples of these unspoken words, and how do they affect both men throughout Danny's life?
- In a moment of anger, Frank tells Danny, "Not every mistake turns into a foul ball." How do these words come back to haunt both characters?
- Danny's relationship with baseball is different from his father's. How does it differ, and how does it change throughout the course of the book?
- Ellie's memory haunts Frank and Danny in different ways. How are father and son affected differently by her loss?
- Baker pays close attention to Danny's tie, which Danny removes soon after his father's secret is revealed. What does this tie represent, and what does it symbolize when Danny removes it in the waiting room?
- This story is told in two parts, spanning nearly sixty years, with each chapter capturing one pivotal day in the characters' lives. What are the advantages and disadvantages of this unique structure?